SUPPORTING SERVICE LEVEL AGREEMENTS ON IP NETWORKS

Dinesh Verma

MACMILLAN
TECHNICAL
PUBLISHING
U·S·A

Supporting Service Level Agreements on IP Networks

By Dinesh Verma

Published by:
Macmillan Technical Publishing
201 West 103rd Street
Indianapolis, IN 46290 USA

Copyright © 1999 by Dinesh Verma

International Standard Book Number: 1-57870-146-5

Library of Congress Catalog Card Number: 98-89585

03 02 01 00 99   7 6 5 4 3 2 1

Interpretation of the printing code: The rightmost double-digit number is the year of the book's printing; the rightmost single-digit number is the number of the book's printing. For example, the printing code 99-1 shows that the first printing of the book occurred in 1999.

Composed in Galliard and MCPdigital by Macmillan Computer Publishing

Printed in the United States of America

Trademark Acknowledgments

All terms mentioned in this book that are known to be trademarks or service marks have been appropriately capitalized. Macmillan Technical Publishing cannot attest to the accuracy of this information. Use of a term in this book should not be regarded as affecting the validity of any trademark or service mark.

Warning and Disclaimer

This book is designed to provide information about service level agreements. Every effort has been made to make this book as complete and as accurate as possible, but no warranty or fitness is implied.

The information is provided on an as-is basis. The authors and Macmillan Technical Publishing shall have neither liability nor responsibility to any person or entity with respect to any loss or damages arising from the information contained in this book or from the use of the discs or programs that may accompany it.

Feedback Information

At Macmillan Technical Publishing, our goal is to create in-depth technical books of the highest quality and value. Each book is crafted with care and precision, undergoing rigorous development that involves the unique expertise of members from the professional technical community.

Readers' feedback is a natural continuation of this process. If you have any comments regarding how we could improve the quality of this book, or otherwise alter it to better suit your needs, you can contact us at `network-tech@mcp.com`. Please make sure to include the book title and ISBN in your message.

We greatly appreciate your assistance.

PUBLISHER
David Dwyer

EXECUTIVE EDITOR
Linda Ratts Engelman

MANAGING EDITOR
Patrick Kanouse

ACQUISITIONS EDITOR
Karen Wachs

DEVELOPMENT EDITOR
Lisa M. Thibault

PROJECT EDITOR
Jennifer Nuckles

COPY EDITOR
Barbara Hacha

INDEXER
Tina Trettin

PROOFREADERS
Elise Walter
Megan Wade

ACQUISITIONS COORDINATOR
Jennifer Garrett

MANUFACTURING COORDINATOR
Brook Farling

BOOK DESIGNER
Anne Jones

COVER DESIGNER
Aren Howell

PRODUCTION
Amy Parker

About the Author

Dinesh Verma is currently manager of the Enterprise Networking Group at the IBM T. J. Watson Research Center. He has been working in the area of extending Quality of Service (QoS) support for more than a decade, and played a key role in developing one of the first QoS architectures for support of real-time communication in high-speed networks at the Tenet Research Group at Berkeley in the late 1980s. He has subsequently worked on network control in IBM's Network Broadband Services, a control architecture for switched networks. Currently, Dinesh is involved in exploring different ways to support SLAs in IP networks and to exploit developing standard techniques for SLA support. Dinesh has published more than 30 articles and has more than 10 patent applications in the area of computer networks. He has been an active member of consortiums such as IETF and the ATM Forum, and he has worked with leading network strategists, network operators, and researchers in this field.

Dinesh received his Bachelor of Technology degree in computer science from the Indian Institute of Technology, Kanpur, India in 1987, and was the recipient of the President's Gold Medal. He obtained his Ph.D. in computer networks in 1992 from the University of California, Berkeley, and an M.S. in management from the Brooklyn Polytechnic University in 1998.

Dedication

Dedicated

To my late mother, Chanda Devi,

Who gave me life and the courage to undertake new ventures

To my father and to Bhaiya, Didi, Baby Di, and Guddu,

Who stood by me as I grew up

To my wife, Paridhi, and kids, Chitu and Riya

Who gave me all their support during my work on this book.

Acknowledgments

I would like to express my thanks to the two sets of people who made this book possible: those who helped me learn all about SLAs and those who helped me write this book.

I owe most of my knowledge about computer networks to Professor Domenico Ferrari, who introduced me to performance evaluation of computer networks. I am fortunate to work with a wonderful set of colleagues at IBM. Special thanks are due to the managers who supported my research on the topic of SLAs: Hamid Ahmadi, Arvind Krishna, John Tavs, and Dilip Kandlur, and to the colleagues who worked with me on different aspects of SLAs: Edward Ellesson, Raymond Jennings, Mandis Beigi, Srinivasa Rao, Ashish Mehra, Vishal Bhotika, Lap Hunyh, and Kenneth White.

For the book itself, I was lucky to work with a great team at Macmillan. Special thanks are due to Karen Wachs, who helped in developing the proposal for the book, and to Lisa Thibault, who took great pains in refining the presentation. I am also greatly indebted to the technical reviewers, Edward Ellesson and Robert Cahn, whose comments and patient revisions helped immensely in improving the contents of the book.

About the Technical Reviewers

These reviewers contributed their considerable practical, hands-on expertise to the entire development process for *Supporting Service Level Agreements on IP Networks*. As the book was being written, these folks reviewed all the material for technical content, organization, and flow. Their feedback was critical to ensuring that *Supporting Service Level Agreements on IP Networks* fits our readers' need for the highest-quality technical information.

Ed Ellesson is a Senior Engineer at IBM. He is currently responsible for IBM's technical direction in the areas of service level agreements, policy-based management, and Quality of Service for TCP/IP implementations across IBM's product divisions. Ed chairs the Service Level Agreement Working Group within the Desktop Management Task Force (DMTF), which is extending the Common Information Model (CIM) to support policy. Ed also co-chairs the Policy Framework Working Group within the Internet Engineering Task Force (IETF) international standards organization. Ed has 28 years of engineering and technical marketing experience in a combination of voice and data communications technologies with such companies as ROLM Corporation, TRW, and GTE, prior to joining IBM. He is a member of the IEEE and the ACM, and he completed his undergraduate work in EE at Cornell University, Ithaca, NY.

Robert S. Cahn is a network architect for AT&T Global Network Services. He is active in the areas of network design and new network services. He received his B.S. from the University of Chicago and a Ph.D. from Yale University, both in mathematics. After teaching at a number of universities, he joined the IBM T.J. Watson Research Center in 1985. There he began a research project in network design and network economics that continues to this day. In 1998, he joined the IBM Global Network and transitioned to his current position with the sale of the network to AT&T in 1999.

Overview

CONTENTS

Foreword

The Internet is maturing from a research testbed to an essential part of the infrastructure. Within a few years, most people will expect to receive Internet services, such as email and World Wide Web access, as easily and reliably as electricity, water, sewage, and telephone service. The current Internet, however, leaves much to be desired in terms of its availability and responsiveness. Frequent disruptions in service and long delays are all too common. A critical step in the transformation of the Internet into a ubiquitous, reliable infrastructure is the establishment of Service Level Agreements (or SLAs) that quantify the service expectations between a service provider and its customers. In the near future, I envision a web of SLAs spanning the Internet, allowing Internet service to be provisioned and efficiently provided to all its users.

This book is perfectly positioned to help IT managers, Internet service providers, and network operators to understand and deploy SLAs. It provides not only a quick tour of the necessary theoretical background but also a detailed guide to creating SLAs for each of these user constituencies. The technical content of the book is leavened with detailed case histories that reinforce important concepts. A careful reader will get a first hand look at SLA terms, the state-of-the-art mechanisms for implementing SLAs, and learn about unresolved questions in the area.

The author, Dinesh Verma, is one of the leading experts in the area of Internet quality of service and SLAs. His thesis work on guaranteeing network quality of service was the pioneering effort in the field and much of the work since has built on this solid foundation. In this book, Dinesh has brought to bear his enormous knowledge of the field as well as a decade of experience in building real protocols and systems. The result is a thorough and authoritative treatment of the area.

I am sure that this book will play a significant role in transforming the Internet from its current state to a robust, reliable, infrastructure.

S. Keshav
CTO, Ensim Corporation

Introduction

Any relationship that you may have with an organization or another individual is invariably associated with a set of expectations as well as a set of obligations. The expectations and obligations may be implicit, but it is almost always better that these be made explicit, especially in a business context. A *service level agreement (SLA)* is an explicit statement of the expectations and obligations that exist in a business relationship between two organizations: the service provider and the customer. *Bilateral SLAs* can also be defined among organizations that have a symbiotic relationship, with each being a customer of the other's services.

SLAs have been widely used in many businesses; they define the expectations and obligations of different business units to each other. They have been deployed extensively in functions such as help desks, call centers, facility management, and in I/T departments. Typical expectations and obligations specified in an SLA include conditions such as requiring that a database server be available 99% of the time, that 90% of problems be resolved within 2 hours of the complaint, or that the maximum waiting time a customer is put on hold be less than 3 minutes for 90% of the calls received at a help desk.

SLAs have become especially important because of an increasing tendency among businesses to outsource functions that are not considered part of their core competency. One function that is often outsourced in this manner is the operation and management of the phone and computer networks that link different sites of the organization. Computer networks in a typical business are usually operated by a special business unit or outsourced to a service company such as IBM Global Services..

CIOs overseeing the operation of their computer networks and the support of their customers often have to sign up specific SLAs regarding the performance and operation of their computer networks. Creating formal SLAs among different business units has been the standing recommendation of several management consultants.

Despite the wide acceptance of SLAs in business and management circles, the concept of SLAs is relatively new in the data networking community. This book describes the different technologies for supporting SLAs in an IP network. It is my hope that the book will bridge this gap between the management community and the technical community in the area of SLAs.

Who Will Benefit from This Book?

This book is intended for operators of IP networks who want to implement support of SLAs in their network. If you are a network operator who has signed SLAs with your customer, and if you are looking for techniques to automate the various processes related to SLA management, this is the book you want. Conversely, if you are a customer of a network service and are thinking about implementing SLAs to aid in managing your expectations of the performance of that network, and if you want to figure out what that means, this book is for you.

If you are not a network operator, but develop network management software and tools, this book will be useful for you. It explains the different techniques that can be used for SLA management.

This book will also be beneficial to management consultants whose clients include operators of IP networks who are thinking of outsourcing those clients to a service provider. If you are a management consultant and would like to understand the technical issues associated with support of SLAs in the network, this is the right book for you.

Finally, if you are a technical professional in the area of IP networks, with an interest in areas such as quality of service, performance monitoring, policy enablement, or traffic engineering, you may find this book of interest. If you want to examine how these different, focused research areas can be combined to support a business need such as SLAs, this is the right book for you. If these terms are new to you, you can find a brief discussion of these topics in Chapter 4, "Service Differentiation and Quality of Service in IP Networks."

Who Is This Book Not For?

If you are looking for an overview of the business processes and practices associated with SLAs in a network, you may find this book to be too technical. Although this book can help you determine what can or cannot be done within an IP network, the book does not explain the legal or business issues associated with SLA management in the network.

If you are looking for an introduction to IP network management, this book is not intended for you. This book addresses only those aspects of network management that relate to SLAs.

Finally, if you are looking for specific details on how to manage service levels using a specific vendor product, this book is not for you. This book describes the general techniques in this field, but it does not describe any specific product intended for service level management.

The Organization of This Book

This book has been organized into eight chapters:

Chapter 1, "Service Level Agreements Overview," introduces the concept of SLAs and provides an overview of SLAs as used in the industry. It describes the contents of an SLA, the steps needed to comply with SLAs, and reasons for supporting SLAs by the network provider.

Chapter 2, "IP Networks and SLAs," introduces the use of SLAs in a computer network. It describes the useful metrics to include in an SLA and the common ways to measure reliability and availability in a computer network. It also describes the use of SLAs in the context of different applications that may be running on the network.

Chapter 3, "Network Design and SLA Support," describes how network design and capacity planning may be used to support SLAs in a network. It explains how to determine SLA parameters for a network, and how to design a network with a given SLA.

Chapter 4, "Service Differentiation and Quality of Service in IP Networks," introduces the different current approaches to service differentiation and quality of service that are found in IP networks. This includes a discussion of the integrated services and differentiated services defined within the Internet Engineering Task Force (IETF) and a comparison of IP quality-of-service initiatives with the corresponding ones in network architectures such as SNA and ATM.

Chapter 5, "A General SLA Architecture," introduces a general approach to handling service level agreements in an IP network. The approach includes the basic framework of service differentiation, performance monitoring, and network adaptation based on the performance measurements. It also describes SLAs in three typical deployments—a network operator, an enterprise I/T department and a web hosting service.

Chapter 6, "SLA Support in Different Network Environments," describes how the architecture described in Chapter 5 applies to different types of IP networks—ones that support an integrated services approach to quality of service, ones that support a differentiated-services approach to quality of service, and the traditional, best-effort IP networks.

Chapter 7, "Network Monitoring and SLA Verification," describes the general topic of network performance monitoring in the context of IP networks, as well as the various tools and techniques that can be used to monitor the performance on an IP network.

Chapter 8, "Advanced Topics," discusses some advanced topics that are related to the concept of service-level agreements, including a discussion of how SLAs can be used for IP virtual, private networks, how SLAs can be defined and used for IPV6, and how IP tag-switching can be exploited to support SLAs.

Topical Information on SLAs

In addition to the contents of this book, some topical information on SLAs can be found on the Web site for this book, at http://www.macmillantech.com/verma. The Web site contains information on vendor products that offer support for SLA management, pointers to different reports on SLAs available on the Web, as well as information on companies offering courses and training programs in the area of SLA management.

1

Service Level Agreements Overview

A *Service Level Agreement (SLA)* is a formal definition of the relationship that exists between two organizations, usually between a supplier of services and its customer. The supplier organization may be an I/T organization providing computing services to its customers, an intranet operator who provides network connectivity services to its customers, a telecommunications company providing phone services to its customers, a services company providing computer maintenance and administration support to its customers, or an Internet Service Provider (ISP) providing Internet access to its customers. SLAs can be defined and used in the context of any industry in which a provider-customer relationship exists. Two service providers that are customers of each other's services could have bilateral SLAs defining the agreement between themselves.

The SLA provides a means of defining the service required by the customer. It specifies what the customer wants and what the supplier is committing to provide. It defines the standards for the quality of services provided, setting performance objectives that the supplier must achieve. It also defines the procedure and the reports that must be provided to track and ensure compliance with the SLA.

In an environment where noncritical functions of corporations are outsourced to other organizations, SLAs play an increasingly vital role. The operation and management of the computer networks that link different sites of the organization are often subject to such outsourcing. Even when the function is not outsourced, these networks are typically operated by a dedicated reporting to the CIO of the corporation.

CIOs overseeing the operation of their computer networks and supporting their customers often have to sign up specific SLAs regarding the performance and operation of their computer networks. Creating SLAs among different business units has been the standing recommendation of several management consultants [CHATTERTON] [WALDER]. Some prominent network operators such as UUNET [UUNETSLA], IBM Global Services [IGSSLA] and UKERNA [UKERNASLA] have adopted formal SLAs for their networks.

1.1   Contents of a Service Level Agreement

A service level agreement typically contains:

- The type and nature of service to be provided, which includes the description of the service to be provided, such as facilities management, network services, or help-desk support. Within the context of a computer network, the service to be offered may include dial-in access, leased-line access, security services, Web-hosting services, and so on.

- The expected performance level of the service, which includes two major aspects: reliability and responsiveness. *Reliability* includes availability requirements—when is the service available, and what are the bounds on service outages that may be expected. *Responsiveness* includes how soon the service is performed in the normal course of operations. In the context of a computer network, reliability is usually measured in the uptime of the network, and responsiveness is measured as bounds on round-trip delays between two customer sites.

- The process for reporting problems with the service, which forms a big part of a typical SLA. It includes information about the person to be contacted for problem resolution, the format in which complaints have to be filed, and the steps to be undertaken to resolve the problem quickly. The agreement also typically describes a time limit by which a reported problem should be responded to (someone would start to work on the problem), as well as how soon the problem would be resolved.

- The time frame for response and problem resolution, which specifies a time limit by which someone would start investigating a problem that was reported. The start of the investigation is typically marked by a representative of the supplier contacting the customer who reported the problem initially. A time limit by which the problem would be resolved may also be included. For example, an SLA may specify that a failed link would be recommissioned within 24 hours.

- The process for monitoring and reporting the service level, which outlines how performance levels are monitored and reported—that is, who will do the monitoring, what types of statistics will be collected, how often they will be collected, and how past or current statistics may be accessed. Some network providers may allow the customer to directly access part of the network through a network management tool. Typically, the customer is provided access to monitoring and statistics information, but may not be allowed to modify the configurations or the operation of the network.

- The credits, charges, or other consequences for the service provider in not meeting its obligation (that is, failing to provide the agreed-upon service level). It is customary to extend some credits to the customers when the service expectations are not met. Other consequences of not meeting the obligation may include the ability of the customer to terminate the relationship or to ask for reimbursement of part of the revenues lost due to loss of service. The consequences of not meeting the SLA may vary depending on the nature of the relationship between the customer and the supplier.

- Escape clauses and constraints, including the consequences if the customer does not meet his or her obligation, which qualifies access to the service level. *Escape clauses* are conditions under which the service level does not apply, or under which it is considered unreasonable to meet the requisite SLAs—for example, when the service provider's equipment has been damaged in flood, fire, or war. They often also impose some constraints on the behavior by the customer. A network operator may void the SLA if the customer is attempting to breach the security of the network.

Note

An SLA may consider other aspects not covered here—for example, when the SLA is a part of a larger contract between the customer and the service provider. We are assuming that other aspects of the agreement between the customer and the service provider, such as payment expected for services, are part of some other business contract.

The hope in most cases is that the service provider would be able to meet the performance expected of it, and large portions of the SLAs would never be invoked. In this book, we describe the techniques that can be used to meet the desired service level in an IP network, as well as techniques to continuously monitor the network performance to validate its compliance with the SLA.

A more detailed discussion of the contents of SLAs, especially from a business perspective, can be found in the books by Hiles [HILES] or LaBounty [LABOUNTY].

1.2 Service Level Agreements in Computer Networks

In the context of a computer network, service levels have become exceedingly important for business customers. Providers of network connectivity to consumers (ISPs, for example) can also use SLAs to attract customers. In this section, we discuss the structure of a computer network and show how SLAs can be supported within these networks.

Note

In this book, we assume that computer network means an IP network. Non-IP computer networks are referred to explicitly by their protocol (for example, SNA networks or ATM networks).

1.2.1 The Structure of a Computer Network

A simplified view of the network supported by a typical network provider is shown in Figure 1.1.

Figure 1.1   A typical IP network.

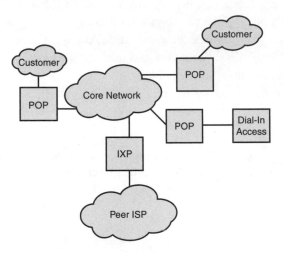

The cloud shown as the core network is the domain of a single network operator or ISP. An ISP would have multiple points of presence (POP) at various cities. The POPs are sites that could be used to access the ISP network. Customers may connect to POPs using leased lines or dial-up lines. Dial-up access requires modem banks that terminate in a local office of the ISP and are connected to the POP using high-speed links (typically T1). For access to other customers, the ISP may place a router on the customer's premises (called a *customer site router,* or *CSR*) and connect it to the POP using a metropolitan area network or a leased line. In addition to the POPs, the ISP needs to partner with other peer ISPs to connect to the global Internet. These peering points are known as Internet Exchange Points, or IXPs. An IXP can connect a regional ISP to a national ISP or act as a conduit among several ISP networks. Different ISPs have peering agreements among themselves as to which traffic they accept from other ISPs at an IXP. Very large service providers also have private peering arrangements with each other.

> **Note**
>
> An exchange point is also known by several names other than IXP. Common equivalent terms include NAP (Network Access Point), MAE (Metropolitan Area Exchange) and FIX (Federal Internet Exchange).

An ISP provides specific SLAs to its customer organizations. The connectivity to the customer networks is maintained through an access router. It is customary for the ISP to enter into a bilateral SLA with peer ISPs and provide mutual assurances about the performance of their networks. However, from the perspective of a single ISP, the obligations for handling traffic emanating from a peer ISP are similar to the obligations for treating traffic that emanates from a customer organization. The POPs and IXPs supported by the ISP are interconnected by its core network. The core network of the ISP consists of several routers connected by means of high-bandwidth circuits, which may be owned by the ISP or leased from other bandwidth vendors.

> **Note**
>
> The public Internet consists of all the ISP networks and the different servers provided by the ISPs or their customers. The IXPs provide the gateways by which a user on an ISP network can access servers provided by a customer of a different ISP.

A customer may use the ISP network in one of three ways:

- To access the public Internet
- To interconnect two or more of its sites
- To access proprietary, industry-specific networks

Most customers in the real world would probably want to do a combination of all three methods. However, the terms of SLAs that govern different types of access may be quite different.

When a customer wants to connect between two of its own sites, SLAs can be defined to assure some performance level on the network communication between the pair of access routers that connect those two sites. When accessing the public Internet, the customer is present at one of the access routers, but may communicate to any of the other public access routers present at the network operator (except those access routers that are for the exclusive use of the locally connected customer). The end objective of the customer communication on the Internet is quite likely to be outside the administrative domain of the network operator. Although the network operator cannot honestly offer any assurances about the performance level of the network outside his domain, he can provide some assurances about the communication within his own domain.

> **Note**
>
> The performance levels assured for public Internet communication are essentially identical for all the customers on a best-effort IP network. On the other hand, the performance levels assured for interconnecting customer sites may vary from customer to customer.
>
> Another scenario in which SLAs play a role is in extranet relationships. That is, a performance level may be assured for communication between two customers of the same ISP that have an extranet between them. These differentiated service scenarios could potentially be extended to multiple ISPs, but would require bilateral SLAs between one ISP and another, further complicating the management of end-to-end SLAs.

The service levels of the network are defined by the performance of the network between a pair of access routers in the network. The metrics for performance include the delay and loss rate between a pair of access routers, as well as the maximum amount of throughput a customer can get across an ISP network. For the dial-in access points, the assurances about call blocking at the dial-in server should also be included.

In addition to assurances about the basic service provided to all its customers, some ISPs may want to offer different SLAs to different customers. Business customers may be offered a premium access with better promises on communication quality of service at a higher cost than residential customers.

1.2.2 Support of SLAs in a Network

The support of SLAs in a computer network, as in any other context, requires the following steps:

1. Identify the type of customer and associated service level.

2. Monitor network performance.

3. Issue SLA reports, possibly including periodic meetings with the customers to discuss the status of SLA compliance.

4. Revise system configuration and operations, including taking steps to augment bandwidth on specific links, if necessary, to maintain agreed-to service levels (this is called service provisioning).

5. Revise service level agreement.

Different SLAs may have been provided to different customers. The network operator needs to identify the type of packets coming into the network so that they can be dealt with the appropriate degree of urgency.

> **Note**
>
> Identification of packets with different urgency is not always necessary. If the network is designed to meet the most stringent SLAs, all packets can be treated identically. However, this works only if requirements of different SLAs are similar.

After the SLA has been agreed upon, the network operator needs to monitor the performance of the network. The SLA determines which network performance metrics ought to be monitored, as well as the operating ranges of the performance metrics. Some of the monitoring tools and techniques that can be used in computer networks are described in subsequent chapters of this book.

The creation and filing of periodic reports is an important step in the process of supporting SLAs. The reports on monitored performance must be available for examination by the customer. A side benefit of storing reports is that the historical information can be used to extrapolate trends in network traffic and thus be used as input to the service-provisioning process.

If monitoring indicates that all the SLAs are being satisfied, there is cause for rejoicing. However, you may want to check whether it is possible to satisfy the same SLA constraints with possibly a cheaper or a simpler configuration. If so, the operational constraints of the network might need to be changed. A worst case scenario would be when the SLA objectives are not being met. In this case, the network configuration must be changed, through the service-provisioning process, so that the objectives can be successfully met. Service provisioning is discussed in more detail in Chapter 3, "Network Design and SLA Support."

As the last step in the customization process, you must examine whether the agreed-to SLAs can be satisfied. If experience shows that the SLAs cannot be met, you may want to revise the performance objectives to ones that are feasible to meet. You can also revise SLA objectives to become more stringent, if that is likely to attract new customers and new streams of revenue.

The big differentiator in SLA support in networks from other fields such as help desks or facilities management is that the bulk of the SLA operations in a computer network can be automated. The goal of this book is to define how such an automated process to monitor and track SLAs can be developed in an IP network.

1.3   Further Information

From a business processes perspective, SLAs are a relatively mature topic. You can find detailed business-oriented discussion on different aspects of SLAs and the use of SLAs in different industries in the books by Hiles [HILES1] [HILES2] (information technology), LaBounty [LABOUNTY] (information technology), Brill [BRILL] (facilities management), and Hallows [HALLOWS] (computing and telecommunication). Chorleywood Consulting has published a comprehensive manual of SLAs [CHORLEY] focused on the telecommunication industry.

Discussions on SLAs and their applicability to networks can also be found in articles such as [CHATTERTON], [MERSED], and [WALDER]. Courses on defining SLAs are available from several training organizations.

1.4   Endnotes

[BRILL] Brill, Kenneth G. "Facility Infrastructure Service Level Agreements: Case Studies." Brookfield, CT: Rosenthein Associates. Publication number DR-127, 1992.

[CHATTERTON] Chatterton, Ruth and Rebecca Wetzel. "Service Level Agreements Key Feature for ISPs." *Interactive Week*, May 4, 1998. Also available at
`http://www.zdnet.com/intweek/print/980504/313656.html`.

[CHORLEY] Chorleywood Consulting Ltd. *The Manual of Service Level Agreements*, April 1998. Available at `http://www.chorleywood.com/manuals/ccb/sla/sla.htm`.

[HALLOWS] Hallows, Richard T. *Service Management in Computing and Telecommunications.* Boston: Artech House, 1995.

[HILES1] Hiles, Andrew. *The Complete Guide to I.T. Service Level Agreements: Matching Service Quality to Business Needs.* Oxford, UK: Elsevier Advanced Technology, 1991.

[HILES2] ———. *Service Level Agreements: Measuring Cost and Quality in Service Relationships.* London; New York: Chapman & Hall, 1993.

[IGSSLA] "Service Level Agreements Announced for IP Remote Access Dial to the IBM Global Network." Press Announcement April 21, 1998; available at `http://www.ibm.com/globalnetwork/p210498c.htm`.

[LABOUNTY] LaBounty, Char. *How to Establish and Maintain Service Level Agreements.* Help Desk Institute Bookstore, Publication Number PF09.

[MERSED] Mersed, Bobby. "Service Level Agreements." *Quality Times Newsletter*, June 1996. Also available at `http://199.240.192.40/quality/QualityTimes/June96ServiceLevel.htm`.

[UKERNASLA] UK Education and Research Network Service Level Agreements, at `http://www.jisc-tau.ac.uk/sla98-99/intro.html`.

[UUNETSLA] UUNET Service Level Agreement, available at `http://www.uu.net/lang.en/customers/sla/terms`.

[WALDER] Walder, Bob. "Service Level Agreements." *Connections Newsletter from the NSS Group*, March 1998. Also available at `http://www.nss.brand.co.uk/March98.htm`.

CHAPTER 2

IP Networks and SLAs

An SLA is used in an IP network to make assurances about the performance and availability of the network to a customer organization. Although the network performance (including reliability and availability) is the only factor that the network operator can control, the customer may often be looking for a slightly different aspect of performance—namely, the performance (reliability and availability) of the application that is running over the network. SLAs can be specified in terms of application performance or in terms of the performance of the network.

Even when network performance is the only target, some control of application performance is required. The proper operation on an IP network requires supporting several applications, such as the domain name service. Without adequate performance and reliability assurances regarding these applications, network performance is hard to control.

Note

The *domain name service* is an application used to translate human-readable machine names into 32-bit numeric addresses..

In this chapter, we discuss the different aspects of network performance that may be covered in an SLA. We also examine the requirements of an SLA in a corporate intranet and for transport of Voice over IP (VoIP) networks. We also look at some sample SLAs offered in companies in the I/T industry.

2.1 SLA Performance Specifications

SLA performance may be specified in terms of application-level performance or in terms of network-level performance. Depending on the nature of an organization, one or the other of these SLA performance specifications is more appropriate.

Application-level SLAs are much closer to customer requirements than a network-level SLA. However, a network provider who does not have control over the end hosts cannot provide application-level SLAs and can provide SLAs only at the network level. Operators of an enterprise I/T department that controls both the enterprise network and the enterprise servers are capable of providing application-level SLAs.

Figure 2.1 shows a simplified model of a corporate intranet. The corporate intranet shown consists of three components: a client network, a core network, and a server network. Each component can potentially be administered and operated by a different organization. The client network consists of different user workstations, personal computers, and the local area networks interconnecting them. The server network consists of the mainframes, databases, other application servers, and the networking infrastructure interconnecting them. The core network interconnects the client network and the server network. Note that routers may be present within all three types of networks, as well as at the borders between these networks.

Although the I/T department, in the case of an enterprise network, is responsible for the operation of all three components, it may choose to outsource the operation of individual components to other organizations. The I/T department has to provide application-level SLAs to its customers, which it needs to build up from network-level SLAs that are provided to it by the organizations administering the different components of the network. The operator of one of the components (that is, the core network operator) will not be able to provide application-level SLAs to its customers and can provide only network-level SLAs.

Figure 2.1   Simplified model of an I/T network.

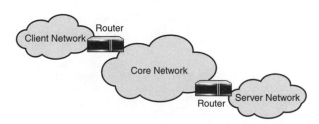

In a real corporate network, the organization would be much more complex than the model shown in Figure 2.1. However, the observations regarding application-level SLAs and network-level SLAs still hold true.

At both the network layer and the application layer, the two most important aspects of performance in an SLA are availability and responsiveness. *Availability* refers to the percentage of time that the application or the network is available and usable by the customer. *Response time* is a measure of the latency that is considered acceptable by the customer.

2.1.1 *Application-Level SLAs*

An application-level SLA specifies performance requirements in terms of a specific application. Examples of such performance specifications may include statements such as the following:

- The database server will have a response time of less than 100ms with a maximum load of 100 clients.

- The time to download a file of less than 1MB will be less than 5 seconds.

- The server will be available 99% of the time during normal business hours and 97% of the time during other hours.

In a corporate I/T department responsible for the networking and the computing infrastructure of the organization, application-level SLAs come closest to the performance requirements of computer users. The application-level SLA specifies the performance in terms of application units that the user cares about (for example, the time it takes for a transaction to complete or the time it takes to obtain a specific response from the system).

The performance limits specified in an application-level SLA are dependent on the number of concurrent application clients, as well as on the capacity of the application servers and the capacity of the network that connects the clients with the application server. The number of concurrent application clients can be specified in the SLA. When the I/T department is also responsible for all the client workstations in the organization, the number of concurrent application clients can be forecast, based on the expected level of business activity and the number of workstations budgeted to handle that activity.

Case Study: IBM Site I/T Department

International Business Machines (IBM) is a global company and one of the leading manufacturers of computer hardware and software, with offices, software development laboratories, and manufacturing units in several countries. A typical software development site in California has a large I/T infrastructure comprising mainframes, AIX workstations, OS/2 servers, and PCs running various versions of Windows. The site has more than 50 LAN segments and a complex network infrastructure comprising SNA (Systems Network Architecture), as well as TCP/IP networks. A variety of servers and applications are supported by the I/T department, including database servers, workstation and PC backup servers, code servers, network license servers, news servers, and remote-access gateways.

The site's computing facilities have been outsourced to another division of IBM, which operates and supports the site's network, workstations, and servers. An SLA put into place by the I/T department in May 1996 defined the performance expectations of the various servers, applications, and the network. Different performance goals are specified for different applications and servers. A typical performance objective for applications running on a mainframe is described next.

Availability

Monthly total availability is determined by dividing total minutes available by total minutes scheduled for the month. *Monthly prime availability* is determined by dividing total prime minutes available by total prime minutes scheduled for the month. Prime hours are from 8 a.m. to 6 p.m. Pacific time, Monday through Friday. Total hours are 24 hours per day, 7 days per week, less the maintenance window scheduled for each system. The availability objective for each system is 99.0% for prime time and 97.0% for total time.

Response Time

The I/T department has determined the following quantitative objectives on the basis of the current and planned capacity of the networks and performance measurements of the host server:

- 90% of all local transactions will be less than or equal to a total time of 1 second (.5 seconds for the host and .5 seconds for the network).

- 90% of all remote transactions within the United States will be less than or equal to a total time of 2.5 seconds (.5 seconds for the host and 2 seconds for the network).

The I/T department continuously monitors the performance of the server and the transaction response time to ensure that the SLA targets are being met. Monthly reports are generated using network management tools to validate compliance with the SLA specifications.

2.1.2 Network-Level SLAs

A network-level SLA specifies its objectives in terms of network performance between one or more exchange points on its network, as described in Chapter 1, "Service Level Agreements Overview." An application-level view of response time is difficult to provide in such a case because the servers may not be in the administrative domain of the network operator. SLA specifications are then described in terms of the delays or loss rates on logical tunnels between the exchange points.

As shown in Figure 2.2, a network-level SLA may specify network performance using one of the following three approaches:

- *The tunnel approach*: Network-level performance is specified for two specific exchange points on the network. Performance is specified for all traffic that enters the network through one of the exchange points and that exits through another. The specification of the ingress and egress exchange points specifies a logical tunnel for network communication across the provider's network. For example, an SLA may state that all traffic between a California site and a New York site will experience a delay of no more than 0.5 seconds.

- *The funnel approach*: Network-level performance is specified from the view of one exchange point only. Performance is specified for all traffic that enters the network at one of the exchange points. Packets entering the ingress exchange point may then spread through the network, exiting through any of the other exit points. The traffic distribution forms a funnel shape with the stem of the funnel at the specified exchange point. For example, an SLA may state that network delays between the California site and any other site within the U.S. will be no more than 2.0 seconds.

- *The cloud approach*: Network-level performance is specified in a uniform manner across all the exchange points. The limits on network reliability and responsiveness apply to traffic that may enter at any exchange point and leave at any other exchange point. For performance purposes, the entire network is an opaque cloud with a bound on the worst-case performance. For example, an SLA may state that network delays between any two exchange points within the U.S. will be no more than 85ms.

Among the three approaches, the tunnel approach is the easiest one to support in a network, but the hardest one to specify. When the traffic load and performance limits on each of the tunnels is known, network design can be optimized to meet the SLA requirements. However, specifying the characteristics on all the possible tunnels is a daunting task for a network of any moderate size. The funnel approach is the one that is often used when SLAs are offered to a specific site. The example taken is from an actual SLA offered to an IBM site by its I/T department. Network providers such as UUNET have taken the cloud approach to SLA performance specification.

Figure 2.2   Different types of SLAs in a network.

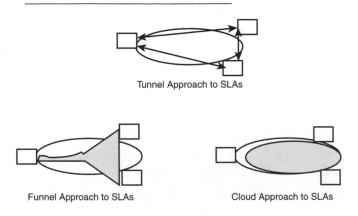

Tunnel Approach to SLAs

Funnel Approach to SLAs

Cloud Approach to SLAs

Case Study: UUNET

Formed in 1987, UUNET Technologies, Inc., was the first commercial Internet service provider in the world. In 1996 it was acquired by MCI WorldCom, and since then it has expanded to become one of the largest ISPs in the world, with more than 1,000 POPs worldwide. It offers a wide variety of services, including dial-up access, high-speed leased access, Internet fax, and audio/video multicasting. In August 1998, UUNET announced one of the first public SLAs for its network connectivity to customers who purchase leased-line services for Internet connectivity.

As of this writing, UUNET's SLA guarantees its customers four elements:

- 100% availability of UUNET backbone and customer access circuit, with credits offered to customers for the time that the network is unavailable

- Average monthly latency of no more than 85ms roundtrip within UUNET's backbone in the contiguous U.S. or the European sections of the network, and of no more than 120ms on the transatlantic link between New York and UUNET's international gateway hub in London

> **Note**
>
> Are you surprised by the low bound on network delays specified in the UUNET SLA (85ms) compared to the bound in the IBM site SLA (0.5 seconds)? The UUNET bound is a monthly *average* across several sites, whereas the IBM SLA specifies a strict upper bound on the *maximum* network delay for a transaction.

- Proactive outage notification that guarantees customer notification by UUNET operations within 15 minutes of an outage

- An upper limit on the installation date, which will be not more than 40 business days for Frame Relay, 56Kbps, and T-1 customers, and 60 business days for T-3 customers in the U.S.

UUNET collects latency statistics via the Network Time Protocol (NTP). Data is collected from designated routers in 15-minute intervals. A monthly latency value is derived from averaging all the 15-minute samples in the previous month. A description of the UUNET SLA can be found on the Web at http://www.uu.net/lang.en/customers/sla/terms.

> **Note**
>
> *NTP* is a protocol designed to synchronize clocks of computers connected to the Internet. In addition to its main function, it can also be used to measure delays in the network. Details of how this delay measurement can be done are provided in Chapter 7, "Network Monitoring and SLA Verification."

2.2 SLA Performance Metrics

In the context of both application-level SLAs as well as network-level SLAs, the two main performance aspects covered in an SLA are system availability and responsiveness. The case studies of UUNET and the California site illustrate some of the performance metrics that are specified and measured in an SLA.

In the following sections, we discuss some other metrics that are commonly used in existing SLAs. We also give a brief description of how these performance metrics can be measured in an IP network. The description of monitoring techniques in this chapter provides a short overview of the techniques. A more detailed discussion of network monitoring techniques is provided in Chapter 7.

2.2.1 Availability Metrics

Several metrics can be defined to measure service availability in an IP network. Some of the most common metrics include the system uptime, network connectivity, outage count, outage resolution time, error rates, and packet loss rates within the network.

System Uptime

A system's availability is measured by the number of minutes it is available and accessible to the customer. The system uptime can be measured by monitoring the server by using a specific server-monitoring program. A common way to measure the availability of servers has been to use a program that pings the server periodically and monitors the number of lost packets.

Note

ping is a program available on almost every platform. It sends an ICMP echo request to the destination system and measures the response time to obtain an echo reply. The advantages and limitations of using ping for network monitoring are discussed further in Chapter 7.

An alternative approach is to analyze system logs to determine whether the system was available and operational. Most servers log the time they were booted up and shut down. These logs can be analyzed to determine the amount of time that a server was unavailable. Some tools to analyze these logs are available from platform vendors, and other tools need to be developed by the server administrator.

Measuring server unavailability by pinging or analyzing system logs is not a very accurate measure of application availability, for the following reasons:

- Some applications may be unavailable even if the system is nominally up and responding to pings.

- The application may be supported by multiple servers, with load balancing among the servers.

Probing mechanisms can be developed for specific applications to measure the availability of specific application servers. Passive measurement tools can also be developed to analyze the packets going to and from the server and to determine whether an application is operational by analyzing these packet traces.

The measurement of uptime is most appropriate for an application-level SLA.

Network Connectivity

Network connectivity measures the percentage of time when one exchange point on the network is reachable from another exchange point, or a POP. In the context of network-level SLAs, connectivity is the analog of uptime for application-level SLAs. A common method to measure network connectivity is to send ping packets from one site in the network to another, to ensure that the packets are not getting lost in the network.

Outage Count

Outages in network connectivity can also be monitored and detected using network management tools. IP routers are usually configured to send an alert to a network management tool when an interface or an adapter becomes inoperable. A log of these alerts can be monitored to determine the outages in the network and to determine whether connectivity has been lost between two points in the network.

Network outages can be classified into two categories:

- Ones whose effects would be perceived by the customer as a disruption in the service

- Ones whose effects would not be perceived by the customer, or that would be perceived only as a temporary glitch or as reduced performance by the network

A network link failure in an IP network can be worked around by most IP routing protocols in a relatively short amount of time. From an SLA perspective, only outages whose effects would be perceived by a user should be counted. The outage of a network node or a network link that constitutes the only connection between two segments of the network would definitely be perceived by the customer. Proper network design can identify such elements in the network.

Outage Resolution Time

A common performance metric used in SLAs deals with limits on how soon network problems are resolved. The time between the resolution of the problem is within a small number of days (or hours) after the problem is reported to the provider, either by a customer or by automated network monitoring tools. Some of the outages could be automatically corrected, (for example, routing around minor network failures, such as a single failed link). In these cases, network routing protocols would automatically reroute traffic to new routers, and service will continue (perhaps with a slightly increased delay) to the customer.

Other types of outages may require other courses of action, such as bringing up a back-up link to replace a failed link or borrowing capacity from other service providers.

Outage-resolution time can be specified for application-level SLAs as well as network-level SLAs. The management of this aspect of network/server performance is more dependent on proper procedures followed in the network department. Nevertheless, quick problem resolution is an important aspect in customer satisfaction, and steps must be taken to conform within the limits specified by the SLA.

Error Rate

An error in the network or an application server may be measured in several ways. Some of the common methods to measure errors in systems include

- Measuring the number of failed transactions in the network in a given interval of time

- Measuring the number of packets dropped in the network in a given interval of time

- Measuring the number of packets corrupted in the network in a given interval of time

The number of packets that are dropped because of network buffer overflows and corruption are recorded by the network routers as part of the standard Management Information Base (MIB) definition. They can be collected and analyzed by most network management tools.

Note

Different network elements collect and store performance and configuration information in structures known as *Management Information Bases (MIBs)*. Information in the MIBs can be collected by a network management tool using the Simple Network Management Protocol (SNMP).

The measurement of failed TCP connections or transactions is an end-to-end performance metric that is not collected as part of standard MIB definitions. However, they can be collected using a packet sniffer that can log the packets flowing through the network. By analyzing the packet traces collected in this fashion at exchange points or POPs, the number of aborted TCP connections or specific application flows can be identified.

Error rates can be used in the context of network-level SLAs as well as application-level SLAs.

Packet Loss Rate

The packet loss rate in the network can be measured as the fraction of packets that fail to reach their destinations. A local count of lost or corrupted packets is maintained at each IP router. However, this information does not indicate the packet loss rate on individual tunnels.

When SLAs are specified using the tunnel approach, the customer is primarily interested in the loss rates between two specific exchange points. The number of lost packets can be measured by pinging the specific destinations at random intervals and collecting statistics about lost packets. More advanced network monitoring tools using active probes can also be used for this purpose; they are described in Chapter 7.

Packet loss rates are most appropriate for network-level SLAs.

2.2.2 Responsiveness Metrics

Some of the common metrics used to measure responsiveness of the network include the application response time, one-way or roundtrip delays, and the delay jitter in the network.

Response Time

The *response time* is a metric commonly used in measuring application performance. The response time is the interval perceived by the user of the system to complete a command given to the computer. It is also the time the user typically needs to wait before issuing the next command to the system.

Most user interactions with a computer system can be identified as a request-response transaction. The user requests a specific file to be transferred between two sites and has to wait until the system responds with a message that the transfer has been executed. The user requests the download of a specific page from the Web and has to wait until the system has displayed that page. A clerk swipes a credit card at a checkout line and has to wait until the back-end server has verified the credit of the customer. In all these transactions, a specific request-response exchange is needed.

> **Note**
>
> This characterization of all applications as request-response is perhaps an oversimplification. However, a large number of applications can be put into this category, and this serves to illustrate the importance of the response time as a performance metric. This metric is also extremely important to commercial use of the Internet.

In an ideal world, response time would be measured as a regular and standard feature by all the applications. Unfortunately, most of the popular IP applications (for example, file transfer, Telnet, Web browsers) neglect to do so. Some applications that have focused on the business world do monitor response time (for example, tn3270 implementations can keep track of response time for user requests).

Note

tn3270 is a program used to gain access to SNA applications hosted on mainframes over an IP network. It emulates an IBM 3270 terminal. The tn3270 program sends and receives a screenful of information (or changes to current screen information) at a time.

Given the lack of consistency in measuring application response time, the I/T administrator may resort to analyzing packet traces to measure the application response time. A packet analyzer that is capable of understanding the application format would be able to determine the response time of various applications.

One-Way Delay

If the administrative authority of an organization covers only part of the network between the client and the server, response times of applications cannot be assured. However, analogs of response time could be measured in terms of one-way delays and roundtrip latency of the network.

The one-way delay of the network can be measured between any two pairs of exchange points (using the tunnel approach), between one specified exchange point and any other exchange point (using the funnel approach), or as a bound on the one-way delay between any pair of exchange points (using the cloud approach).

One of the challenges in using one-way delay between the different machines in the network is that the clocks between the different routers are relatively poorly synchronized. One network operator has worked around this problem by putting in clocks synchronized by satellite signals and measuring the one-way delays accurately.

Case Study: ANS and the Surveyor Project

Advanced Network and Services (ANS), Inc., was formed in September 1990 by a group of network researchers who were interested in the deployment and development of the Internet infrastructure. The company was responsible for operating and maintaining the core Internet. It was acquired by America Online in 1994. People at ANS have been participating in different aspects of IP network performance measurements through the IPPM (Internet Protocol Performance Metrics) working group at IETF. ANS is also the company responsible for the deployment and support of the next-generation Internet, the so called Internet-2 project.

As an effort to measure the performance of the global Internet, ANS has played a key role in measuring the performance of the network in the context of its Surveyor project. The Surveyor project was initiated in June 1997 with three measurement points, but it had grown by the end of 1998 to 38 nodes at different university sites throughout the continental United States. Each of the surveyor nodes sends two probe packets every second to other surveyor nodes. The probe packets contain the time when the packet was created. The receiving surveyor node can compute the one-way delays in the network and the loss rates experienced by the probe packets. All the surveyor nodes are synchronized using GPS signals and permit accurate measurement of one-way delays. Network performance metrics are collected and represented as described in the guidelines of the IETF IPPM Working Group [IPPM].

Note

GPS, or *Global Positioning System*, is a method to precisely determine the location of an object using signals from multiple satellites. By combining the exact location of a router, timing signals from satellites can be adjusted accurately for propagation delays, and very precise synchronized times can be maintained.

Although the Surveyor project is relatively academic in nature, it offers a technique to measure SLAs in IP networks that can be deployed by an ISP. It is also one of the first uses of GPS signals to synchronize network clocks.

Roundtrip Latency

An approach to work around the clock synchronization issue is to measure roundtrip delays in the network between network access points. Like the one-way delay, the roundtrip delays can be measured between any two pairs of exchange points (using the tunnel approach), between one specified exchange point and any other exchange point (using the funnel approach), or as a bound on the one-way delay between any pair of exchange points (using the cloud approach).

One problem with the measurement of roundtrip time is that the forward paths followed by packets in the network between two points are not necessarily the same as the reverse paths between the same points. Studies conducted over the Internet have shown that about 40% of the reverse paths in the network follow a different route than the forward path.

Delay Jitter

Whereas delays and roundtrip times measure how much time a packet spends in the network, *delay jitter* measures what the variation in the time spent in the network could be. For many applications, the delay jitter is a more important aspect of network performance than the actual delay. For example, applications that retrieve and play stored audio/video clips from the network allocate buffers to smooth out the delay jitter in the network and are more sensitive to delay jitter than the actual delay in the network.

Delay jitter can be measured for one-way delays or for roundtrip latencies. The issues and comments related to delay measurements also apply to the measurements of delay jitter.

Allowable Bandwidth

Some SLAs offered by network providers allow customers to inject a specific amount of data into their network with an assured delay and loss characteristic. Sometimes, the SLA simply allows the sender to send up to a specified amount of traffic into the network with a guarantee that it will not be lost at the access router, as long as the agreed-upon source traffic amount is not exceeded. Bandwidth may be specified using either the tunnel or the funnel approach.

One common technique employed among many network service providers is to connect the client using a network whose physical capacity matches the bandwidth allowed in the SLA. The characteristics of the physical link ensure automatic compliance with the terms of the SLA.

2.3   SLA Requirement Examples

Having explored the different types of performance metrics that can be specified for a network, let us explore the types of performance specifications that would be desired by the customers of an IP network. We consider two types of customers and their expectations from the IP networks:

- The customers who are migrating their legacy SNA networks to an IP backbone

- The customers who want to provide voice services over IP networks

For both types of customers, we start with the overview of the related technologies and then outline the requirements that must be satisfied for these networks to operate over an IP backbone.

2.3.1 *SLA Requirements in SNA Over IP Environments*

Corporate intranets are internal networks that are used to interconnect different sites in large enterprises. The structure of a corporate intranet usually consists of several campus networks connected by a core network made up of relatively lower-speed links. The primary aim of the corporate intranet is to facilitate the deployment of business applications to different sites of the corporation.

The predominant applications in corporate networks tend to be business applications that run on mainframes. These applications may target functions such as corporate work flow management, transaction processing, data warehousing, or payroll. Historically, mainframe applications have been developed to run on SNA.

Evolution of Corporate Intranets

In the late 1970s, corporate networks largely consisted of mainframes connected by an SNA network. The SNA architecture tends to be relatively static, and it permitted easy capacity planning, support for four different qualities of service, and support of SLAs within the business units. As IP networks evolved and became more ubiquitous, corporations were faced with the prospect of running two parallel core networks: one for SNA and the other for IP connectivity. Because the dominant factor in the cost of running a network is the expense of leasing bandwidth, the solution was relatively expensive. As shown previously in Chapter 1, Figure 2.3 illustrates the typical enterprise network in the mixed SNA and IP mode.

Figure 2.3   Parallel IP and SNA backbones in enterprise networks.

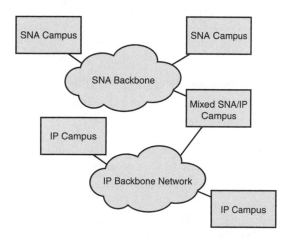

Note

SNA, or Systems Network Architecture, is a network architecture developed by IBM in the mid 1970s. It defines a layered architecture that can connect a wide range of equipment—from dumb terminals to mainframes—into a hierarchical network structure.

In the early 1990s, techniques to encapsulate and deliver SNA traffic over IP were developed. These techniques, such as *Data Link Switching*, or *DLSw* [DLSWREF], allowed the corporate intranet operators to run a single core IP network and leverage the better price-to-performance ratio of IP routers and gateways. However, the gains in cost were associated with some losses in terms of capacity planning and SLA support [JANDER]. Figure 2.4 illustrates the typical enterprise network when using SNA encapsulated in IP.

Figure 2.4   SNA over IP in enterprise intranets.

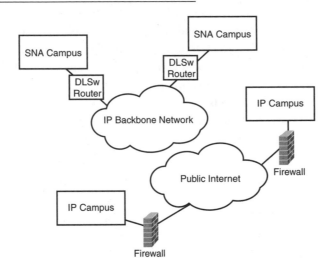

A recent trend has been to eliminate the need for an IP intranet as well, and replace it with a Virtual Private Network (VPN) offered by an ISP. The savings in cost from such a service would be immense for any large customer.

Such a configuration is shown in Figure 2.5. Two main issues that need to be resolved before the configuration shown in the figure becomes widespread are security and QoS. VPN services based on IPsec and SSL protocols offer solutions in the security domain. QoS issues can be addressed to some extent by using SLAs in the ISP network. Deployment of SLA and security support in ISP networks would promote the replacement of private networks using VPNs.

Figure 2.5   A virtual private IP intranet using the Internet.

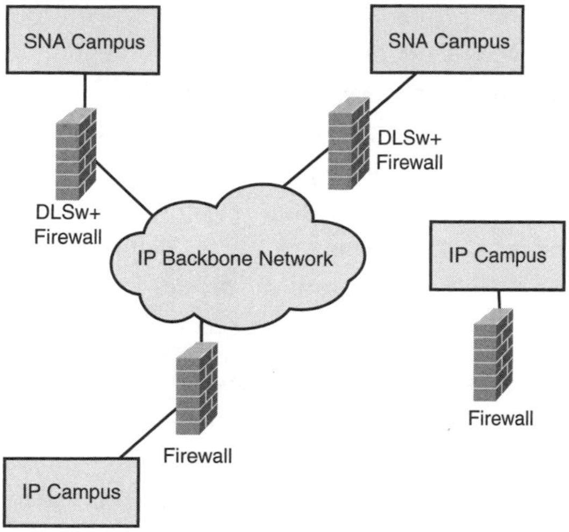

SLA Support in SNA Networks

Several features within SNA networks are helpful to the network operator for the purpose of defining SLAs:

- *Static configuration*: The most commonly deployed sub-area SNA follows a relatively static configuration in how packets flow through the network. The routes of end-to-end connections are statically defined by means of configuration files. As a result, the capacity requirements on each link in the network are known, and determining whether SLAs are being satisfied or whether a network upgrade is needed is straight-forward. SNA also permits distributing the traffic between two nodes among several alternate paths, which exploits the capacity available in the network.

- *Limited Traffic Types:* SNA networks tend to be used only for commercially significant traffic. That is, they tend to be used to support applications such as transaction processing (that is, order entry, inventory, accounting, payroll, data center backup, printing, and so on). SNA networks tend not to be used for applications such as casual Web browsing or games. Because the traffic capacity requirements of the commercially significant applications are tied to the level of business activity, enterprises can do a fairly accurate job of forecasting required SNA network capacity. IP networks, on the other hand, are used for a larger range of application types, many of which generate traffic levels that are not directly tied to the level of commercial business activity. SNA networks thus tend to be less volatile, and thus present a less difficult capacity-forecasting problem when compared to IP networks.

- *Classes of Service (CoSes)*: All flavors of SNA permit four levels of transmission priorities in the network (Network, High, Medium, Low). Transmission priority is used to determine the queuing priority for the given session on the given path that is chosen. SNA configuration allows the network operator to define multiple CoSes using the Network transmission priority. A CoS defines performance limits such as throughput, delay bounds, security requirements, bounds on reconnect time after network failures, network transmission priority, and so on for a session using the specific CoS. Most products ship with an "architected" set of a dozen or so preconfigured CoSes and allow customers to modify them as well as define their own customer CoSes. Within the network, CoS is used to select the session path that matches the application's needs (low delay, high throughput, secure links only, and so on).

- *Rate control and pacing*: SNA builds in network rate control at several layers in its protocol stack, limiting the rates at which data can be transmitted to specific upper limits. This avoids network congestion and results in a more predictable performance of the network. TCP, in contrast, attempts to maximize the utilization of the network by trying to send packets until it begins to detect losses in the network. As a result, the performance of TCP tends to be more erratic compared to SNA.

- *Response-time monitoring*: SNA includes hooks for the network and the application to continuously monitor its own performance. Thus, SNA applications can continuously monitor their response time; for example, a transaction server can log the response time for each transaction. It is easy to monitor these logs and to identify when service levels have become unacceptable.

- *Reliability features*: Dynamic flavors of SNA (that is, APPN and HPR) allow a nondisruptive path switch, which routes around network failures. Higher-layer protocols in SNA permit restart of applications after an end-host failure, allowing active sessions to be resumed after the end host restarts or its functions are switched over to a standby host. These features improve the reliability and availability of the SNA network. In comparison, IP probably does a better job at routing around network failures using its routing protocols and built-in connectionless architecture. However, it is difficult for sessions to persist after the failure of an end-station.

Note

Three flavors of SNA architecture exist. The most common deployment is *sub-area SNA*, which is statically configured, assumes a hierarchical relationship among different network elements, and requires reliability at the link level. A more dynamic version, called *APPN (Advanced Peer to Peer Networking)*, permits a peer-to-peer relationship like TCP/IP, but still requires reliability at the link level. A flavor of APPN called *HPR (High Performance Routing)* permits unreliable links, building end-to-end reliability in the same manner that TCP does over unreliable IP networks.

Management of SNA is typically done using IBM *NetView*, a series of programs that takes diagnostic data from subsystems running on the mainframe operating system. NetView contains its own response-time monitor and network configuration tools, as well as automation capabilities for fixing problems as they occur.

User SLA requirements in terms of SLA can be used to define network topography and to compute the host capacity, link speeds, aspects of SNA network controllers, and configuration of software on the hosts that would support the desired performance results [RANADE].

2.3.2 SLA Requirements in Voice Networks

Voice is traditionally carried over the telephone system. Since the early 1980s, various researchers have attempted to build an effective method to carry voice (music as well as telephone conversation) over an IP network. In the second half of the 1990s, IP telephony has become a commercial reality, with several companies using IP networks and the Internet to offer a cheaper alternative to telephone networks. Furthermore, the increasing number of audio clips available on the Internet indicates that voice data will form a non-trivial part of Internet traffic.

Audio clips are commonly available from the Web sites of most radio and television stations (www.cnn.com, for example), as well as from sites that sell music CDs and cassettes online and sites that offer music clips of different CDs for preview by Net surfers.

Typical Voice over IP Architecture

The transport of voice data over an IP network may be classified into one of three categories [CLARK]:

- Two POTS users communicating using the IP network as an intermediate link
- One POTS user communicating to a computer user over an IP network
- Two computer users exchanging voice information over an IP network

The three classes are illustrated in Figure 2.6.

Figure 2.6   Three types of voice data over an IP network.

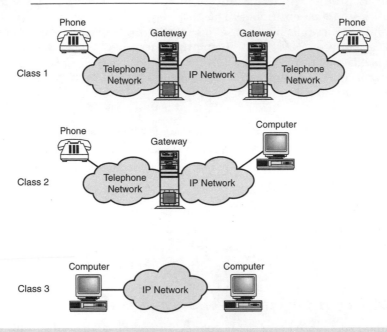

Note

POTS is an acronym for *Plain Old Telephone Service*. A POTS user is one who uses a conventional telephone set at his end for conversation.

When two POTS users communicate using the IP network as an intermediate transport method, each of the users connects to a VoIP gateway. The two VoIP gateways act as bridges between the IP and the telephone network. A user dials into the local gateway using the phone line, waits for a dial tone, and punches the destination telephone number. The gateway determines the voice over IP gateway that would be closest to the destination user, and contacts it. The second gateway calls the destination telephone number using the telephone network. In addition to call setup functions, these gateways perform the necessary voice packetization and depacketization for the purposes of transport over the intermediate IP network.

The second class, in which one user has a POTS connection and the other user has computer equipment, can be viewed as a modified version of the first class, when the second telephone connection has been replaced by an IP network. Instead of a telephone set, the second user has a computer application that allows equivalent functionality. When the computer user initiates the call, he specifies the destination telephone number through his application. When the POTS user initiates the call, he needs to specify the computer user's machine address in a format understood by the gateway.

The third class of voice communication can occur when two or more computer users use an application such as Microsoft NetMeeting to communicate with each other. It also occurs commonly when a Web browser loads a page that contains audio clips. Given the large number of Web sites with audio clips and the ever-growing size of the Internet community, this class of traffic is a nontrivial fraction of the overall voice traffic on the Internet.

SLA Support for Voice over IP

When voice is carried over IP networks, the network has to offer real-time performance. The quality of voice communication degrades significantly if roundtrip delays exceed 300ms.

Note

Human factors studies performed by multiple telephone companies [ITU] reveal that one-way transmission times of greater than 150ms, or more precisely, roundtrip times of greater than 300ms, result in unacceptably degraded human-to-human communication. These latency numbers include any delay in the end systems that sample, compress/decompress, and code/decode the voice communications. The reason delay becomes such an important factor in real-time voice communication lies in the dynamics of human speech patterns and the unspoken rules that we all follow in our daily conversations.

Human speech patterns are characterized by pauses, during which time the speaker unconsciously waits to see if a reaction occurs on the part of the listener. If the speaker hears no reaction during the pause, the speaker often continues the conversation, assuming the listener is waiting to hear more. When greater than 300ms of roundtrip delay is introduced into the conversation, two things happen when a listener tries to "get a word in edgewise." First, by the time the speaker hears the listener's attempted verbal interjection, he or she has often already resumed speaking and unconsciously becomes irritated at the listener's perceived rudeness in trying to interrupt in mid-sentence. Second, the listener unconsciously gets upset at the speaker for his or her perceived rudeness in not responding to the listener's interjection and in talking over the listener's attempt to interject.

continues

The reality of these human factors has very real economic consequences to which many can attest—in particular, those who attempted to make a large-scale commercial success out of two-way voice communications via high-earth-orbit geosynchronous satellites. These same factors apply to real-time voice communications over packet networks, such as VoIP. The acceptable roundtrip time for playback of recorded voice or music is less stringent than for real-time communication between two or more humans; however, delay and delay jitter are still important factors in these applications, as well.

Human factors studies on traditional voice telephony networks show that the delays incurred in communication of voice over an IP network should not exceed a 150ms one-way latency limit. To account for delays in the POTS section of the network, as well as the latency introduced by capturing the voice sample, compressing/coding/packetizing it at the source, and then performing the reverse functions at the receiver, the SLA requirements for VoIP networks are likely to be much more stringent. One advantage that VoIP networks have is that an occasional lost or delayed packet beyond the playout bound can be disguised through clever interpolation at the receiver because the typical real-time voice sample size in each packet is quite small—on the order of 10ms to 30ms.

If you look at the SLAs in the two case studies of this chapter, you discover that both companies are inadequate for supporting voice traffic over an IP network. The maximum bound on delays offered in the IBM site SLA are too large for effective transmission of voice data. On the other hand, the UUNET SLA does not offer an upper bound, but only an average delay—which may or may not be quite acceptable for voice transmission, depending on the distribution of the delays. The same bounds are quite acceptable for most data communication. Thus, the network operator would, in general, need to create two SLAs: one for voice traffic and the other for data traffic.

To support voice traffic, a network operator needs to take the following steps:

- Distinguish the voice packets from data packets at the access router

- Deal with voice packets in a manner different from the treatment offered to data packets so that the desired SLAs are met

The network operator may determine which packets are voice packets by maintaining a list of VoIP gateways and identifying packets originating from or destined to such gateways. However, it is difficult to determine the originating voice packets because of references embedded in Web pages using these mechanisms. The use of traffic filters, as explained in Chapter 4, can help in the differentiation of voice packets from data packets.

To treat the voice packets differently, the network operator may choose one of the following three options:

- Route the voice packets over a different IP network that is specifically designed for this purpose. Thus, voice packets traverse an IP network dedicated to their use. Although this redundancy is relatively expensive, it is the only practical approach feasible in a traditional IP network that does not distinguish among different classes of traffic.

- Use a signaling protocol such as RSVP [RSVP] to signal the establishment of a voice connection, and reserve resources for the call. This approach comes close to the traditional POTS mechanism of establishing a call, and it can work very well for the cases in which the number of voice calls are small. However, if the number of voice calls at a gateway or the network approaches a large number (for example, more than a thousand calls per second), the signaling itself imposes a significant load on the network elements, and SLAs are likely to be violated. RSVP is described in more detail in Chapter 4 of this book.

- Give voice packets a higher transmission priority over normal data packets in the network. This requires marking the voice packets in some manner so that core network routers can identify them and support multiple priorities in the network. A generalization of this approach is found in the differentiated services architecture for the Internet and is further discussed in Chapter 4.

By a judicious use of these techniques, it may be possible to provide SLAs to voice traffic with SLAs that are feasible in IP networks.

2.4 *Further Information*

Several SLAs for network operators and I/T organizations are available on the World Wide Web. The detailed SLA for UUNET is available at http://www.uu.net/lang.en/customers/sla/terms [UUNETSLA]. More information on the Surveyor project and their results can be found at the ANS site on the Web at http://www.advanced.org/surveyor [ANS].

A more detailed discussion of SNA architecture, including its support for SLAs, can be found in the book by Ranade [RANADE]. The relationship between the different flavors of SNA and IP is discussed in books by Matusow [DLSWREF] and Sackett [SACKETT].

An overview of technologies and issues involved in VoIP networks can be found in the books by Goncalves [GONCALVES] and by Minoli [MINOLI].

2.5 Endnotes

[ANS] Advanced Network and Services, Inc. Surveyor Project Home Page, available at `http://www.advanced.org/surveyor`.

[CLARK] Clark, David. "A Taxonomy of Internet Telephony Applications." Paper presented at the Twenty-fifth Annual Telecommunications Policy Research Conference, Alexandria, VA, 27-29 September 1997. Also available at `http://itel.mit.edu:/itel/pubs/ddc.tprc97.pdf`.

[DLSWREF] Matusow, David. *SNA, APPN, HPR & TCP/IP Integration.* New York: McGraw-Hill, 1996, pp. 249-267.

[GONCALVES] Goncalves, Marcus. *Voice Over IP Networks.* New York: McGraw-Hill, 1998.

[IPPM] Internet Protocol Performance Metrics Work Group Charter, available at URL `http://www.ietf.org/html.charters/ippm-charter.html`.

[ITU] ITU-T Recommendation G.114, *One-Way Transmission Time.* March 1993.

[JANDER] Jander, Mary. "SNA and IP: Managing the Mix." *Data Communications Magazine*, July 1998.

[MINOLI] Minoli, Daniel and Emma Minoli. *Delivering Voice Over IP Networks.* New York: John Wiley & Sons, March 1998.

[RANADE] Ranade, Jay and George Sackett. *Introduction to SNA Networking*, 2nd ed. New York: McGraw-Hill, 1994, pp. 266-268.

[RSVP] Braden, B., Ed., et. al., Resource Reservation Protocol (RSVP)—Version 1 Functional Specification, IETF RFC 2205, September 1997.

[UUNETSLA] UUNET, SLA Terms and Conditions. Available at `http://www.uu.net/lang.en/customers/sla/terms`.

[SACKETT] Sackett, George and Nancy Sackett. *Internetworking SNA with Cisco Solutions.* Indianapolis, IN: Macmillan Technical Publishing/Cisco Press, 1999.

CHAPTER 3

Network Design and SLA Support

Network topology is probably the single most important factor determining the performance of a computer network. Finding a good network topology that satisfies the anticipated traffic load on a network is the goal of network design.

Two types of problems must be considered when we look at the interaction between network topology and SLAs. You can start with a network with a known topology and determine the performance and reliability bounds that could be satisfied using the given network. These bounds then provide the parameters that you can offer to customers in an SLA. In these cases, the SLA parameters are derived from the network topology. Alternatively, an ISP may first determine the parameters of the SLA that it wants to support—and then look for a network topology to meet those performance requirements.

Before discussing the approaches to solving these two problems, we need to present an overview of some prerequisite fields. The design of a network draws heavily from concepts in statistics, queuing theory, and graph theory. These prerequisites are described in Section 3.1. After going over the prerequisites, we examine how a network can be modeled as a graph and develop models to determine the delays and losses in the network in Section 3.2. Section 3.3 provides an overview of network design with and without SLA constraints. Section 3.4 describes the use of network design for a typical corporate intranet environment. Finally, Section 3.5 discusses the limits of network design as an approach to support SLAs in networks.

3.1 Prerequisite Information

The three areas related to network design are statistics, graph theory, and queuing theory. This section covers the basics of each of these fields that are necessary to explain aspects of network design.

The only predictable aspect of network performance is its unpredictability. Statistics provide a method to understand the behavior of unpredictable and chaotic metrics such as network delay and loss rates. Queuing theory enables us to predict the performance of a network, making specific assumptions about the nature of traffic at a network router or a link. Finally, graph theory provides a method to correlate the performance and information about all the routers and links that make up a computer network.

3.1.1 Express Tour of Statistics

Statistics is the science of understanding random variables—that is, quantities that do not seem to have a predictable value. A common example of a random variable is the outcome of the toss of a die. A fair die that is thrown will show one of the values between 1 and 6, but you never know which value will show in the next throw. The delays and loss rates in a computer network are similar random variables. Although random variables can be defined in many ways, we are only interested in random variables that take on a numeric value, such as delays measured in milliseconds, losses measured in counts of lost packets, or the number that shows on the face of a die.

Although it is not possible to accurately predict the exact value that a random variable will take, it is possible to understand its behavior in other ways. For a die, we know the bounds on the maximum and minimum value that any throw can show. We know from the physical characteristics of the die that any throw will be between 1 and 6. It is also possible to predict the behavior of the die after a relatively large number of throws and to devise techniques to determine whether a die is indeed fair, or whether its fairness has been compromised in some manner. In a similar manner, use of statistical techniques can enable the network provider or the customer to determine whether their SLA bounds regarding limits on delays or loss rates are being satisfied.

The key concept in understanding a random variable is the concept of probability of an event. An *event* is any outcome of a trial that we are interested in (for example, if the die throw shows 6 or if a packet in the network is delayed less than 85ms). The number of possible events that can occur in any trial may be finite, or even infinite. For an example of an infinite number of events, define the event as the exact distance that a dart lands from the center of a dartboard. An infinite number of events are possible because the number of distances from the center on which the dart can land is infinite.

The *probability* of an event is an estimate of the relative chance that the event will be seen when a sufficiently large number of trials are repeated.

The probability that a fair die will roll a 4, which we denote as p(4), is 1/6. The meaning of this is that if we roll the die a large number of times, say 600,000, we will expect 1/6, or about 100,000, of the trials to produce a 4. The mathematical function that describes the probability that a random variable will take a specific value is known as its *probability distribution function* (or *PDF)* of that variable. The probability of any event is less than 1, with 0 implying that the event is very unlikely to occur, and 1 implying that the event is almost guaranteed to occur.

Associated with the values of a random variable is the concept of the mean, the variance, and the standard deviation. The mean E(X) of a random variable X that can take mutually exclusive values x1, x2, …xn with probabilities p1, p2, …pm is given by

$$\sum_i p_i x_i$$

When the random variable can take a continuous set of values between a lower value of l and an upper value of b (for example, the distance of a dart from the center of the dart-board), the summation is replaced by an integration

$$\int_{x=l}^{x=b} p(x)\,dx$$

where $p(x)$ is the probability that the variable will take the value of x.

The *mean* of the random variable is the value you would expect it to take on average.

The *variance* of a random variable is an estimate of how much the random variable deviates from the mean value. If the mean of a random variable is m, its variance is defined as

$$\sum_i p_i (x_i - m)^2$$

The square root of the variance is called the *standard deviation*. One useful aspect of standard deviation is that it is measured in the same unit as the mean or the random variable, whereas the variance is not. Thus, the standard deviation, mean, and a specific value measured for delay experienced by packets in the network could all be expressed in milliseconds, whereas the variance would be in terms of squares of milliseconds.

For random variables that take continuous values, the summation can be replaced for variance by an integration as was done for the case of the mean.

Two events are called *mutually exclusive* if the occurrence of one implies that the other cannot occur, and vice versa. In the toss of a die, the event that the die shows 1 implies that the die cannot show 2, and vice versa. Mutually exclusive events have a useful relationship in the way their probabilities can be combined. The probability that one of a number of mutually exclusive events can occur is the sum of their probabilities. If the random variable is taking continuous values in a range, rather than discrete values, we could perform a continuous summation (that is, an integration) over the range of values to determine the probability that the outcome is in a specific range.

Suppose that we have defined a set of mutually exclusive events for a trial and that no more events can be defined. One of these mutually exclusive events is guaranteed to occur, so the sum of probabilities of all these mutually exclusive events should be 1.

Two events are called *independent* if the occurrence of one cannot influence the occurrence of other one, and vice versa. When two events are independent, the probability that they will both occur can be determined by multiplying their probabilities together. Let us assume that the probability that a packet is not dropped at the first node along its path is p1, the probability that the packet is not dropped at the second node is p2, and so on. If the dropping of packets at one node is independent of the dropping of packets at the other nodes, then the probability that the packet is not dropped along a path of n nodes is given by

$$p1 \times p2 \times ...pn$$

Suppose a random variable X and another random variable Y are independent, in that the values taken by one have no effect on the values taken by another (and vice versa). A new random variable Z can be defined by adding these two together:

$$Z = X + Y$$

Then, the mean of Z is the sum of the means of X and Y, and the variance of Z is the sum of the variances of X and Y. If the PDFs for X and Y are known, then it is possible to obtain the PDF of Z.

As an example, consider the simultaneous toss of two dice, with X being the outcome of the toss of the first die and Y being the outcome of the toss of the second die. The outcome of the simultaneous toss (Z) is the sum of X and Y. Assuming that the dice are fair, the PDF of X and Y is identical. They can both take a value between 1 and 6, with each outcome having a probability of 1/6. Z can take a value between 2 and 12. The probability that Z would take any specific value can be calculated by enumerating the different values that X and Y will need to take for this to occur. Thus, Z can take the value of 3 if X=1 and Y=2, or if X=2 and Y=1. Both of these have the probability of 1/36, and the probability that Z would take the value of 2 has the probability of 2/36 or 1/18. The PDF for Z is shown in Figure 3.1.

Figure 3.1   Probability distribution function for Z.

v	2	3	4	5	6	7	8	9	10	11	12
p (Z=v)	1/36	2/36	3/36	4/36	5/36	6/36	5/36	4/36	3/36	2/36	1/36

Sometimes we are interested not in the precise value of the random variable, but in the fact that the random variable will be less than a specific limit. This is often the case for network delays, where we want the delay to be less than a specific limit. The probability that a random variable will be less than a specific value is known as its *cumulative distribution function*, or *CDF*.

The cumulative distribution function is used to define the notion of the percentile. If the probability that a random variable takes a value less than a limit L is y/100, then we say that L is the yth percentile value for X. Thus, the delay in the network is less than 10ms with a probability of 0.99 (or 99/100), then 10 ms is the 99th percentile of the delay.

Note

Several excellent books can provide a much more detailed overview of the field, including texts by Ross [ROSS], Freedman [FREED], and Stone [STONE].

3.1.2 Express Tour of Queuing Theory

Queuing theory is the study of the queues that you see forming everywhere in daily life, whether it is the queues at the bank teller's line or the airline ticket counters. A *queue* is an organized sequence of entities that are waiting their turn to receive a service of some type. A queue may have a limit of how many entities can join it, or it may grow without any limits. Within a computer network, queues of packets build up at routers and link adapters waiting for appropriate hardware or software to process them and dispatch them along the right path. Queuing theory provides a way to model and estimate the delays at the routers and links in the computer network. The theory can apply to queues of any type, but we are primarily interested in the queues of packets. A queue is usually represented as shown in Figure 3.2, where the line with squares represents the packets (or other entities) waiting in the queue.

| Figure 3.2 | Representation of a queue. |

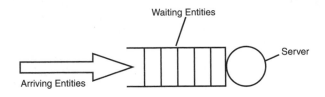

Stochastic Process

A *process* is a description of repeating events that occur in time, often including a description of the times when the events will occur. When the time interval at which the events occur is a random variable, the process is called a *stochastic process.*

> **Note**
> Mathematicians will probably cringe at this hand-waving definition of a stochastic process, but this will suffice for our purpose in the context of this book.

A queuing system (that is, the system containing the queue and the server) is characterized by two stochastic processes, one describing the addition of new packets and the other describing the time spent processing the packets by the servers in the system. In order to model and analyze the behavior of queues, it is often assumed that the time intervals between packet arrivals are independent, identically distributed random variables. The independence assumption implies that the time spent serving one packet in the queue does not influence the time spent serving any other packet in the queue, and the arrival of one packet in the queue does not impact the arrival of any other packets in the queue. The identical distribution assumption implies that the same PDF applies to the inter-packet interval between the first and the second packet, the second and the third packet, and so on between any two consecutive packets. Limitations of the stochastic modeling approach are discussed in a later section of this chapter.

The time spent processing the packets in the queue is also a stochastic process (the service process). If the queue models the behavior of a transmission link, the service time of a packet is the duration needed to transmit it on the link, and it depends on the length of the packet. Some packets require additional processing because they may carry options for special handling, which is another factor contributing to the stochastic nature of the service process.

Poisson Process

The behavior of queues has been analyzed for a variety of arrival and service processes. One queuing system that is easy to analyze consists of a queue in which the arrival and services processes are Poisson processes.

A *Poisson process* consists of independent, identically distributed random variables with the CDF given by

$$Pr(X < x) = 1 - e^{-\lambda x}$$

where λ is the mean rate of the process, and $Pr(X < x)$ represents the probability that the random variable is less than x. The average inter-arrival time between events is $1/\lambda$.

Let us take a closer look at what a Poisson process looks like. The PDF for inter-arrival times for a Poisson process with a mean rate of 1 packet per second is shown in Figure 3.3. The probability is highest around the inter-arrival time of 0, implying that many packets are likely to arrive fairly close together. At the same time, the probability remains a small positive number even for relatively large values of inter-arrival time. This indicates that big gaps could occur between packet arrivals, although the likelihood of a bigger gap is correspondingly smaller.

Figure 3.3   PDF of exponential process.

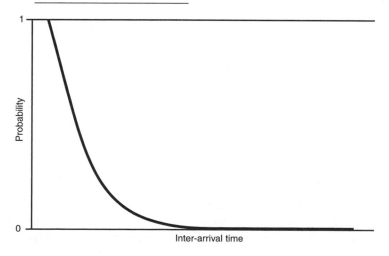

A queue (in which the arrival process is Poisson and the service process is Poisson) is tractable, and its behavior can be expressed in a closed-form mathematical expression. It is conventional to use a Poisson process with a mean rate of λ to model packet arrivals, and to use a Poisson process with a mean rate of μ to model the servicing process of the queue.

Analyzing Queues

In addition to the mean arrival rate and the mean service rate, a queue is characterized by two other significant parameters:

- The number of servers

- The buffer space available at the queue

A queue with multiple servers behaves like the number of clerks at an airline counter. People waiting in the queue can be served by any one of the clerks who become available. The number of people who can wait in the queue may also be limited. This is especially true with packets switches or routers, where each router/switch has only a finite capacity to hold packets still waiting to be forwarded.

It is typical to express the behavior of a queue using a shorthand notation that describes the arrival process, the departure process, the number of servers, and the buffer space at the queue. A queue with Poisson arrivals and departures with a single queue and 50 buffers would be expressed as a M/M/1/50 queue. The M stands for *Markov process*, which (for the purpose of this book) is the same as a Poisson process. When a queue has a large number of buffers so that it can effectively be modeled as having infinite buffers, the last term is dropped, and we can refer to it simply as a M/M/1 queue.

The load on the queue is expressed as the ratio of the mean arrival rate and the mean service rate—that is, λ/μ. It can be shown that the delay of a packet in a M/M/1 queue is characterized by a Poisson process with the mean value of

$$(\lambda - \mu)$$

The average utilization of the M/M/1 queue (or the offered load on the queue) is λ/μ and the average length of the queue is

$$\lambda/(\lambda-\mu)$$

Figure 3.4 illustrates the length of the queue for a M/M/1 queue as a function of the utilization (λ/μ). As the figure shows, the queue lengths are small at low utilizations but start to increase exponentially as the utilization becomes closer to 1. When the arrival rate exceeds the service rate of the queue, the queue length can become excessively large.

Mathematically, the queue length becomes infinite in those conditions, and the system is said to be unstable. In any real queue, the buffer space is finite, so packets will start getting dropped after the queue length exceeds the buffer size.

Figure 3.4   Queue length as a function of the offered load (λ/μ).

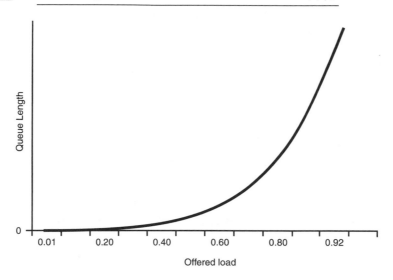

The probability of packet loss in a queue with a fixed size of buffers can also be computed as a *closed form expression*. Figure 3.5 plots how this function would look for a queue with space for 16 buffers (that is, a M/M/1/16 system). At low values of the offered load (for example, when the offered load is less than 70%), the probability of packet loss is fairly small. However, as the load starts increasing and comes close to 1, the packet loss rate becomes very high, coming fairly close to 1.

Figure 3.5   Loss rate as a function of the offered load (λ/μ).

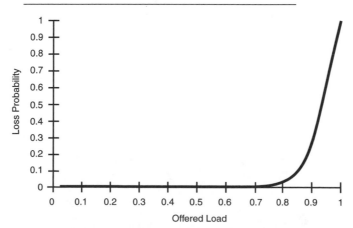

The behavior illustrated by the queue length and losses in Figures 3.4 and 3.5 are typical of many queuing systems. Regardless of the type of arrival process or service process, the average queue length increases exponentially with the utilization of the queue. Similarly, the packet loss rate increases dramatically with the offered load on the network.

One useful property of the M/M/1 queue is that the packets that depart from the queue still form a Poisson process with the rate of λ. This is very useful when we have to study a network of queues in which the packets coming out of one queue are fed into another queue. We can assume that the arrival rate is Poisson with all queues in the network. The Poisson process also has very good summation and distribution properties, which allows us to compute the arrival rate at all the queues. If we combine two packet arrival processes, one that is Poisson with a rate of $\lambda 1$ and one that is Poisson with a rate of $\lambda 2$, then we get a Poisson process with a rate of

$$(\lambda 1 + \lambda 2)$$

Furthermore, if we divide a Poisson process with a mean rate λ into two different processes in a random manner such that any event in the original process has a probability p of being in the first output process, and the second event has a probability q of being in the second output process, then the first output process is Poisson with rate $p\lambda$, and the second process is Poisson with rate $q\lambda$.

Of course, we also have the relationship in which p + q must equal 1.

Note

The randomness property of distribution is really important for dividing the rates. If the packets were divided in a nonrandom manner (for example, by looking at specific fields of the packets), then the Poisson property would not be strictly preserved.

The implication of this behavior is that we can model the distribution of the packets in a network in a convenient manner. Consider a hypothetical ISP that connects the four cities of Albany, Boston, Cambridge, and Dublin. The ISP has a healthy customer base, and the routers at the four sites are somewhat overloaded, resulting in a queuing network as illustrated in Figure 3.6.

Figure 3.6   Queuing model for simple ISP.

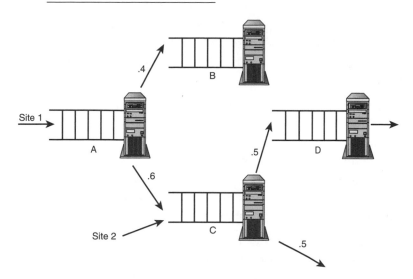

The ISP is hosting a very popular Web site in Albany, which is accessed by customers in the other three cities. The average size of the packets transferred from the server is 384 bytes. Another server is located at Cambridge and is used heavily by the users at Dublin. The Cambridge server generates traffic at the rate of 0.6Mbps. The bulk of the packets in the network originate from Albany at the aggregate rate of 1.2Mbps. Fourty percent of packets from Albany go to Boston, whereas 60% are headed to Cambridge. Of the packets received at the Boston router, 70% are forwarded to local receivers and 30% are forwarded further to the router at Dublin. Of the packets received at the Cambridge router, half are consumed locally, and the rest go to Dublin. The router at all the sites can handle 500 packets per second (or 500pps). Buffer space at the routers is sufficiently large so that the packets are almost never dropped. As consultants to the ISP, we want to determine the delays that would be experienced by the users at the three sites in the network.

Assuming that the arrival process as well as the service process can be modeled as Poisson processes, the router at Albany can be modeled as a M/M/1 queue. With an average rate of 1.2Mbps and an average packet size of 384 bytes, we get an arrival rate of 400pps. Thus, the queue has a λ of 400pps and an μ of 500pps. The average delay at the Albany router would be $1/(\mu-\lambda)$ or 10ms.

How about the routers at Boston and Cambridge? Assuming that packets arriving at the two destinations are randomly distributed, we see that Boston would get packets as a Poisson process with a rate of 160pps, whereas Cambridge would get packets as a Poisson process with a rate of 240pps. The router at Boston would have a λ of 160pps and a μ of 500pps. This results in an average delay of about 3ms using the same calculation that delay equals $1/(\mu-\lambda)$.

The router at Cambridge would have input from two streams: one from Albany, which is Poisson at $\lambda 1$ of 240pps, and the other from the Cambridge Web server, which is Poisson at $\lambda 2$ of 200pps (0.6Mbps at an average packet size of 384 bytes). Using the additive property of Poisson processes, the router at Cambridge receives packets as a Poisson process with λ of 440pps, whereas its μ is 500pps. The resulting average queuing delay is 16ms. The router at Dublin also has an input stream at λ of 440pps and μ of 500pps, resulting in an average queuing delay of 16ms.

By summing up the average queuing delays along the path of the packets between any two sites and the propagation delay along the links connecting them, we can determine the average total delay that would be expected by the users of our ISP at any given site. The propagation delay is determined by the speed of light (or electromagnetic signals) and is approximately 5 microseconds per kilometer of distance. Section 3.2 discusses how to account for propagation delays in a general network.

Of course, modeling the behavior of traffic in a network using Poisson arrival processes and Poisson arrival rates is an oversimplification. Furthermore, the assumption that traffic gets randomly divided among the links is not true in general; the traffic actually gets divided based on the destination of the packets. However, the model does provide a first approximation of the behavior of the network. Other, more sophisticated, models of queues have been studied in the field of queuing theory. These include queues with non-Poisson arrivals, queues with non-Poisson service rates, as well as queues with limited buffer sizes. Although the more sophisticated models come closer to modeling the behavior of the real networks, it is easier to learn the principles of network design using the simpler, closed-form solutions of the M/M/1 queue. After the principles have been understood, it is easy to switch to the better models.

Note

For more details on the queuing theory, refer to the two books authored by Kleinrock [KLEIN1] [KLEIN2], which are considered the authoritative references in the field.

3.1.3 Express Tour of Graph Theory

The third field that we need to understand is the theory of graphs. A *graph* is a mathematical concept that can be used to study the topology of computer networks. A graph consists of two types of entities: a set of nodes and a set of edges. The edges connect pairs of nodes in the graphs. A simple graph is shown in Figure 3.7. It is common practice to name the nodes (or vertices) in the graph for easy reference.

Figure 3.7   A simple graph.

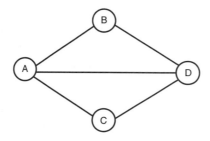

When modeling an IP network, the routers in the network can be modeled as nodes in the graph, and the communication links can be modeled as edges. Each of the nodes or edges in a graph can have attributes; for example, an edge will have the attributes of transmission capacity and the propagation delay, whereas a node may have the attributes of buffer space and processor speed.

The edges in the graph could have an associated direction attribute, which is shown using arrows on the edges. In this case, the graph is said to be *directed*. In other types of graphs, the edges may be bidirectional and have no arrows shown with them. In this case, the graph is said to be *undirected*. An undirected graph can be converted easily into a directed graph by converting each undirected edge into a pair of directed edges in opposite directions between the same pair of nodes. The number of edges that a node has is called the *degree of the node*. When modeling telecommunication links, full-duplex links are often represented by two directed edges.

Note

A node in the graph is also called a *vertex*, and an edge is also called a *link*. We use the terms *node* and *vertex* interchangeably in this book. Similarly, the terms *edge* and *link* are used interchangeably.

A path between two nodes in the graph is a set of nodes that can be traversed to move from one node to the other one; each consecutive pair of nodes along the path must be connected by edges. When multiple edges exist between two nodes in the path, the specific edge has to be specified. A graph is said to be connected if every node in it has a path to another node in the graph. If the graph is not connected, then a maximal connected subset of the edges and nodes of a graph is called a *component* of the graph. Any graph thus consists of a number of connected components.

When using a graph to model the connectivity between two sites, it is more common to choose an undirected graph. It is much simpler to say that an edge connects two sites than to show two directed edges between the two sites. On the other hand, when you analyze the amount of bandwidth available on a link, a network would typically be modeled as a directed graph because the amount of traffic in the two directions of the link may be quite different.

When you can follow a set of edges from a node in a graph and return back to the same node, you get a *cycle* in the graph. A graph without any cycles is an *acyclic graph*. An undirected acyclic graph is called a *tree* (more precisely, an *undirected tree*). If n nodes are in a tree, then the tree has n–1 edges and exactly one path between any two points in the tree. A directed acyclic graph is called a *DAG*. A DAG with a special root node such that there is exactly one path from the root to any other node in the DAG is called a *directed tree*.

In any connected graph, you can find embedded spanning trees that consist of a subset of edges of the graph that connect all the vertices of the graph. When the graph links have associated attributes of weight or cost, you can also find one (or more) spanning trees with the least amount of weight. The weight of a tree is the sum of the weight of all the edges in it. Such a tree is a called a *minimum spanning tree*.

When the links in a graph have weights associated with them, you can find paths between two nodes that have the least weight. This is called a *shortest path* between the two nodes.

Note

For more discussion on graph theory, look up the works of Shimon Even [EVEN]. Other books include those by Wilson [WILSON] and Thulasiraman [THULASI].

3.2 *Determining SLA Performance Bounds in a Network*

Given an operational network (or the design of a proposed network), you can use the concepts of statistics, queuing theory, and graph theory to determine the performance bounds that can be used in the SLAs related to the network's operations. As you may have guessed by now, we will model the network as a graph and consider the queuing behavior at each node in the graph. The queuing behavior at different routers can then be combined to determine the end-to-end delays and loss rates in the network.

You may be wondering about what exactly is being modeled by the queues at each of the nodes. The structure of the queue depends on the type of routers that are installed in the network.

Many low-end and access routers are single-processor routers. These routers have one dedicated processor that obtains packets from the different input interfaces and stores them in the memory of the processor. The processor parses the header, determines on which outgoing interface to place the packets, and gives them to the link hardware for transmission. The link hardware buffers the packets until the outgoing link is available for packet transmission, and then it transmits the packet on the link.

There are two places where queuing occurs in the router described previously:

- One for the processing of the packets by the processor of the router

- The other for the transmission of the packets on the outgoing link

These queues are connected as shown in Figure 3.8. In most cases, the model can be further simplified. Usually, one of the following two cases occurs:

- The processor is fast enough so that queues at the processor are not significant.

- The link speed is fast enough so that the queues at the output links are not significant.

In the latter case, the only queues of significant size occur at the processor, and the entire model can be collapsed to a single queue representing the processor. In the other case, the queue at the router can be eliminated, and the model will consist of several queues, with each queue representing one of the outgoing links.

Figure 3.8   Queuing model of a single processor router.

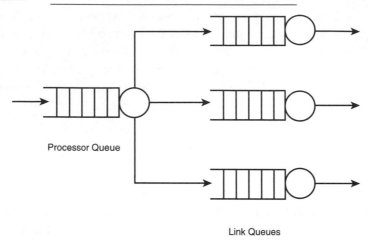

Processor Queue

Link Queues

The other common type of router architecture consists of deep adapters. In a *deep adapter*, an embedded processor is dedicated to each of the link interfaces. An additional processor may be available to handle control flows and configuration of the entire router. Packets are received at an adapter and a forwarding decision is made. The packets then contend for access to a switch fabric to reach the outbound adapter, from where they are transmitted out on the link. In many cases, the packets are stored in a common memory shared by all the adapter processors, and only packet headers or a small amount of header information is transmitted on the shared bus (or other switching fabric).

This header information is sufficient to determine the output adapter for the packet, and the output adapter then fetches the entire packet from the shared memory for transmission on the link. In other cases, the shared bus is used to transmit the full packet to the output adapter, and no shared memory is needed. The former architecture (shared memory) makes sense when the speed of the shared bus is relatively low compared to the output link speeds. The latter (no shared memory) is more appropriate when the shared bus can operate at speeds larger than that of output links.

These routers can be modeled as a pair of queues modeling the input and output queuing at each of the adapters, and one additional queue modeling the behavior of the access to the switch fabric. However, it has usually been observed that the bulk of queuing in these systems occurs at the processing associated with the output queues, and thus they can be modeled by one queue for each of the adapters. This model is shown in Figure 3.9.

Figure 3.9   Queuing model of a deep adapter router.

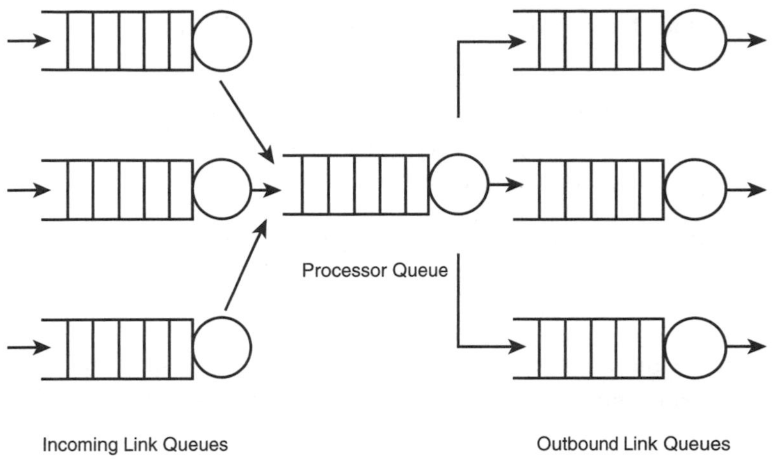

Incoming Link Queues   Outbound Link Queues

Thus, a deep adapter or a single-processor router with a high-speed processor is modeled as a set of queues representing the queuing delay at each of the links. An access router with a single, slow processor can be modeled as a single queue.

3.2.1 Estimating Queue Parameters

Because the network can be modeled as a graph with different types of queues, we can easily analyze the performance of the network provided we know the traffic load and service rate at each of the queues. In this section, we examine how to obtain the load on the different links in the network.

We begin the process by assuming that a traffic matrix is available for the access routers in the network. The *traffic matrix* specifies the amount of traffic that is expected to be present between the pair of access routers. From the traffic matrix on the network, the load on each link and router can be computed. The load may be characterized by a simple average rate or by a more complex traffic descriptor, such as a peak rate, as well as an average rate. Chapter 4, "Service Differentiation and Quality of Service in IP Networks," discusses an example of such a complex traffic descriptor used for resource reservation in IP networks.

Packets are typically routed in IP networks according to a shortest path algorithm (OSPF).

Each of the links in the network is assigned a weight that reflects how expensive the link is for the purpose of determining network routes. The weight may be determined on a number of factors, such as the monthly cost for the link, the link capacity, the length of the link, and so on.

Links with lower weights are preferred over links with higher weights. It is quite common for the weight to be set at 1 so that the resulting routing pattern in the network picks the shortest hop path between any two nodes.

Determining the shortest length path among all pairs of nodes can be done by several algorithms, the simplest one being Floyd's algorithm. The algorithm is most easily described by means of the following pseudo-code:

Step 0: Create a length matrix such that $C[i,j]$ contains the length for nodes containing the length between pairs of nodes in the graph. For other pairs, the matrix contains a large number.

Step 1: Create a path matrix P such that $P[i,j]$ contains j if a link occurs between nodes i and j, and a dummy node otherwise.

Step 2: For node j from 1 through N, repeat steps 3 through 5.

Step 3: For node i from 1 through N, repeat steps 4 through 5.

Step 4: For node k from 1 through N, repeat step 5.

Step 5: If $C[i,k] + C[k,j] < C[i,j]$ then assign.
$C[i,j] = C[i,j] + C[k,j]$
$P[i,j] = P[i,k]$

At the termination of the algorithm, the matrix element $C[i,j]$ contains the lowest possible length of a path between nodes i and j, and the matrix element $P[i,j]$ contains the node that is the next node along the shortest path from i to j. The path from node i to node j consists of nodes i, $P[i,j]$, $P[P[i],j]$, and so on.

After the shortest paths in the network are known, you can determine how the traffic in the network flows. At each node or link in the network, the intensity of all the traffic flows that traverse the node or link can be obtained to determine the traffic arrival rate at the node or link.

Sometimes, multiple shortest paths of equal length exist between two access nodes in the network. During the operation of the network, any of the possible paths may be used by the network routing algorithms. If we are looking for bounds on delays, then one way to approach this situation is to consider one configuration of the shortest paths at a time and compute delays for the queues in the selected configuration. The worst-case configuration can then be selected from all the possible shortest path configurations. If several alternatives exist, this approach may become computationally expensive. A more practical option in those cases would be to look at the paths that a real routing algorithm such as OSPF uses, and consider only those shortest paths in the network.

We now need to determine the service rate at the queues that are modeling the routers and the links along the path. For a queue representing a router, the *service rate* is the rate at which the router can forward packets. The rate can be determined by looking at manufacturer specifications or by measuring the maximum rate at which the router would forward packets through it in a test configuration. The latter is the preferred approach because manufacturers' performance numbers typically tend to be higher than ones usually observed in the field.

The average service rate at a queue that is modeling a link depends on the time it takes to transmit one packet on the link. It depends on two factors: the capacity of the link and the average length of the packet. The service rate is given by the capacity divided by the mean packet length. When predominant queuing at a network occurs at the links (rather than the routers), the service rate and the arrival rate are better expressed in bytes per second rather than in packets per second.

3.2.2 Analyzing Network Delays

The delays in a computer network arise because of several factors. Part of the delay is due to the propagation delays in the network. The *propagation delay* is characterized by the properties of the underlying graph in the network. As an example of the propagation delays involved in a network, consider the network topology illustrated in Figure 3.10. It shows the intranet backbone of a hypothetical company that has linked its sites at various cities in the U.S. The links have been obtained as T-3 connections for various telecommunication providers. All the links have propagation delays associated with them, as shown in Figure 3.10.

Note

The propagation delays would have a lower bound as the time required for light to propagate between the two sites. Even though the link appears as a single leased line between two sites to the intranet operator, the telecommunications provider needs to go through a number of multiplexors, switches, and repeaters to provide this connectivity. Thus, the actual propagation delay is likely to be much higher than the lower bound.

Figure 3.10   Propagation delays in networks.

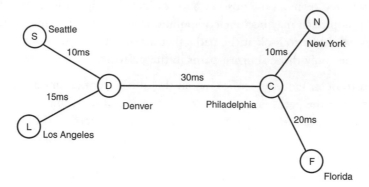

By looking at the propagation delays in the network, it is easy to see that the propagation delay for any packet between Seattle and New York is the sum of the propagation delay between three links: between Seattle and Denver, between Denver and Philadelphia, and between Philadelphia and New York. Thus, the propagation delay is going to be 50ms.

Let us further assume that the 99th percentile queuing delay at Seattle, Denver, Philadelphia, and New York is 40ms each. The 99th percentile delay is the bound on delay that is likely to be met by 99% of the packets. The 99th percentile delay for the communication between Seattle and New York would then be 210ms†. If you now consider the fact that most customers are interested in round-trip latency rather than one-way latency, the 99th percentile delay for round-trip becomes 420ms. Thus, any SLA for such a communication would offer a delay bound of about 420ms, or more likely, round it up to the bound of 0.5 seconds.

Additional delays may be incurred because of processing at the servers, but this is outside the scope of what we are considering.

The question that still remains is the mechanism to determine the 99th percentile queuing delays; for this, the analytical models such as the M/M/1 queue (or some other type of queuing model) can be used.

An alternative approach that helps determine an upper bound on the delay is to look at the physical characteristics of the queue modeling the router or the link. The buffer space in any router is limited. Therefore, the maximum delay in any router can be the amount of time that it takes to drain out the contents of the entire buffer into the network. For example, consider an access router that typically operates in a configuration shown in Figure 3.11. The router has one LAN interface and another interface that can connect to one or two wide-area serial links.

---

†We have simply added the 99th percentile delays at the nodes to get the end-to-end 99th percentile delay. This is not entirely accurate, but is not too far off from the correct answer.

Examples of such access routers are the Cisco 700 series routers and the IBM 2210 access router. Suppose the wide-area link consists of a T-1 line, and the router has buffer space for packets of 250KB equals 2Mb. Then, the maximum delay is that the router cannot exceed the value of 2MB/1.5Mbps or 1.3 seconds. No packet in the router can have a delay exceeding the upper bound. Packets that would otherwise exceed this delay are dropped because no buffer space would be available for them.

Figure 3.11   Typical access route configuration.

Although the bound obtained from physical characteristics is a hard deterministic limit, it is also fairly large, as illustrated in the previous examples. The observed delays in the routers would typically be much smaller than the worst-case results. That is the reason why the analytical modeling approaches might present a more realistic bound on maximum delays.

The average and maximum delays at various routers in the network can be summed up to obtain the end-to-end average or maximum delay along a path in the network. When you examine percentile bounds on delays, you cannot sum up the bounds and end up with the percentile bound on the end-to-end delay. The correct way to obtain this bound is to perform an operation called *convolution* on the individual delay distributions to obtain the percentile bound on the sum. The description of convolution can be found in most texts on statistics and is outside the scope of this book.

Most of the delay distributions in the network are fairly well behaved. As a result, if you simply summed up the percentile bounds on the individual queuing delays (assuming percentiles are on the order of 99%), you will get an answer that is not too far from the real answer, and you are very likely to get a safe answer; that is, the 99th percentile of the cumulative delay is less than the sum of the 99th percentiles of the individual delays. It must be kept in mind, however, that this summation is just an approximation.

3.2.3 *Analyzing Loss Rates*

The loss rate in a computer network can also be modeled similarly to that of delays. The losses in the network can be attributed to two main causes:

- Overrun of buffers in intermediate routers and link adapters

- Errors in the transmission links

In most fiber-optic networks, the errors in the transmission links are relatively small (about 1 error for every 10^{10} bits transmitted) and can be ignored for most practical purposes. This leaves the main culprit for losses in the network as buffer overruns in the routers.

Suppose a packet in the network takes a path that causes it to traverse N queues in the network, and let p^i be the probability that the packet will be lost due to buffer overrun at the ith queue. If we assume that the packet loss rates at the different queues are independent, then the probability that the packet will make it through to the end is given by the product of the probability at each individual node—for example, $\prod (1-p^i)$. If the packet loss rates are relatively small in the network, this can be approximated as

$$1 - \Sigma\, p_i$$

So, the end-to-end loss rate is approximately $\Sigma\, p^i$. In other words, losses at the queues can be summed up to obtain the total loss rate along a path.

Armed with the knowledge of delay and loss characteristics in the network, we are ready to analyze the performance of real computer networks.

Let us consider the example of a two-node network that connects the sites of a hypothetical young and upcoming enterprise, foo.com. The corporation has two sites, one in Austin and the other in Boca Raton. At both of these sites, the company's local network consists of a 10Mbps ethernet. The CIO of the company had leased a T-1 line between the two sites for connectivity. The young entrepreneurs in the corporation did their computation on a Windows platform and did not wish to learn the intricacies of managing a new access router. Therefore, they simply used a Windows NT platform to forward packets between the two sites as both ends. Based on their initial measurements, they believe that their hardware is capable of handling 500pps. They have observed that the average size of packets on their networks is about 200 bytes. They have also noticed that they have been sending about 250pps or 400Kbps from Austin to Boca Raton and about 225pps from Boca Raton to Austin.

The first step in analyzing the performance of this network is to determine the queuing points in the network. The queuing model can consider the queues at the routers as well as the link adapters between the two cities. However, let us consider the processing load on the two routers and the link adapters. The link from Austin to Boca Raton is relatively lightly loaded, with only 400Kbps being used out of the maximum possible 1,500Mbps. The other direction also uses only 360Kbps and is even more lightly loaded. On the other hand, the routers at both sites have to process 475 packets out of a total capacity of 500pps. Therefore, it makes sense to model this network as one in which the bottleneck queues are at the nodes. Let us assume that the M/M/1 model can be applied; then, each of the queues has an arrival rate of 475pps and a service rate of 500pps. The average delay at each of the routers thus turns out to be 40ms, and the users of the network would see round-trip delays of 80ms on average. However, the routers have an average utilization of 95%, so the actual delays can be substantially above the average.

3.2.4 Analyzing Reliability

The reliability of the network is a measure of how it reacts to the cases of node or link failure. One of the ways to define the reliability of the network is to determine the number of node or link failures that need to occur before a service disruption occurs in the network.

The Internet Protocol is fairly good at handling isolated link or node failures. If a link or router fails in the network, the routing protocols detect the failure of the link and readjust the routing tables in the different nodes to route around the failed node. This rerouting typically occurs within a few seconds or minutes (depending on the size of the ISP network). Therefore, the only cases you need to worry about are those in which network connectivity would be disrupted.

The way to determine the reliability of the network is to count the number of links or nodes that need to fail before connectivity between two pairs of nodes is disrupted. A set of links that can be removed from the graph and cause two nodes to be disconnected is called a *cut* in the graph. The problem then is that of finding the minimum cut between a pair of specified nodes in the graph. We solve the problem by finding the maximum number of disjoint paths between the two pairs of nodes. The algorithm is presented in the context of a directed graph. As described in Section 3.1.3, an undirected graph can be readily converted into a directed graph. The algorithm works as follows:

Step 0: Find one shortest path from the source to the destination. If no such shortest path exists, go to step 3.

Step 1: Remove the directed links along the path from the graph and replace them with "dummy" edges in the opposite direction of the original links.

Step 2: Repeat steps 0 through 1. When a dummy edge is used in the shortest path, replace it with the original rather than another dummy edge.

Step 3: Collect all the dummy edges in the network and find the corresponding original edges. These edges constitute all possible edge-disjoint paths between the source and destination. The number of paths thus formed is the size of the minimum cut.

You can repeat the process for all pairs of source and destination nodes to determine the minimum number of links that must fail before any of the nodes in the network become disconnected. The algorithm, as presented, is a special case of the Ford-Fulkerson algorithm, which is a common one used to determine minimum cuts in graphs. The minimum cut problem is also often stated in terms of maximum flow problem, where you attempt to find the maximum information that can be pushed between two nodes in a graph with link capacities, and is commonly stated as the *maximum flow—minimum cut problem.*

The number of nodes that are required to fail before communication is disrupted can also be calculated using the above algorithm. Simply replace each node in the network with two auxiliary nodes connected by a directed edge, with the first node receiving all the edges that were coming into the original node, the second node originating all the edges that were going out of the original node, and the directed edge leading from the first node to the second one. The size of minimum cut determined on this modified graph is the minimum number of routers required to fail before communication is disrupted.

Not all links or routers in the network have the same level of reliability. Each link or node may fail with a different probability. In those cases, we may want to find the maximum probability of communication being disrupted. In other words, rather than finding the minimum cut, we want to find the cut with the largest probability of failure. The probability of the failure of a cut is the product of the failure of individual links or nodes included in the cut, assuming that the link and node failures are independent.

To solve this problem, we assign a weight or capacity to each of the directed edges, which equals the absolute value of the logarithm of the probability of the link failure. For the probability of node failure, the weight is assigned to the internal directed edge connecting the two auxiliary nodes that replace it. The problem then reduces to that of finding the cut with the minimum weight. This problem is readily solvable if the weights are integers. Although our probability values are not integral, we approximate them with integers obtained by scaling them with a multiplying factor (for example, multiply by 1,000).

The problem of finding the minimum weight cut is solved in a manner quite similar to that of finding the minimum cut, which is a special case of the following general algorithm:

Step 0: Find one shortest path from the source to the destination. Find the edge along the path with the lowest weight (such as w). If no such shortest path exists, go to step 3.

Step 1: Reduce the weight of directed edges along the path by w, and introduce new "dummy" edges of weight w in the opposite direction of the original link.

Step 2: Repeat steps 0 through 1. When a dummy edge is used in the shortest path, modify the weight of the corresponding original edge rather than introducing another dummy edge.

Step 3: Collect all the dummy edges in the network and find the corresponding original edges. These edges constitute all possible edge-disjoint paths between the source and destination. Find the minimum weight along each path and sum them up to get the minimum weight cut.

The weights or capacities have been computed so that the resulting minimum cut gives the cut corresponding with the highest probability.

A network may be connected, but may have excessive delays in the presence of node or link failures so that the connectivity is not useful. The probabilities computed using the above analysis are not a true measurement of the network's availability, but only of the network connectivity. Despite this limitation, the probability of link connectivity serves as a useful metric of network availability and is found in many SLAs.

3.2.5 *Simulation-Based Performance Evaluation*

The analysis in previous sections had assumed that the network characteristics can be represented using the M/M/1 model. This assumption is bound to raise eyebrows among several people who would point out that the assumption is wrong for various reasons. Some of these reasons are enumerated in the next section. Although several other models can be used to model the delays and loss rates, all of them are based on assumptions regarding specific arrival patterns. An alternative approach to determine the performance of a computer network is to simulate the behavior of the network under specific traffic loads.

The simulation of the network consists of modeling the network as a system of multiple queues and feeding a synthetic workload through the queues. The synthetic workload could be generated from traces collected from real network loads or may be generated by means of a traffic generator function. The traffic generator function could model the behavior of packets conforming to a probability distribution function that is not easy to analyze. Thus, questions regarding network performance can be analyzed and answered by means of computer simulations.

Simulations provide a better answer to determining the performance in a more realistic fashion. However, the simulation of a network in itself makes several assumptions about the operation of the computer systems and is only as good as the validity of the assumptions made in the simulation model.

An overview of computer simulations and their use in analyzing network performance can be found in the book by Robertazzi [RTZZ].

3.2.6 Determining SLA Bounds by Network Monitoring

Perhaps the best way to determine reasonable bounds on the performance limits that can be specified for an SLA is by monitoring the performance of an existing network. Because you need to monitor the performance of a real network for a while before drawing meaningful estimates about delays or loss rates, this method can only be used to determine the appropriate SLAs after a network has been operational for a while.

The biggest advantage of this approach is that you do not need to make any of the unrealistic assumptions inherent in any type of analytic network model (see Section 3.2.7). Even the most well-designed simulation may fail to take into account some of the idiosyncrasies of real routers in the network.

The delays and loss rates in the network can be monitored using a variety of techniques. Some of these monitoring techniques are described in Chapter 7, "Network Monitoring and SLA Verification." By keeping a historical log of network delays and loss-rate information between access points in the network, you can estimate the delay limits that are likely to be found in the network under typical operating environments. You can determine the 99th percentile of total network delays observed empirically and decide to offer it as part of the SLA terms.

One of the assumptions associated with the use of empirical measurements to determine SLA bounds is that the traffic distribution during the measurement period would remain relatively constant over the lifetime of the network. Because network traffic has grown and changed significantly over time, you need to periodically assess whether the current network SLA performance limits are likely to remain with a modified traffic load. When the SLA limits are in danger of being violated, it is a good time to explore a redesign of the network and consider increasing the capacity of links and/or upgrading the routers in the network.

3.2.7 *Models and Reality*

The M/M/1 model has several limitations. In real life, neither arrivals nor service rates are Poisson. In the case of IP networks, most routers need to spend only a fixed amount of time to process the bulk of the packets. A few packets contain special processing options and take more time. However, the behavior of the service process is far from Poisson. Similarly, analysis of traffic traces in the Internet [PAXSON] shows that the arrival process of IP packets is not Poisson.

Several models have been used to characterize the performance of a single queue. These include different traffic arrival patterns as well as different service processes.

However, the analysis of a network of those queues using the sophisticated models poses a difficulty when we need to determine the arrival process at different queues.

When the arrival process is Poisson, but the service process is not, then the departure process from a queue is not Poisson. This means that the arrival process at the next queue in a network has to be analyzed using some different non-Poisson arrival model. The same problem would arise if the arrival process was not Poisson, but the service process was Poisson. In general, if the queuing behavior does not reflect characteristics referred to as a *Jackson Network* [ROSS], it is fairly hard to analyze a network of queues in a significant manner. However, some characteristics of any general arrival process would remain unchanged as it passes through a queue (for example, the average rate of the process).

You can take two approaches to work around the problems associated with the queuing theory limitations:

- Determine the average arrival rates at the different nodes using the sophisticated models at all nodes; using an average-case analysis, assume that the general model can still be used and obtain a bound on the delays.

- Use the M/M/1 model to determine the delays in the network, but multiply all delays and loss factors by a "fudge factor" (for example, double all the delays) to account for the assumptions in the model that are unrealistic.

None of the approaches are on solid mathematical ground, but they can provide a reasonable estimate of network delays. As network providers, these estimates are what we need to support SLAs.

Even when a better model is used, you should be aware of the following limitations of any model used to predict performance of the network:

- All queuing models assume packets arrive independently of one another. In most real networks, packet arrival is highly correlated with past packet arrivals; for example, request packets generate response packets, lost packets result in retransmission after a timeout period, and so on. If network traffic is aggregated so that each individual connection with correlated requests and responses is only a small constituent of the overall traffic, the independent arrival assumption can be justified. However, evidence also shows that traffic on some packet networks may exhibit *self-similarity* [LELAND], which is a long-term correlation in packet arrivals that is exhibited at multiple time-scales, and which is extremely difficult to model and analyze using traditional queuing theory techniques. Another nasty fact about self-similar traffic is that even aggregation does not result in an aggregate process with independent arrivals.

- Typical queuing models assume that the packet arrival process and service processes are stationary; that is, the process describing the arrival or service remains unchanged (in a probabilistic sense) regardless of the time that you are observing the queue. Typical networks show variations in packet arrivals that are very much dependent on the time of day. Networks are usually designed for the busy traffic hours to accommodate for the time-of-day changes.

- All queuing models assume packet service rates are independent of each other. Depending on the architecture of the router forwarding the packet, this assumption may or may not be reasonable.

- All queuing models assume that traffic arrival rates and service rates are known in advance. In most real networks, the rate of packet arrivals and rate of services are rather vaguely defined and can only be determined after the network is in operation.

Given the various limitations, we must keep in mind that the results predicted by queuing theory are simply estimates, and they should not be treated as deterministic bounds.

3.3 Network Design Overview

The aim of network design is to determine the topology most appropriate for meeting a specific traffic load on the network. Most network design problems are formulated in terms of finding the lowest cost graph to connect a number of sites, where the estimated traffic generated at each of the sites is known.

The design problem may be specified with constraints on network performance or without any such constraints. The former case is the constrained network design problem, whereas the latter one is the unconstrained network design problem.

The immediate question is. What is the best graph? The usual definition of the best graph is one that minimizes the cost of the resulting network. The cost of the graph is the cost of the telecommunication links represented by the edges. If you or your organization owns fiber, this is the cost of digging the trenches and laying the fiber. More commonly, you or your organization will lease bandwidth. In this case, the cost of the graph is the recurring or monthly fees paid to the provider.

It is usually common in network design problems to come up with not only the lowest cost graph, but a few enumerations of possible network topologies that meet the specific performance constraints and traffic loads. As a matter of fact, nobody knows how to design the best network. Each design tool does its best to solve a problem to the best of its capabilities.

The choice among these designs is made using subjective trade-offs among the cost, the performance, and the reliability achieved by the alternate designs. For example, the network operator may want the lowest cost network but may be willing to pay 10% more if an alternate topology reduces the network delay by 50%.

In many cases, you are looking for a tree network. This is the case when you are designing an access network for an ISP.

In other cases, you are looking for a mesh design that need not necessarily be tree-structured. Mesh design is common in ISP backbone networks and the wide-area component of corporate intranets.

We refer to the network design problem formulation in Section 3.3.1. Then, we discuss some common algorithms used for design of tree-structured networks in Section 3.3.2 and the algorithms for mesh network design in Section 3.3.3. Because the field of network design is too complex to cover appropriately in a single chapter, we restrict ourselves to provide an overview of a selected few algorithms that illustrate the basic concepts behind network design. For a more thorough coverage of the issues, many excellent books in this area are available, such as the ones by Cahn [CAHN], Kershenbaum [KERSH], and Schwartz [SCHW2].

3.3.1   Network Design Problem Formulation

The typical formulation of a network design problem consists of a description of participating sites, a traffic matrix, and a cost matrix.

The participating sites are the sites that need to be connected. These sites are the nodes of the graph resulting from the design. In this section, we make the simplifying assumption that we need to consider only the specified nodes to generate the final graph.

In the general network design problem, other secondary nodes may also need to be introduced for a better solution. For example, consider the three sites shown in Figure 3.12 (refer to A). Without using any intermediate nodes, you may be forced to use one of the network topologies shown in Figure 3.12 (refer to B, C, or D). However, it may be quite possible that the best way to interconnect these three sites would be to use a secondary node such as that shown in Figure 3.12 (refer to E). Approaches that include secondary nodes for network design can be found in the texts dealing with network design mentioned in the previous section.

Figure 3.12   Network design using intermediate nodes.

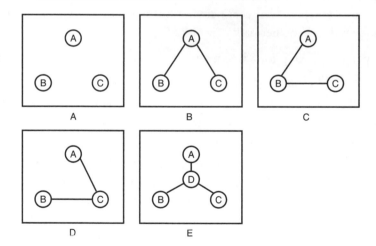

For each of the sites in the network, we assume that the amount of traffic that is to flow from that site to any other site is known. Thus, for the interconnection of N sites, we assume that a NxN matrix specifying the amount of traffic flowing between the two sites is known. If we are trying to redesign and restructure an existing network, this traffic can be estimated by measuring the distribution of traffic in the network. When a new network has to be designed, the entries in the traffic matrix need to be predicted. A number of prediction schemes that account for the population at each site and the distribution patterns of traffic are described in Chapter 4 of Cahn's book [CAHN].

In addition to the traffic among the different sites, you need to determine the cost of connecting the different sites. The cost is also represented as a matrix, with each element in the matrix specifying the cost of connecting the two sites. The cost may measure the monthly charges associated with operating a direct line between the sites (including, perhaps, an amortized term dependent on the one-time expenses of creating the site). The cost depends on many factors, including the distance between the sites, the amount of traffic to flow between the sites, and the location of the sites. Determining the traffic, especially if the sites being connected are in different countries, is not a trivial task. However, commercial tools that estimate the costs of creating a line are available.

The performance constraints on the network are represented by yet another matrix. If the SLA specification is done for specific tunnels, we need to have a performance matrix that would specify the performance limits between any pair of sites that needs to be connected. If the SLA specification is done using the funnel approach described in Chapter 2, "IP Networks and SLAs," then the performance matrix could be reduced to a performance array, with each entry in the array specifying the performance constraints pertinent to a specific site. Finally, if the SLA specification is done using a cloud approach, then a single performance specification needs to be satisfied by the network design.

Armed with traffic, cost, and performance matrices, we are ready to embark on the task of network design, which is to determine the lowest-cost network that supports the specified traffic while meeting the performance constraints on the network. However, there is one small fly in the ointment. The network design problem can be shown to be within the class of what are called *NP-complete problems.* This is a class of problems in which no known way exists to solve the problem using a software program that is more efficient than enumerating all the possible solutions. Such enumerations tend to take an immense amount of computer time. A more detailed description of NP-completeness and its implications can be found in the book by Garey and Johnson [GAREY].

The fact that the network design problem is NP-complete should not be a setback. Many important problems are known to be NP-complete. A common approach to solving these problems is to use a heuristic. The *heuristic* is an algorithm that is not guaranteed to give the best network, but that comes fairly close to the best network you could have obtained using enumeration.

All the network design approaches mentioned in the following sections are heuristics. However, they have been shown to yield networks that are within 5%–10% of the best solution in the network; that is, the cost of the network generated by the heuristic is no more than 5%–10% beyond the network cost of the optimum solution. If this cost difference is significant, you should consider investing in the additional programming time required to obtain the optimum solution by means of enumeration. This is assuming that the cost of performing the enumeration is smaller than the expected savings due to the improved network design.

Because network design problems are hard to solve, it is quite common to come up with a network topology without the performance constraints, and then to modify the resulting topology with SLA performance requirements in mind. In Sections 3.3.2 and 3.3.3, we present network design algorithms that are unconstrained. Then in Section 3.3.4, we provide an overview of techniques that can be used to modify the unconstrained network designs to meet the specific SLA performance limits.

3.3.2 Design of Tree Networks

The design of a tree network requires us to find a tree topology that meets the constraints of the performance matrix. In many cases, the root of the tree is known. The traditional method to solve the tree design problem is to use an algorithm called the *Esau-Williams algorithm* [ESAU], named after the two inventors of the algorithm. The algorithm's input consists of the specification of N nodes, one of which is the designated root of the tree.

The algorithm starts out with an initial solution in which each of the nodes is connected directly to the root. It keeps track of a trade-off function; the *trade-off function* is the difference between the cost of connecting a node directly to the root and connecting the tree to another node in the network. At each stage of the algorithm, the algorithm determines the node that would result in the maximum cost savings by connecting it through another node rather than directly to the center. It terminates when no more cost savings occur by connecting any other node. The algorithm can also enforce constraints that limit the links on the network to use no more than a specific amount of bandwidth on the link.

The steps involved in the algorithm are as follows:

Step 0: Create an initial tree with several components, with each component consisting of a single node. Each component is connected directly to the root node.

Step 1: Compute a trade-off matrix for all the components; the trade-off function $T_{i,j}$ is defined as $C_{i,j} - C_{i,root}$, where C is the cost matrix.

Step 2: Select the entry in the trade-off matrix with the smallest trade-off function. If no entry has a negative trade-off, we have the desired solution. Suppose the smallest trade-off is given by the entry i,j.

Step 3: Validate that the capacity constraints in the network are satisfied by connecting the ith node with the jth node instead of directly to the center. If not, replace the trade-off entry for i,j with a large value, and repeat the process starting from step 1.

Step 4: Connect component i to component j. Update the trade-off and cost matrixes to update the new cost and trade-offs associated with selecting this link. Then repeat from step 1.

A detailed description of the code required to implement the Esau-Williams algorithm and an overview of the algorithm is given by Cahn [CAHN]. Variations on the Esau-Williams algorithm that allow the use of multiple centers are also provided in the same book.

The Esau-Williams algorithm was designed for serial multidrop lines and may not produce very good trees when designing a LAN topology. Two other common heuristics can be used to design tree topology networks: *Prim's algorithm* and *Kruskal's algorithm*. Prim's algorithm for designing tree topology with capacity constraints works as follows:

Step 1: Start with a spanning tree containing only the root.

Step 2: Select the node that has the smallest cost link connecting it to the tree.

Step 3: Validate that the capacity constraints on the link are satisfied. If not, mark the cost of the link as a large value, and repeat from step 2.

Step 4: Include the node selected in step 2 to the tree. If all the nodes have been connected, stop the algorithm. Otherwise, repeat from step 2.

The algorithm proposed by Kruskal operates in the same manner as the algorithm by Prim. However, Kruskal's algorithm selects the lowest cost link in the network as the starting point of the tree, rather than starting with the root, and the difference is only in the initial step.

Step 1: Start with a spanning tree containing the lowest cost link.

Step 2: Select the node that has the smallest cost link connecting it to the tree.

Step 3: Validate that the capacity constraints on the link are satisfied. If not, mark the cost of the link as a large value and repeat from step 2.

Step 4: Include the node selected in step 2 to the tree. If all the nodes have been connected, stop the algorithm. Otherwise, repeat from step 2.

If the capacity constraints are removed, all three of the algorithms produce a minimum spanning tree in the network.

All three algorithms presented above can be considered special cases of a unified heuristic proposed by Kershenbaum and Chou [KCHOU]. The *unified heuristic* is a generalized algorithm that is capable of handling more complex constraints on capacities (for example, supporting links with different capacities) and having more than one root at the access router.

3.3.3 Design of Mesh Networks

The *MENTOR algorithm* [MENTOR] is an example of a typical algorithm used to design a mesh network. The following are the steps taken by the MENTOR algorithm to design a mesh network:

Step 0: Divide all the nodes in the network into two sets: edge nodes and backbone nodes.

Step 1: Assign each edge node to a backbone node, resulting in a set of clusters. Each cluster consists of one backbone node as well as several edge nodes.

Step 2: Connect all the node clusters with a spanning tree using Prim's algorithm.

Step 3: Connect all edge nodes in a cluster to the backbone node using one of the tree algorithms described in Section 3.3.2. Compute the capacities needed at each link that is dependent on the traffic load distribution on the network.

Step 4: Introduce additional links between nodes to balance traffic load along different routes on the network. Compute the capacities of the links that would satisfy the traffic load on the link using the shortest-path routing algorithm.

Steps 2 and 3 can be implemented in an alternate manner by doing a Prim spanning tree over all the nodes with the restriction that no two edge nodes can be connected together at any stage of the algorithm. The only links allowed are those connecting two backbone nodes or one connecting an edge node to a backbone node.

The above description is a much simplified description of a relatively complex series of steps. A detailed description of the algorithm, including several variations and nuances, can be found in Chapter 8 of Cahn's book [CAHN].

Each of the steps described above can be done in a variety of ways. The division of nodes into edge nodes and backbone nodes is done by assigning them a weight that is proportional to the traffic load expected in the network and selecting nodes in which the weight is below a user-specified threshold as edge nodes. Additional nodes may be classified as backbone nodes to ensure that the distance between any edge node and a backbone node is below a specific threshold distance. These additional backbone nodes are selected on a merit function, which is dependent on the traffic load on the node and its proximity from the center of the network.

The basic network that results from step 3 of the algorithm is a tree in which only one path exists between any pair of nodes. The addition of new links introduces a more balanced traffic distribution. When introducing new links, the MENTOR algorithm uses an approach that accounts for the fact that routing in IP networks tends to route packets along the shortest-length paths. It introduces additional edges between two nodes by taking a factor that takes the traffic on the edge and the cost of the edge into account. It also determines the edge lengths that should be used by a routing protocol to come up with a traffic distribution in the operational network that corresponds to the one assumed during network design process.

Note that a network designer would typically experiment with different values of the parameters (for example, thresholds to determine edge nodes and backbone nodes) used by the algorithm to come up with a few alternative designs. One of these designs is then selected by the network operator as the one that is most appropriate for the operational environment at hand.

Another interesting network design algorithm is the *cut-saturation algorithm* [GERLA]. The cut-saturation algorithm starts with an initial network topology, the traffic matrix and the cost matrix, and refines the topology in each iteration. Each iteration performs the following steps:

Step 0: For the given network topology, use shortest-path routing and the traffic matrix to determine utilization of each network link.

Step 1: Sort the links in decreasing order of link utilization. Remove the links, one at a time, until the network becomes disconnected. The set of removed links is the saturated cutset.

Step 2: Add the least-costly links to the network that will divert traffic from the saturated cutset. Nodes that are at least two nodes away from the endpoints of a removed link in the cutset are used to add the links.

Step 3: Determine the link with the highest value of cost multiplied by its idle factor (the idle factor is 1–link utilization). Eliminate this link from the network.

Step 4: Validate that the traffic requirements of the traffic matrix are satisfied. If not, repeat step 2.

At the end of each iteration, the resulting throughput possible between two pairs of nodes is checked. If it is within specific lower and upper ratio of the corresponding bounds in the traffic matrix, the algorithm terminates. Otherwise, the algorithm goes through another iteration.

A more detailed description of the cutset saturation algorithm can be found in Chapter 10 of Schwartz's book [SCHW2].

As with the MENTOR algorithm, the cutset saturation method can result in several alternative topologies, with each iteration producing one feasible topology. The designer would then choose one of the many possible topologies.

3.3.4 Adjusting Network Topology for Performance Constraints

When performance constraints are specified in the network design problems, you would typically follow an approach in which an unconstrained design is determined first, and then modifications and adjustments are made to accommodate the existence of the performance constraints. The following are the techniques that can be used to ensure that a network design satisfying the specific performance constraints is obtained:

- *Culling*: As mentioned previously, network design produces several alternative topologies depending on the selection of several parameters in the design process. For each of these topologies, you can determine whether the performance constraints are being satisfied. You can then prune the space of possible solutions down to the ones that meet the performance constraints.

- *Capacity increment*: If a topology fails to meet the specific delay or loss targets that are desired, you can increase the capacities of the links resulting from the design to reduce the resulting delays and loss rates in the network. If the delay constraints are exceeding the bounds between two nodes, you need to investigate the cause of the delay. If the propagation delays between the two nodes are less than the associated SLA bound, you would increase the capacity of the links (or routers) along the path to reduce the queuing delay and bring it within the required bound. A useful heuristic in incrementing the capacities of the links is to try to keep the load on all the links in the network roughly equal so that the link with the highest utilization is the first candidate for an increase in capacity. The process is iterated until all the performance bounds are met.

- *Augmentation of links*: If a topology fails to meet reliability constraints or the delay constraints due to the propagation delays in the network, you need to augment the network with additional links to meet the performance requirements. Assuming that the propagation delay has to be reduced between two nodes, you can introduce a direct link between the two, bringing the edges of the link successively closer to the center of the path until the propagation delay requirements are satisfied. To meet the reliability constraints, you could determine the minimum cut between two nodes that fail to meet the reliability criteria and introduce an additional edge between two nodes on different sides of the cut to improve reliability.

- *Cost modification*: One way to ensure that the unconstrained network design generates solutions that are likely to meet the performance requirements is to modify the cost matrix in the original problem specification. The cost of each link is incremented by a factor that is proportional to the propagation delay or the reliability of the link. You would then generate network designs that would be likely to minimize delays in the network and that are likely to satisfy SLA requirements.

An alternate approach to obtaining the performance constraints is to formulate the network design problem as an optimization problem. An *optimization problem* attempts to minimize a function (for example, the overall cost of the network) subject to specific constraints that reflect the SLA bounds requirements, as well as capture the characteristics of the traffic flow on the network. The cost of a link could be a generic function dependent on the capacity of the link. Optimization techniques such as linear programming are then used to come up with an appropriate network design. A detailed introduction to this approach in the context of network design can be found in the book by Girard [GIRAR].

3.4   *Designing a Corporate Intranet*

Having understood the basic issues regarding network performance, let us examine how we can design a network to meet specific SLA targets. SLA objectives can be met by ensuring that the different components of the network have adequate capacity to meet the performance requirements of the offered traffic.

Figure 3.13 illustrates the different parts of the network that need to be considered when you design a network to meet a specific SLA limit. The communication is shown as occurring between a client workstation and a server. The client and server connect via a local area network (LAN) to an access router, and the access routers are connected by means of a wide area network (WAN).

Figure 3.13 Structure for a corporate intranet.

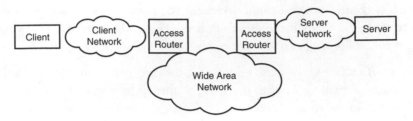

The three types of network components that you need to consider for performance purposes are

- The LAN
- The WAN
- The server

Each of these components must be designed to meet the target performance levels. The same three components would need to be designed adequately to meet SLAs even in the case of a peer-to-peer communication. Notice that two other components are shown in the figure that are not mentioned in the previous design. The two components are *access routers* and *client workstations*. The performance of desktop workstations is improving at such a rapid rate that the best way to satisfy a desktop requirement is to upgrade a slow machine to a faster one. Therefore, the design problem for desktops is not a tough one to solve. The same applies to the design on an access router. Assuming that the amount of traffic to be processed is known, you need to select an access router that is capable of processing packets at the required speed or higher. If the access router needs to implement mechanisms for Quality of Service (QoS) or service differentiation (see Chapter 4 for some examples of such mechanisms), then it needs to be configured appropriately.

Design issues become important for servers because the workload at that site is large enough so that simply upgrading to faster machines is not always the best solution. Similarly, the design of LANs and WANs to meet specific performance requirements requires more careful thought. A related issue is that of determining the appropriate location of the server to meet the performance and reliability constraints imposed by SLAs.

3.4.1 Designing a Local and Wide Area Network

The LAN is the infrastructure that connects the different machines to the access router. It is common practice to design the LAN with a hierarchical tree-like structure with one root at the access router. Given both of these factors, it is natural to use one of the tree design algorithms to design the LAN.

The presentation of the tree design network was done in the context of point-to-point links. However, the original version of the Esau-Williams algorithm was done to design for multidrop lines (that is, a single line that could connect multiple terminals). The concept is not too far removed from that of LANs, which connect multiple machines. Thus, the Esau-Williams algorithm can be readily adapted to design an appropriate configuration of LANs.

To meet the reliability requirements for connectivity, you may want to have more than one access router at the site. In that case, you could need to use the multicenter variation of the Esau-Williams algorithm. An alternative scheme is to have more than one router on the same backbone LAN. That would be much simpler and provide adequate reliability for most practical purposes.

The design of the WAN is done using the mesh network design outlined in Section 3.3.3. Of particular interest in the WAN design is the cost and capacity of the access lines to the WAN, particularly when wide-area service is being provided by an ISP with backbone resources that are vast compared to the often constrained capacity of the last mile link to the customer premises.

3.4.2 Designing a Server to Meet SLA Constraints

In addition to making the network design in accordance with SLA requirements, many corporate I/T departments need to operate application servers to meet the same requirements. These requirements often state lower bounds on the performance expected of the server, as well as constraints on the availability of the service.

Examples of servers needed with network operation and maintenance include the domain name servers, routing daemons, the authentication servers, and the proxy servers (for example, the Web caching servers or socks servers used within firewalls). Non-networking servers that need high availability and performance include transaction servers and database servers, as well as high volume Web servers. Servers that are critical for the operation of the business must be available during normal business hours. The downtime costs of such mission-critical servers can be enormous. If the server processing credit card transactions in a department store chain is down, a significant volume of sales can be lost.

The first approach to meeting server SLA requirements is to simply use a machine that is sufficiently fast to satisfy the user requests. However, several situations occur in which even the fastest available machine is not adequate to meet the load generated by the clients of the servers. When one machine is not adequate, you need to use multiple machines to spread out the load on different servers. Using multiple servers improves availability and speed, provided the system can operate even when one or more servers fail. Four common approaches to obtain high availability servers are the following:

- *Client configuration with redundant servers*: The clients of many applications can be configured with several servers. One of these servers is the primary server that the client would normally communicate with. However, if the primary server is not available, either because the primary server is down or the network connectivity to the primary server has been lost, the client can connect to one of the secondary servers to obtain the same services. Examples of such applications include the domain name service and the mail service.

- *Clustering*: Many servers come together in the form of a cluster that offers a single system image (that is, it appears and behaves like a single system). These clusters appear to be like a single machine, yet contain many individual servers internally to the cluster. Clients may obtain services from any of the servers in the cluster. When one server in the cluster becomes unavailable, clients can be switched over to another server. The switchover usually requires the client to reconnect, although schemes are available that can eliminate this requirement as well. Clustered servers are used in high-volume call centers and data processing centers. The reliability and gain in performance that is achievable by the servers is impressive; for example, a cluster of IBM S/390 servers usually has a downtime of less than 10 minutes in a year.

Server clusters tend to be relatively expensive, and not all applications have clients that can be configured to support redundant servers. The two approaches that follow can be looked upon as the poor man's approach to clustering:

- *Name service round robin*: In this approach, multiple servers are placed at different points in the network. When a client needs to communicate to the server, it usually needs to contact the domain name server to determine the location of the server (details on the domain name server can be found in Chapter 4). The domain name server can be configured to return the address of one of the many redundant servers in the network on every client request in a round-robin fashion. This distributes the load from the clients onto different servers in a uniform manner. If one of the servers becomes unavailable, the domain name server can exclude its addresses from the list.

- *Front-end dispatcher*: The front-end dispatcher approach does not rely on a modified domain name service to distribute the requests. It relies on the efficiency of a fast processor that acts as a front-end interface for the servers. The front-end dispatcher selects one of the servers that a client must communicate with and dispatches those messages to the appropriate server. The front-end dispatcher needs to process requests at the combined rate of all the servers. However, because it is only dispatching requests to one of the servers rather than processing the message completely, the goal can be achieved by an efficient software design.

For some applications, the front-end dispatcher can use application-specific commands to direct the clients to a specific server. Web browsers support a mechanism wherein one server can direct that a page be loaded from another server. This mechanism can be used to efficiently redirect Web pages to multiple servers. Other types of dispatchers do not rely on application-level mechanisms but direct the messages to the right server based on message headers.

3.5 Limitations of Network Design for SLAs

Although network design is a crucial and necessary step toward supporting SLAs, it cannot be the only step involved. Some limitations of network design exist, including the divergence of traffic estimates used in design from the actual load on the network and its inability to support multiple SLAs at the same time.

The network topology that you may end up implementing after coming up with an appropriate design may or may not meet the target performance objectives for many reasons: The network design algorithms used models that may not quite match the real traffic behavior in the network, and the heuristics used to find path and cost may not have yielded the best possible topology. Other practical issues may come up after the network design is completed. Equipment such as routers may arrive at varying schedules, which could cause the real network deployment to differ from the designed one. Furthermore, some of the routers may have some idiosyncrasies that may make their processing rate much different than the one assumed during the design phase. Other nontechnical issues, such as reliability of vendors, financing, staff turnovers, and interoffice politics can cause the real network to differ from the designed one.

Robert Ellis, the author of one of the earlier books on network design [ELLIS], described network design as an attempt to patch a bucket with 10 leaky holes by using 4 bandages. The metaphor reflects the difficulties in converting the desired network design into a practical one that satisfies the requirements of the users.

Even if the practical network is designed to match the goals of network design perfectly, the goals themselves may not be phrased appropriately. Consider the case of an ISP that has to support two customers at the same access points. One customer wants to have a network with delays of less than 100ms and a loss rate of 10^{-2}, whereas the other customer wants to have a network with delays of less than 250ms but a loss rate of 10^{-3}. What should the goals of network design be? You could design a network that has delays of less than 100ms and a loss rate of 10^{-3}, which is stringent enough to satisfy both customers. However, that may not be the best possible use of network resources and could result in expensive designs.

The difficulty arises from the different requirements of different users; in addition, IP networks tend to be best-effort and cannot distinguish among packets with different performance requirements. Chapter 4 discusses some of the approaches that are used within IP networks to support service differentiation and quality of service. These approaches can augment network design to come up with an efficient method to support SLAs in networks.

Despite the limitations of network design, it is quite an effective solution for SLA support in cases where different user demands are similar. If the network does not support any service differentiation, network design is the only approach that would work to support SLAs.

3.6 Further Information

This chapter has attempted to provide an overview of several topics related to SLAs. Each of these fields has several excellent books. For a more detailed discussion of probability and statistics, we recommend the book by Freedman [FREED] for an easy-to-read introduction. Various other books have also been published on the topic, and we mention the books by Ross [ROSS] and Stone [STONE] as ones that cover material adequately for most problems related to networks. For queuing theory, the excellent books by Kleinrock [KLEIN1] [KLEIN2] are the bibles of the field. I also found the books by Gross [GROSS] and WOLFF [WOLFF] to be useful in clarifying many concepts related to that topic. For graph theory, I have found the book by Even [EVEN] to be an excellent and authoritative reference. The book by Wilson [WILSON] provides an excellent introduction, and the book by Thulasiaman [THULASI] is a good textbook.

For the performance evaluation and modeling of computer networks, the book by Bertsekas and Gallagher [BERTS] is considered the standard reference. Other excellent books are available by Schwartz [SCHW1] and Robertazzi [RTZZ].

For a detailed discussion on network design, the book by Cahn [CAHN] gives a very good introduction to practical approaches to the problems. Schwartz [SCHW2] and Girard [GIRAR] have a somewhat more theoretical discussion of the issues. Another book worth mentioning in the field is the one by Kershenbaum [KERSH].

For a much more practical approach to network design and advice on the process for developing a corporate network, the book by Rhodes [RHODES] provides some useful and practical advice.

3.7   Endnotes

[BERTS] Bertsekas, D., and R. Gallagher. *Data Networks*. Upper Saddle River, NJ: Prentice Hall, 1992.

[CAHN] Cahn, Robert S. *Wide Area Network Design*. San Francisco, CA: Morgan Kaufmann Publishers, 1998.

[ELLIS] Ellis, R. L. *Designing Data Networks*. Upper Saddle River, NJ: Prentice Hall, 1986.

[ESAU] Esau, L., and K. Williams. "On Teleprocessing System Design: A Method for Approximating the Optimal Network." *IBM Systems Journal* 5 (1966): 142-147.

[EVEN] Even, Shimon. *Graph Algorithms*. Computer Science Press, 1979.

[FREED] Freedman, David, Robert Pisani, and Roger Purves. *Statistics*. New York, NY: W. W. Norton & Co., 1997.

[GAREY] Garey, M., and D. Johnson. *Computers and Intractability: A Guide to the Theory of NP-Completeness*. Salt Lake City, UT: W. H. Freeman & Co., 1979.

[GERLA] Gerla, M., H. Frank, W. Chou, and J. Eckl. "A Cut-Saturation Algorithm for Topological Design of Packet-switched Communication Networks." Proc. IEEE National Telecommunication Conference (1974) 1074:85.

[GIRAR] Girard, Andre. *Routing and Dimensioning in Circuit-Switched Networks*. Reading, MA: Addison-Wesley, 1990.

[GROSS] Gross, D., and Carl M. Harris. *Fundamentals of Queuing Theory*. New York, NY: John Wiley & Sons, 1997.

[KCHOU] Kershenbaum, A., and W. Chou. "A Unified Algorithm for Designing Multidrop Teleprocessing Networks." *IEEE Transactions on Communications COM-22* 11 (1974): 1762-1772.

[KERSH] Kershenbaum, A. *Telecommunication Network Design Algorithms*. New York, NY: McGraw Hill, 1993.

[KLEIN1] Kleinrock, L. *Queuing Systems: Theory*. New York, NY: John Wiley & Sons, 1975.

[KLEIN2] ———. *Queuing Systems: Computer Applications*. New York, NY: John Wiley & Sons, 1976.

[LELAND] Leland, W.E., M.S. Taqqu, W. Willinger, and D.V. Wilson. "On the Self-similar Nature of Ethernet Traffic." *IEEE/ACM Transactions on Networking* 2 (1994): 1-15.

[MENTOR] Kershenbaum, A., P. Kermani, and G. Grover. "MENTOR: An Algorithm for Mesh Network Topological Optimization and Routing." *IEEE Transactions on Communications* 29 (1991): 503-513.

[OSPF] Moy,.J. "The OSPF Specification." *Internet Engineering Task Force Technical Report* IETF RFC 1131, October 1989.

[PAXSON] Paxson, V., and S. Floyd. "Wide-Area Traffic: The Failure of Poisson Modeling." *IEEE/ACM Transactions on Networking*. Vol. 3, No. 3. (June 1995: 226-244.

[RHODES] Rhodes, Peter D. *Building a Network: How to Specify, Design, Procure, and Install a Corporate LAN*. New York, NY: McGraw Hill, 1996.

[ROSS] Ross, Sheldon M. *Introduction to Probability and Statistics for Engineers and Scientists*. New York, NY: John Wiley & Sons, 1987.

[RTZZ] Robertazzi, Thomas G. *Computer Networks and Systems: Queuing Theory and Performance Evaluation*. Secaucus, NJ: Springer Verlag, 1994.

[SCHW1] Schwartz, M. *Telecommunication Networks: Protocol, Modeling and Analysis*. Reading, MA: Addison-Wesley, 1987.

[SCHW2] Schwartz, M. *Computer Communication Network Design and Analysis*. Upper Saddle River, NJ: Prentice Hall, 1977.

[STONE] Stone, C. *A Course in Probability and Statistics*, Pacific Grove, CA: Duxbury Press, 1996.

[THULASI] Thulasiraman K., and M. N. S. Swamy. *Graphs: Theory and Algorithms*. New York, NY: John Wiley & Sons, 1992.

[WILSON] Wilson, R. *Introduction to Graph Theory*. Reading, MA: Addison-Wesley, 1997.

[WOLFF] Wolff, Ronald. *Stochastic Modeling and the Theory of Queues*. Upper Saddle River, NJ; Prentice Hall, 1989.

Service Differentiation and Quality of Service (QoS) in IP Networks

As discussed in Chapter 3, "Network Design and SLA Support," network design is a good model for supporting service level agreements (SLAs) when the customer requirements are similar, but it may not be the best possible approach when customer requirements differ in a significant manner. Service differentiation allows the network to identify packets with different requirements and deal with them appropriately.

When the network supports service differentiation, this capability can be exploited to support SLAs. In this chapter, we look at the types of service differentiation that are available in IP networks. Service differentiation is closely related to Quality of Service (QoS) in IP networks, which strives to give assurances about network performance to end applications.

We begin this chapter with a definition of QoS and how it differs from network design. We present an overview of IP architecture in Section 4.2, followed by the description of some common building blocks used to provide QoS solutions in Section 4.3. Section 4.4 and 4.5 describe two major approaches to supporting QoS in IP networks. Finally, in Section 4.6, these two approaches and their strengths and weaknesses are compared.

4.1   What Is QoS?

The *Quality of Service (QoS)* of a network refers to the properties of the network that directly contribute to the degree of satisfaction that users perceive, relative to the network's performance. QoS can be considered good or poor on the basis of many factors such as network delay, loss rates in the networks, load on the servers, and so on.

The perceived QoS depends on the type of application the user is running; the same network can have a poor quality if you want to hear RealAudio on the Web but can be sufficient to download a text file relatively quickly. Different applications that are running on a network make different assumptions about the environment and the network. The field of QoS deals with the mechanisms that can meet the performance requirements of different applications.

Both QoS and network design are approaches to managing the performance of a network. The key differences between the two are the following:

- *Online versus offline mechanism*: Network design provides an offline mechanism for managing performance, whereby you determine the right set of links and routers with the right capacities to meet the performance goals of the network. QoS, on the other hand, explores online mechanisms that can be used to manage the performance of the network.

  An offline mechanism is one that does not involve a change in the operations of the traditional best-effort IP network. IP networks continue to operate with the traditional protocols when network design is used to configure a new network or reconfigure an existing protocol. No new aspect is introduced into the operation of the network. The offline approach has the great advantage of avoiding complexity. However, offline also implies that network behavior has to be analyzed, while making some modeling assumptions about how the network performance can be affected by the offered load, determining the paths a set of network flows can take, and so on. Even the best of these assumptions are quite unrealistic. Packet networks are not very friendly toward modeling and analysis. IP networks, in particular, are known to be downright hostile toward any attempt to model their behavior.

  For example, network design may assume that the traffic generated at a specific site does not exceed 1.4Mbps. This assumption is used to plan the capacities of the links; however, no mechanism is put into place to ensure that the assumption is satisfied. You can put in a rate-control mechanism (some such mechanisms are described in Section 4.3) as an online mechanism to ensure that the traffic from the site does not exceed 1.4Mbps. However, installing and configuring the rate-control mechanism adds complexity to the operation of the network.

  To process the packets, online mechanisms such as QoS introduce additional network tasks (for example, determining their class of service, specifying queuing behaviors at links and routers, and signaling mechanisms to communicate applications performance to the network elements). These online mechanisms introduce a lot more complexity to the operation of the network. However, they can make relatively few assumptions about the network models. They can measure the actual delays and traffic load in the network and react to these measurements. For example, an admission-control mechanism may detect that the load on a server is too high and refuse the establishment of any more connections to the server.

- *Network-centric versus application-centric*: Network design is usually done to manage the network performance as an aggregate and to manage the performance of an average packet in the network. QoS mechanisms, however, take an application-centric view of the network and try to manage the performance of individual applications (or classes of applications) on the network. For example, if you have multiple file transfers in the network, network design ensures that the average file transfer happens within a specific amount of time. QoS mechanisms could ensure that an individual file transfer—or a specific class of file transfer—happens within a specific amount of time.

Network design strives to optimize some of the network-related features, such as the cost of the network, the average utilization of links in the network, the average delay in the network, and so on. It does not make any assurances about the delay that may be seen by an individual application communicating across the Internet. A QoS approach attempts to meet this assurance about the performance of the connection, or at least about the performance of a class of connections.

- *Homogeneous versus heterogeneous performance requirements*: Because network design looks at the aggregate performance of the network, it implicitly assumes that the QoS needs of all applications on the network are similar. QoS mechanisms, on the other hand, assume that different applications have different performance requirements and implicitly support heterogeneity in the network.

This difference in the capability to support homogeneous and heterogeneous applications is more a statement about the areas emphasized by the two approaches, rather than a fundamental difference between the two. Network design algorithms can be extended to handle the needs for a heterogeneous mix of traffic. Similarly, QoS mechanisms can be used successfully in a network that supports only a single type of application, such as a network dedicated to Voice over IP (VoIP).

Note

Keep in mind that QoS mechanisms and network design supplement each other, and both can (and should) be used together to manage the performance of the network.

We will examine two approaches to supporting QoS in IP networks. We can loosely describe the first one as the *signaled approach* and the second one as the *provisioned multiclass approach*. In the signaled approach, applications communicate (or signal) their QoS requirements to the network routers and the remote workstations. Each router that is signaled reserves enough local resources (link bandwidth or buffer space) to support the QoS requirements of the application. The other approach is to support multiple preprovisioned and differentiated classes of service in the network. These multiple classes are provisioned to deliver different levels of average performance. Different service classes have different expectations of average network delays and loss rates. With the provisioned multiclass approach, the network decides to map an application's packet flow into one of these preprovisioned differentiated classes of service and schedules them appropriately.

As compared with these approaches, traditional IP forwarding can be described as *best-effort*, in which the network packets are delivered to the destination without any assurances regarding the type of performance it might achieve.

The signaled approach that we examine has been developed within the Integrated Services working group of the IETF and uses RSVP as the signaling protocol. The provisioned multiclass approach that we examine has been developed within the Differentiated Services working group of the IETF. We focus on these two approaches as the ones that will be commercially available and that can be used as building blocks to support SLAs.

Because we are interested in using the services offered by the two approaches, we concentrate more on the service interface offered by them, providing only a broad overview of the issues involved in supporting these QoS mechanisms in routers.

> **Note**
>
> The *IETF*, or *Internet Engineering Task Force*, is a self-organized association of people interested in technical aspects of the Internet and its protocols. Most of the protocols and standards used within the Internet are a direct result of working group activities within the IETF. The IETF has various working groups, each one focused on a specific problem area.

4.2   TCP/IP Architecture Overview

The term *TCP/IP architecture* refers to the networking architecture used in IP networks and is much broader than just the two protocols that are named. This section covers the architecture only to the level required to understand issues related to supporting SLAs. Details relevant for SLAs or QoS are emphasized.

> **Note**
>
> If you are already familiar with architecture and operations of IP networks, you may want to skip to Section 4.3. However, if you are new to IP networks, you may want to supplement the information in this section with a book that describes IP architecture more comprehensively. Comer's book on TCP/IP [COMER] is one of the standard references for learning about IP and associated protocols.

4.2.1 The IP Network View

IP or *Internet Protocol* forms the glue that binds the Internet. It offers a best-effort, connectionless, packet-delivery service.

From the perspective of IP connectivity, the world view is relatively simple. The entire universe consists of millions of machines, each one uniquely identified by a number that is called the *IP address*. The IP address is 32 bits long. Because long numbers are tough for humans to remember, *dotted notation* is often used. The dotted number divides 32 bits into four groups of 8 bits each and separates them by periods. The machine address of 9.2.22.16 refers to the machine whose address has the first 8 bits containing 9, the second 8 bits containing 2, and so on. If we convert the addresses to decimals, it would be machine number 151131614. It is easier to talk about 9.2.22.16 rather than the large number.

To communicate with another machine on the network, you need to generate IP packets in the network. The *IP packet* is delivered to the network, which acts as a courier service and delivers it to the destination.

Imagine you are running a bicycle courier service that delivers packages for people. If you are handed a package, what information do you need on its cover? You should know its destination. You should also know what to do when you arrive at the destination. You may also want to allow some scope for special instructions. It is also useful to know the address of the person who gave you the package, just in case delivery fails or the recipient needs to write back. You may want to determine some maximum distance beyond which you would not bike, or some prankster may have you running in circles with some funny addresses. You should also note how heavy the package is. Suppose the package is too heavy or bulky to fit into some of the narrow alleys you have to travel. You may repackage it into smaller bundles and note on the cover that the contents originally came in one bundle.

In the IP header, the IP packet contains the basic information required on the cover of the package in the above analogy (as well as information needed in a digital representation). The content of the package is the user data that is not supposed to be looked at in normal usage. The information contained in the header is shown in Figure 4.1. Figure 4.1 shows the header layout showing the width of each field in bits (labeled at the top). The header includes the following fields:

Figure 4.1   Internet Protocol header structure.

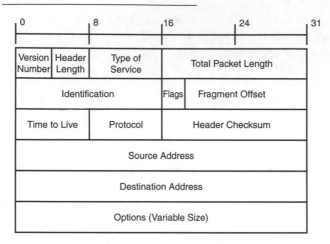

- *Version Number*: This packet identifies the packet as using the IP protocol and also states which version of the protocol. We will be dealing only with version 4 of IP.

Note

The IP that forms the basis of the present Internet is version 4 of IP. The next generation of IP, version 6, has a different header format. However, version 4 is expected to be the predominant version for quite a while. If you are wondering about the missing fifth version, it was assigned to an experimental protocol ST-II. IP version 4 was developed in the 1970s and its current form was defined by an RFC published in 1981 [POSTEL]; IP version 6 was defined by an RFC published in 1998 [DEERING], and the RFC for version 5 experimental protocol was published in 1990 [TOPOC].

- *Header Length*: States how many bytes the information contained in the header is.

- *Type of Service*: Intended to state how important the packet is. This is essentially ignored in most conventional IP networks, but it will be used in Differentiated Services network. (See Section 4.4.)

- *Total Packet Length*: States how long the packet is, including user data. This is the "weight of the package."

- *Identification*: Contains an identity that can be used to identify and reassemble packets that needed to be broken up in the network. A broken-up packet is called a *fragment*.

- *Flags*: Can contain some special directions, such as whether the packet should not be fragmented in the network.

- *Fragment Offset*: Contains information to identify the sequence in which fragments should be ordered when reassembling. Reassembling is done only at the receiving machine.

- *Time To Live (TTL)*:   Contains information that indicates when the packet is running in circles instead of making progress toward its destination. It is a number that is decremented for every node in the network traversed by the packet, with the packet being discarded if the value reaches 0.

- *Protocol*: Tells what to do when the packet reaches the destination—more precisely, what protocol should be used to process the user data in the packet at the destination.

- *Header Checksum*: Contains a checksum over the contents of the packet header to detect any possible corruption in the header.

- *Source Address*: Contains the 32-bit IP address of the machine that generated the packet.

- *Destination Address*: Contains the 32-bit IP address of the machine that is to receive the packet.

In addition to these fields, the IP header can also contain a variable number of options. These options can include directions regarding special processing that needs to be done for the IP packets, such as whether a specific route needs to be followed or whether a record should be kept of the path taken by the packet in the network.

IP packets are forwarded in a fairly simple manner. Each node in the network determines the identity of the next node that should receive the packet and forwards it to that node. If that node is the final receiver, it passes the packet to the correct local entity for further processing. A node in the network whose primary function is forwarding packets is called a *router*.

However, the forwarding of a packet over a single "hop" (LAN or link) can be a relatively complex process. The IP Layer has to depend on some underlying mechanism to deliver the packet over this underlying Layer 2 network. This is done using the *medium access control (MAC)* layer mechanisms.

The OSI Model

Most textbooks on computer networks introduce the network architectures using the seven-layer OSI model. The model provides a conceptual layering that helps in understanding the functions needed to provide the network interconnectivity. Despite the utility in learning about protocols and layering, very few practical networking architectures actually follow the layering suggested in the OSI model. TCP/IP definitely does not.

The layers in the OSI model consist of the following layers:

- *Layer 1*: The Physical Layer provides delivery of electromagnetic signals across a network link.

- *Layer 2*: The Data Link Layer provides delivery of bundles of data (called *frames*) between a source and destination on the same network link or LAN.

- *Layer 3*: The Network Layer provides connectivity throughout the network. This layer needs to be supported at each node in the network.

- *Layer 4*: The Transport Layer provides end-to-end connectivity between two machines in the network. This layer is invoked only at endpoints of a communication.

- *Layer 5*: The Session Layer provides establishment of end-to-end sessions between two hosts. Among other things, it controls the capability to send data and provides checkpoints to protect against failure.

- *Layer 6*: The Presentation Layer is intended to provide reusable modules for functions that are generally reused by many applications, such as a specific way to represent data on the network and translate that to a local representation of data.

- *Layer 7*: The Application Layer is intended to be the final application communicating with the application at the other end.

The TCP/IP protocol stack follows a much simpler layering:

- *Media Access Control Layer*: Combines the Layer 1 and Layer 2 functions and provides access to the hardware of the LAN or link. Ethernet and token rings are examples of Media Access Control Layers.

- *IP Layer*: Corresponds to the Layer 3 of the OSI stack and provides connectionless delivery of packets.

- *Transport Layer*: Includes the TCP and UDP protocols, which provide reliable end-to-end connections and unreliable message delivery, respectively. This corresponds to the Layer 4 of OSI.

- *Application Layer*: Includes all the functions covered in Layers 5, 6, and 7.

The Sockets Layer has traditionally defined the boundary between the Transport Layer and the Application Layer in TCP/IP. However, transport protocols are implemented above the Sockets Layer; a notable example is *Real-time Transport Protocol (RTP)* used commonly in VoIP applications. Another notable protocol implemented above the Sockets Layer is the *Secure Sockets Layer (SSL)*, which provides support for the exchange of encrypted data.

Each of the two models has its merits and drawbacks. However, TCP/IP is the predominant architecture of the day, and it is extremely difficult to find OSI implementations.

The relationship between the layers of each protocol is shown in Figure 4.2.

Figure 4.2   OSI and TCP/IP protocol layers.

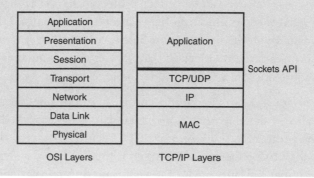

4.2.2 *Transport, Control, and Application Protocols*

The description of the IP network layer in the previous section was overly simple. To operate, the IP protocol relies on various other protocols that perform specific features. The following is a listing of the other protocols that are needed to ensure that IP works as intended.

- *Media Access Control (MAC) protocols*: The MAC protocols are responsible for ensuring that IP packets are carried across a single LAN. An example of a MAC protocol is the Ethernet protocol. When an IP packet is to be sent to another machine on the same LAN, the IP Layer needs to determine an address for the destination that can be understood by the MAC protocol (this is the MAC address). It then forms a MAC packet and relies on the mechanisms used within the MAC Layer to get it through to the destination machine.

- *Address Resolution Protocol (ARP)*: This protocol enables the IP Layer to determine the MAC address of a machine on the local LAN from the IP address of the machine. The reverse function, determining the IP address from the MAC address, is done using a protocol called *Reverse Address Resolution Protocol (RARP)*.

- *Internet Control Message Protocol (ICMP)*: When an error occurs in the transmission of IP packets, the ICMP protocol is used to notify the sender of the packet of that error. For example, if a packet is dropped because the TTL field is 0, the sender will receive an ICMP message with this information. ICMP messages can also be used to check whether a machine is reachable in the network.

- *Transmission Control Protocol (TCP)*: This protocol uses the IP Layer to establish an end-to-end reliable connection between two IP machines. TCP connections look like a pipe of bytes in the network. The sender puts bytes into the pipe, and the receiver gets the bytes out. No structure exists (for example, message boundaries) in the TCP connection.

- *User Datagram Protocol (UDP)*:   This protocol uses the IP Layer to establish end-to-end unreliable communication between two IP machines. UDP has a message structure associated with it. It takes a block of data called the *message* from the sender and gives the same block of data (preserving boundaries) to the receiver. Message boundaries are preserved, but messages may be lost in the network.

- *Application protocols*: Any application protocol can be implemented on top of TCP or UDP. In almost all implementations, a standard interface called the *sockets interface* enables the protocol to work on top of TCP and UDP. Some of the commonly used application protocols include *FTP*, which is used to transfer files; *Telnet,* which enables terminal emulation; *SMTP,* which is used to transfer email between machines; and *HTTP,* which is used to transfer documents on the World Wide Web.

- *Simple Network Management Protocol (SNMP)*: This application protocol is used to manage the operations and configurations of an IP network. Each IP machine and each protocol layer are required to make some of their configuration and performance information available over the network. This information is exchanged using a structure called a *MIB (Management Information Base)*. The SNMP protocol allows for changing and reading of the values in a MIB.

When packets are carried to be sent out on a link, the logical packet structure consists of different headers that are nested inside in the manner shown in the top of Figure 4.3. The second row in Figure 4.3 shows the structure of an HTTP message containing an HTTP header and the data. A single HTTP message may be transmitted as multiple TCP segments. One possible segmentation of the HTTP header and data is shown in Figure 4.3 (the third row). The first segment contains part of the HTTP header. The second segment contains the remaining HTTP header and some of the data. The third segment contains the rest of the HTTP data field. The size of each segment is determined by the congestion-control and flow-control algorithms implemented by TCP.

A single TCP segment could be transmitted as one or more IP packets on the network, as shown in the bottom row of Figure 4.3. Only the first IP packet contains the TCP header.

Figure 4.3   Loss of header information in packet fragments.

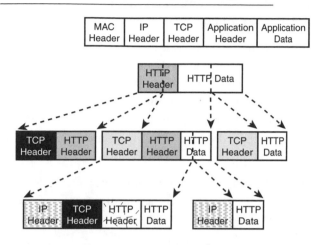

> **Note**
>
> *Congestion control schemes* are mechanisms to ensure that none of the routers in the middle of the network are getting overwhelmed by the traffic. *Flow control schemes* are mechanisms used to ensure that the receiver is not getting overwhelmed by the sender.

The fact that TCP headers may not be present in all packets can cause some practical concerns in building IP firewalls and QoS mechanisms. These concerns are addressed in further discussions of classifiers and access routers in subsequent sections.

Application Communication Process

To understand some of the issues associated with SLAs and QoS, we need to take a closer look at how communication occurs in an IP environment. Specifically, we need to understand how applications talk to each other using TCP and UDP.

At the end hosts, we need some way to distinguish among the different applications that are communicating. In the Internet, each end host is required to support the notion of *ports*. A port is like a mailbox for each tenant in an apartment complex. Each tenant is assigned a mailbox where he or she can receive incoming letters. For outgoing mail, the tenant can simply leave the outgoing letters in an outgoing mailbox (corresponding to the source port in our example), and the carrier will take them from there. The source and destination ports provide this "mailbox" functionality in the computer, which is described in more detail in this section.

The ports are identified by a number at each machine. Each application has to reserve the port it will be using. When an application wants to communicate with another one, it simply needs to send the message to the right destination IP address and the right destination port. Some applications always run on well-known port numbers. Other applications use a *dynamic port number*; that is, they use any port number that is available when they need it.

Communication using TCP transport typically occurs in the following fashion. The application consists of two parts: a client part and a server part. The server part of the application reserves a port number, which is known to the client, and waits for clients to send messages to it (we could say the server is listening on a specific port). The client typically uses a dynamic port and sends an initial message (a connect request) to the server with the identity of the client's receiving port. The server now knows the port number assigned to the client and can accept the request for the connection. Data can be exchanged.

Communication using UDP can occur in the manner previously described, although the connect operation is not always necessary. An application can send messages using UDP to any other application on a known port without necessarily invoking a connect step.

Client applications can know the port number of servers using one of two techniques:

- They know the port number because of an established convention of standard usage.

- They may be given the port number by a user.

When you ask the browser to access a document on the Web, the browser (an HTTP client) assumes that the server is listening on port 80. However, you can also specify another port number when you specify the document. The document identified by `http://9.2.13.4:8080/index.html` tells the HTTP client to talk to a server on machine 9.2.13.4, which is listening on port 8080, and to get the file `index.html` from it. If you had specified the URL as `http://9.2.13.4/index.html`, the browser would have used the convention with HTTP servers to assume it is talking to a server listening on port 80.

TCP and UDP Headers

The header formats of TCP and UDP are as shown in Figure 4.4. The UDP header consists of only four fields; the first two are the port numbers being used at the source machine and the destination machine involved in the communications. Port numbers are 16-bit integers. The third field states the length of the UDP packet, including the 8 bytes of the header. The final field is a checksum over the UDP header fields to guard against packet corruption.

Figure 4.4   TCP and UDP header structure.

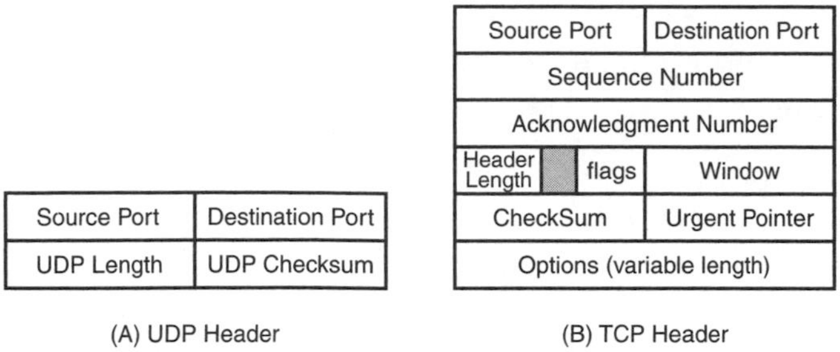

Source Port	Destination Port
Sequence Number	
Acknowledgment Number	
Header Length / flags	Window
CheckSum	Urgent Pointer
Options (variable length)	

Source Port	Destination Port
UDP Length	UDP Checksum

(A) UDP Header   (B) TCP Header

TCP header format is relatively complex compared to UDP because it provides more functions. It begins in the same manner as UDP, with the source and destination port numbers. The next field is a sequence number. The sequence number is needed so that TCP segments can be reassembled at the receiver in the order in which they were transmitted. The acknowledgment number tells the other side how much data has already been received. Acknowledgments are needed for reliable delivery of data. When a TCP user (A) transmits packets to another user (B), the receiver (B) uses the acknowledgment number to tell the sender (A) how much data it has received. This acknowledgment number is carried on a TCP header for packets in the opposite direction—packets being sent by (B) to (A).

Because TCP headers can be variable lengths, a Header Length field is included. Several flags are present in the TCP header. These flags are set in special conditions; for example, the first segment that establishes the TCP connection would have one of the bits in the Flags field set to 1 (this bit is called the *SYN bit*). Similarly, a *FIN bit* in the Flags field marks a segment that indicates the end of data transmission. The Window Size field provides information useful for the flow control scheme and tells the sender how much additional data can be sent in the next segment. A checksum is used for reliability purposes. The urgent pointer is used to point to the location of urgent data in the TCP segment. The urgent data is some information that the sender may want the receiver to obtain ahead of the normal data.

The structure of the TCP and UDP headers are important from the perspective of the SLA and QoS. Information in the header fields enables network devices to determine the applications that may have generated specific packets in the network.

4.2.3 Packet Routing and Routing Protocols

Let us examine how packets are routed within the IP network toward their final destination. Consider a packet that is to be sent to a destination. IP addresses can be up to 32 bits long. Thirty-two bits permit billions of machines to be active at the same time. Most of these machines are many hops away from the destination. For each destination address, each network node just needs to determine which next hop to send the packet toward. Because it is not practical to maintain a table in every node that contains a mapping of all possible IP addresses to the next hop, ways exist to group IP addresses for the purposes of routing and forwarding.

To reduce the size of routing and forwarding tables (and for various other reasons), addresses are clustered into networks. A *network*, in this context, is a group of contiguous IP addresses. The first few bits of IP address represent the network, and the last few bits represent the machine address within the network. The network part of the address could be 8 bits, 16 bits or 24 bits long, resulting in what are called *Class A, Class B* and *Class C addresses*. The first few bits in the beginning of the network address identify the class of the address. Routing entries in a routing table are thus maintained only for every network, not for every address. Each routing entry contains the network address and the next hop router.

Class D Addresses

IP addresses in the range of 224.0.0.0 through 239.255.255.255 are considered *multicast group addresses*, or *Class D addresses*. These addresses identify more than one receiver in the network.

Some of the multicast addresses are considered permanent and are always present. For example, the address 224.0.0.1 reaches all the systems on the LAN, and 224.0.0.2 reaches all the routers on the LAN. Each router receives messages sent on this address. Other multicast addresses are created and managed in a dynamic manner.

Any process on the network can join a group address by contacting a router capable of supporting multicast. The multicast-capable routers periodically exchange group information using a protocol called *IGMP (Internet Group Management Protocol)*. For each group, a spanning tree reaching all known members in the multicast group is maintained. A different spanning tree is maintained for each source and multicast address combination.

When a message is received from a source on one branch of the spanning tree, it is forwarded to all the other branches of the spanning tree. Only routers capable of multicast are included as part of the spanning tree.

On the Internet, routers capable of supporting multicast form an overlay network that runs over all the unicast-only routers in the network. This network of multicast-capable routers is called the *MBONE*.

Multicast group management in IP is well-suited for groups with a large number of receivers and a small number of senders. A very common use of the MBONE has been to transmit video broadcasts of IETF meetings on the Internet.

The transport protocol used on top of multicast IP packets is invariably UDP. The normal TCP assumes that communication is unicast. Multiple efforts have been made to develop a reliable multicast transport protocol, but none have become widely deployed.

Although maintaining routing entries at the network level reduces the size of the routing table, each router still needs a large number of entries for Class C networks. Up to 2 million Class C networks are possible. It is useful to combine multiple routing table entries into one, wherever possible. This is the idea behind *CIDR (Classless InterDomain Routing)*, which does away with the notion of the classes and attempts to combine routing table entries wherever possible. CIDR also comes with recommendations for hierarchical address assignment in the Internet, which can improve the efficiency of CIDR. Each network is identified by the starting address in the network and the length of the *CIDR prefix*, which is the number of bits indicating the network address. An address of 148.2.8.0/21 would cover all the possible addresses from 148.2.8.0 to 148.2.127.255, the equivalent of all 128 Class C networks in that range. If the next hop to all these networks are the same, a single routing table entry can replace 128 equivalent entries for those Class C addresses.

The next hop router to send a packet to is determined by looking at the routing table entry with the longest prefix that matches the destination address of the packet. If no such entry is found, the packet is sent to a preconfigured default router.

The next hop information in the routing table depends on the topology of the network. Because this topology can change as new machines or existing links are added, schemes are needed to keep the routing table information current. These protocols (commonly called *routing protocols*) work as described in the following paragraphs.

The entire Internet is divided into several *autonomous systems (ASes)*. All routers within an AS are in the control of a single network administrative domain. An AS is defined just for the purpose of routing table exchange. An ISP may have more than one AS, or the operator of an intranet may have multiple ASes inside the intranet. All routers within a single AS exchange routing information using an *Interior Gateway Protocol (IGP)*. Different ASes exchange routing information with each other using an *Exterior Gateway Protocol (EGP)*. The EGP determines the most appropriate point to exit from the AS for each network entry outside the AS.

Note

A gateway is an alternative name for a router. Almost all routing protocols use the gateway nomenclature.

A simple network configuration is shown in Figure 4.5. It shows the structure of an AS (numbered AS 4), which interfaces with three other ASes (numbered 1, 2, and 3). AS 4 meets with AS 1 and 2 through a public peering point where router A belonging to AS 1, router B belonging to AS 2, and router 1 belonging to AS 4 are put on a LAN. The three routers A, B, and 1 exchange EGP information with each other. AS 4 and AS 3 have a private peering arrangement. They connect via a serial line using routers 2 and C. Router 2 (in AS 4) and router C (in AS 3) exchange EGP. Furthermore, routers 1 and 2 would use the exterior routing protocol to exchange the information they have learned about routers through other ASes. The routers 1, 2, 3, 4, and 5 will use IGPs to communicate routing information with AS 4 to each other.

Figure 4.5   Routing protocols in an IP network.

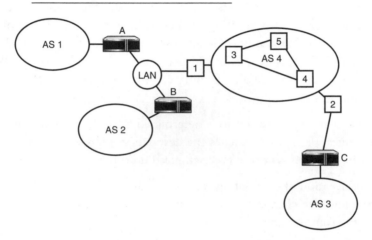

Some examples of an interior routing protocol are RIP, IGRP, and OSPF. *RIP (Routing Information Protocol)* was commonly used in the 1970s and implemented a distributed algorithm to compute the shortest paths among all the routers within an AS. IGRP (Interior Gateway Routing Protocol) is a Cisco proprietary protocol commonly deployed in Enterprise Networks. The current trend, at least in service provider networks, is toward the use of *OSPF (Open Shortest Path First)* . The OSPF protocol exchanges information about link lengths among all the routers within the same AS domain. Each router is able to independently construct a snapshot of the graph representing the entire AS of which it is a part. A shortest path computation is done on this graph to determine which route needs to be followed for each network address. For network addresses that are not in the AS domain, OSPF can use the information about the next AS to come up with the routing table entry.

Routing protocols like OSPF, in which link length is sent to all routers in the administrative domain, are called *link state routing protocols*. In link state routing protocols, each router maintains the topology of the network. In contrast, protocols like RIP and IGRP are distance vector routing protocols. In distance vector routing protocols, each router maintains a table with shortest known lengths to all destinations. Adjacent routers exchange the tables with each other periodically.

RIP computes shortest path in terms of numbers of links traversed to a destination. Each router maintains a table of hop count and the next-hop router towards different destinations. In addition to the periodic exchange, table exchange is triggered on events such as links coming up or down. When an update from a neighbor is received, the shortest path information contained in the new message is combined with the current table information to determine the new table contents. The tricky part with RIP (or any distance vector routing protocol) is to ensure that this combination does not result in a routing loop. RIP uses several techniques for loop prevention, which are generally based on sending a different version of the table to different neighbors. In each version, some of the potential loop-causing paths are given a hop count of infinity, which is the case if RIP means 16 hops. This implies that RIP cannot be used in networks where the path between two routers may involve more than 16 hops.

IGRP is a proprietary protocol developed by Cisco that addresses some of the limitations of RIP. IGRP and its enhanced version, EIGRP (Enhanced IGRP), are commonly deployed in many enterprise networks. Instead of a single hop count, IGRP keeps sophisticated path metrics comprising the sum of transmission delay to the destination, the lowest capacity link along the path, the accumulated error rate (a measure of link reliability) of the links along the path, and a measure of load on the links along the path. The hop count and the maximum packet size of a path are also maintained in the tables. Each router uses a combination of the metrics to determine the shortest length path towards the destinations. IGRP also supports multiple paths towards the same destination, and supports the case of multiple parallel links between two routers. IGRP implements loop prevention algorithms that are similar to ones in RIP, with some variations in the details. One big win over RIP is that IGRP does not have the 16 hop restriction and can be deployed in larger enterprise networks. EIGRP implements a sophisticated loop prevention algorithm called the Diffusion Update Algorithm (DUAL). The details of DUAL and other loop prevention algorithms can be found in the book by Huitema [HUITEMA].

Cisco has patents on portions of IGR; therefore, IGRP and EIGRP can only be deployed in networks consisting solely of Cisco routers. RIP and OSPF are open standard protocols and can be deployed in networks consisting of routers from multiple vendors.

An example of an exterior routing protocol is *BGP (Border Gateway Protocol)*. BGP routers communicate with each other using TCP connections. A program (the routing daemon) implementing the BGP protocol typically runs on each of the access routers at the border of the AS. The routing daemons can communicate with daemons on other access routes within the AS, as well as with routing daemons on any adjacent router that is in a different AS. The BGP protocol requires that each routing daemon exchange the list of network addresses they know, as well as the sequence of ASes that are needed to reach each network address. Each of the BGP routers would then compute the best AS to take for each of the network addresses thus exchanged.

Routing decisions taken by BGP are done in conjunction with routing policies. *Routing policies* allow an AS to specify whether it is willing to act as a transit point for packets originating from other AS domains. A corporation, for example, may not want to deal with any packets except the ones that are sent to or from machines in its domain. An ISP may want to accept packets only from those adjacent ISPs with which it has peering agreements. Restrictions on routing are specified by means of routing policies, which can be specified using a policy specification language [RPSL].

More information on routing in the Internet can be found in the books by Comer [COMER] and Huitema [HUITEMA].

4.2.4   Network Services

The operator of TCP/IP networks requires the use of some servers or applications, such as *DNS servers* and the *DHCP server*. We have selected these servers only because they are basic services or because their presence has an impact upon the support of SLAs in the network.

Domain Name Service

Keeping track of IP addresses as a number is fairly tough, even when they are expressed in the dotted format. As a convenience to human users, the TCP/IP architecture permits applications to identify machines using a character string. The string name is defined in a hierarchical manner. A name consists of a machine name and a domain (just like people have a first name and a surname). The domain itself may be further deconstructed into another level, and so on. The machine with the IP address of 204.146.18.33 has the string name www.ibm.com. This name of the machine is www, and it belongs to the domain ibm.com, which is a subdomain within a larger domain of com.

For the purpose of resolving domain names to IP addresses, name servers are used. The entire domain name space is divided into multiple zones, each zone having a domain name server. The zones are usually (but not necessarily) organized along the same hierarchy as the domains. Each zone has a primary domain name server and possibly some secondary name servers. Each domain name server knows the name servers of its children domains and of its parent. Thus, the domain name server of the com domain would know the children name servers who could resolve any names ending with ibm.com or cisco.com, and so forth.

The translation of string names to IP addresses occurs through an application called the Domain Name Service (DNS). To translate the domain name to an IP address, a local translation file is first checked for the definitions; otherwise, a configured DNS server is contacted. If the DNS server does not know the answer to the query, it contacts another DNS server to obtain the answer. A DNS server first checks whether any of the name servers in the children domain might be able to resolve the name. It does so by comparing the domain name being looked up and the set of names contained in each of the children domains. If the name can be resolved by one of the children name servers, it is passed to that name server. Otherwise, the name is passed to the parent domain name server, which applies the same algorithm recursively. Responses obtained from other DNS servers are cached for a limited period of time to reduce the number of queries.

DHCP Server

A DHCP server is quite often deployed in IP networks for automated configuration of IP workstations. When the IP architecture was originally developed, it was assumed that all machines will have IP addresses statically assigned. It did not account for mobile machines, such as a laptop computer, which may need to be moved across multiple networks. The Dynamic Host Configuration Protocol (DHCP) allows network addresses to be assigned dynamically to the hosts. Of course, DHCP can be used to provide full configuration information to the host, not just the IP address.

During bootup, a machine sends a broadcast to all the machines connected to its physical network looking for a DHCP server. Each physical network has a DHCP server or a relay agent that can relay the requests to DHCP servers on another LAN. The closest DHCP server that obtains the request replies back to the client. After the DHCP server has been identified, the client can communicate with it to obtain the IP address and other configuration information.

DHCP servers are usually configured to give out blocks of addresses to machines belonging to specific subnets. Thus, although the individual addresses of machines may change, the IP network to which the machine belongs does not change. This prevents the need to change IP routing tables whenever addresses are assigned dynamically.

4.3   Basic QoS Building Blocks

The online mechanisms for providing different types of service to different packets are built upon three basic concepts:

- The application states the amount of traffic it expects to send into the network.

- The network ensures that enough resources are available to support the amount of traffic being injected into the network.

- The network identifies the different types of packets in the network and services them in such a way that performance-sensitive packets are serviced first.

Because most applications are not very good at predicting their own performance requirements, you have to make educated guesses about how much traffic an application will be generating. You can use the same techniques to make these estimates as the ones used for network design. You're usually much more likely to get these estimates roughly correct when making them for classes of applications rather than for a specific session of an application.

Because the actual application traffic-generation rate may differ from the ones assumed for capacity planning in the network, you can put mechanisms in place to ensure that the rates being generated are within the assumed limits. These mechanisms constitute the rate controllers or policers in the network.

After the packets are received into the network router, you need to determine the right class of service that is associated with them. This building block is the *classifier*.

After determining the class of service to be applied for all the packets received and waiting to be transmitted, you have to determine the packet to be transmitted first on the outgoing link or to be processed first at the node. This determination is done by a *packet scheduler*, which selects one of the many received and queued packets at the node on the basis of its class of service. The scheduling function is useful only when the node has a queue of packets that need to be processed. If the node is lightly loaded, the scheduling function does not add much value. A lightly loaded network is wonderful for end-user performance. Network operators may, however, find that they have a difficult time making money with a lightly loaded network. The use of a scheduler is intended as an online mechanism to process performance-sensitive packets first when the network nodes and links are experiencing moderate or heavy traffic load, even though the load and, therefore, the congestion, may be transient.

Admission control is the set of rules that can be applied to packet aggregates (application flows, and so on) to regulate how many flows the nodes or links in the network are allowed to experience. If the load on network nodes or links is heavy enough to cause congestion on a regular basis, you need to consider redesigning the network to improve the situation. Otherwise, admission control will cause many flows to be refused.

To explain how the different QoS building blocks work together, we assume a hypothetical model of a router, as shown in Figure 4.6. The router contains two sets of functions; the first set is called *data path functions* and are the operations that have to be performed every time an IP packet is processed by the router. The other set of functions are *control functions*, which include operations that are not done for every IP packet but that may be done on specific types of messages.

In a traditional IP network where packet forwarding is best-effort, the data path function consists of receiving the packet, examining its destination address, looking up the right outgoing interface from the routing table, modifying the fields of the IP header (for example, reducing TTL by one and adjusting its checksum, or fragmenting a packet that is too large to go on the outbound link), and forwarding it along the right output link. The data path function also includes keeping a count of the packets or bytes seen at the router. The control functions include functions such as processing and exchanging routing protocol messages (RIP, OSPF, BGP, and so on) and responding to SNMP queries. These control functions are responsible for managing the information needed for the operation of the data functions.

When QoS support is added to the model router, it performs some additional data functions as well as control functions. A typical data path function includes the steps of classifying the IP packet to determine its QoS requirements, passing it through a rate-control module to ensure rate limits are not being violated, placing the router into a queue from which it is selected for processing on the basis of a scheduling algorithm, and then doing the normal processing of the packet as would be done in the traditional router. The control function may include a mechanism for admission control, assuming that applications are checking with the admission control prior to sending data packets into the network.

The set of functions may be implemented in a different order in different vendors' products. Different types of QoS support implement different subsets of the data and control functions discussed here. In many cases, a control function such as admission control may not be supported. However, the model router is useful for the purpose of understanding the roles of the different QoS building blocks.

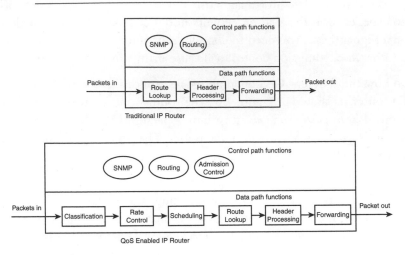

4.3.1 Rate Controllers

The goal of rate control is to ensure that the amount of traffic coming into a network element (node or link) is below a specific amount. Several mechanisms are described here that can introduce such a rate control. *Rate controllers* can be used to delay packets and thus reshape the packet streams being sent into the network. The same mechanisms can also be used for validating whether the packets conform to specific parameter limits—that is, to police the packets. Thus, rate controllers can be used as shapers or policers.

The most basic form of rate control is obtained by the physical capacity of the links that applications are constrained to use. If the physical link that an application can use is a dial-up modem at 28.8Kbps, then the applications are restricted to use no more than that capacity. When the connectivity is through LANs or high-speed serial lines, the speed of the medium may be too high for this to be an effective rate-control mechanism.

When the physical link constraints cannot be counted on for effective rate control, some of the mechanisms described in the following sections can be used. In these sections, we will be focusing on mechanisms that can be implemented in software only.

Token Bucket Rate Controller

The *token bucket rate-control* mechanism requires that every packet arriving at a network interface be assigned a specific number of tokens by the rate-control mechanism before that packet can be sent out into the network. These tokens are kept in a *bucket* assigned for use by the application, hence the name *token bucket*. Each time a packet is transmitted, the appropriate number of tokens is removed from the aforementioned bucket, thus reducing the number of tokens available for subsequent packets. The bucket is refilled with tokens by the rate-control mechanism at a rate determined by the amount of bandwidth to be allocated to the application in question.

For example, assume that we want to restrict an application to using no more than 8Kbps worth of link capacity. Each byte from that application to be transmitted on that link needs to be allocated a token to be transmitted into the network. A packet that is 200 bytes long needs 200 tokens to be sent into the network. Packets have to wait until sufficient tokens (200) are in the bucket, which allows the packet to be transmitted into the network.

Tokens are generated (that is, go into the bucket) according to the desired rate. For the application to be able to use 8Kbps, for example, tokens need to be generated into the bucket for this application at a rate that will support an 8Kbps stream. This is usually done by assigning an appropriate number of tokens at periodic intervals. For example, a rate of 8Kbps (or 1 KBps) can be obtained by generating 100 tokens (one for each byte) every 100ms.

If an application is quiet (that is, does not send any packets) for an extended amount of time, the number of tokens in the bucket can build up significantly. This can, in turn, cause surges of traffic at high rates (up to the link speed) into the network when the application "bursts" a relatively large number of bytes at one time, and the bucket is full of tokens. To prevent this, the total number of tokens that can be accumulated into the bucket is bounded by a limit. This limit is the *bucket depth*. The bucket depth thus limits the number of bytes and, therefore, packets that can be sent into the network at the peak rate of the link.

When a sufficient number of tokens are not available, packets have to wait. Each waiting packet occupies a buffer at the router. If too many packets are arriving and waiting for tokens, the buffer space available may be exceeded, and packets must be discarded.

A rate-control scheme may also follow the scheme that packets not finding the required number of tokens are discarded rather than delayed until a sufficient number of tokens are available.

Timestamp-Driven Rate Controller

The *timestamp-driven rate controllers* operate in a different manner than the token bucket. This approach exploits the capability of many current machines to measure time very accurately using hardware timers.

To restrict an application flow from using a rate in excess of a specific limit (for example, 8Kbps), you can compute the time that would be required to transmit a packet on the link. The difference in timestamps between consecutive packet arrivals can be used to determine whether packets are conforming to the rate limit.

For example, consider a flow of packets that is not to exceed 8Kbps (1KBps, or 1 byte per ms). Suppose a packet 200 bytes long is to be transmitted. At the rate of 8Kbps (1 Byte per ms), this implies that no other packet can be transmitted for another 200ms. You can determine the times when packets are arriving and use that to determine how long the packets need to wait before being transmitted.

As with the token bucket rate controller, each delayed packet requires a buffer at the router. If enough buffers are not available, the packet may need to be discarded. Typically, a timestamp-driven rate controller would have an upper bound on how long a packet can be delayed. If it is determined that the packet needs to wait longer than that time interval, the packet is discarded.

4.3.2 Classifiers

When rate-controlled packets are received at a router, you need to determine to what class of service they belong. This classification can be done in several ways, depending on the granularity of the classes of service into which packets have to be mapped.

One common approach to handling classification has been borrowed from circuit-oriented networks. For each application flow in the network, a *block* is created. This block is created by a control path application that is informed of the existence of the application flow. Some of the fields from the incoming packet are used to identify the correct block associated with the packet. The class of service to be given to the packet is maintained in the block. The block can maintain other information as well, such as parameters needed to ensure rate control. Because blocks have to be created and managed depending on application flow, this approach is most often used with a signaling protocol.

Another approach is to have predefined classes at each router that are identified on the basis of the fields contained in the IP header. In these cases, blocks are predefined. Although this allows only certain predefined classes of services to be supported in the network, the overhead of signaling can be avoided.

The typical fields to be used for the classification process from the IP header include the source and destination IP addresses, the source and destination ports, and the transport protocol. These fields are used in the packet-classification process to identify the appropriate class of service.

The use of port numbers in the classification process implies that packets can only be classified if both the transport and network headers are present in it. If a packet does not contain the transport header, it would be difficult to classify it. To avoid this problem, the transport protocols should attempt to avoid fragmentation. One way to avoid fragmentation is to discover the size of the maximum IP packet that would be supported between a source and a destination, and only generate packets with smaller sizes. A more detailed description of this scheme can be found in [MTUDIS].

4.3.3   Schedulers

The *scheduling process* determines the order in which packets are processed at a node and/or transmitted over a link. The order in which the packets are to be processed is determined by the scheduling policy at the node.

The simplest and most prevalent scheduling scheme is the FIFO queue. In the *FIFO (First In First Out) queues*, the packets that are received first at the node are the first ones to be transmitted out.

The FIFO queue treats all packets as equal. Other scheduling processes treat packets belonging to different classes differently. A variety of other queuing disciplines have been proposed to deal properly with different classes of service. A few common ones are described in the following sections.

Static Priority Schedulers

The *static priority scheduler* consists of multiple FIFO queues. Each queue is assigned a static priority. All packets belonging to the highest priority queue are serviced first. When the highest priority queue is empty, the next queue is serviced. A queue gets to be serviced only when all higher priority queues are empty.

The static priority queues are able to give good performance to the packets in the higher priority queues. However, the packets in the lower priority queues may see a significant degradation in their performance. When this happens, the lower priority queues are said to be *starved* by the higher priority queues because they are denied access to the link.

An issue related to priority is that of *packet preemption*. Suppose a router has two priority levels, and no high-priority packets are present at the current time. A low-priority packet is selected for transmission on the outgoing link. Halfway through the transmission of the packet, a high-priority packet arrives. The router has two choices: it can delay the high-priority packet for the low-priority packet, or abort the current transmission once and transmit the high-priority packet immediately. When the transmission is aborted, the scheduling is called *preemptive*; otherwise, it is called *nonpreemptive*. Most routers implement nonpreemptive scheduling only. The extra delay experienced by the high-priority packet is small compared to the waste of bandwidth associated with aborting a current transmission.

Weighted Fair Queuing

Weighted Fair Queuing is one way to regulate the amount of bandwidth that can be used by each of the different classes of service. Each queue is served round-robin by the scheduler, and the queues are visited with a frequency that is determined by the weights assigned to different classes.

If all the queues are assigned equal weights, then one packet from each queue is serviced in each round. When the link capacity is being fully utilized, this results in an equal division of the link capacity among the different queues.

When each queue is assigned a different weight, a different number of packets are transmitted from each queue during each round of the scheduler. This allows the queues to share the link speed in a different proportion than equally, while avoiding the starvation problem with static-priority schedulers noted in the previous section.

As a simple example, consider two queues that are being served with round-robin weights in the ratio of 2:1. The scheduler servers up to two packets from the first queue on every round and only one packet from the second queue. When several packets are waiting at the router, this would give two thirds of the link bandwidth to packets in the first queue and only one third of the link bandwidth to packets in the second queue. When little traffic is on the link, any of the classes can get the full link capacity.

Weighted fair queuing (or its variants) is found quite commonly in many router implementations and is used for splitting up the link bandwidth into multiple, logical links of separate bandwidth.

4.3.4   Admission Control

Admission control is the process of ensuring that the load on the links is manageable. Usually, admission control determines how many application flows can be mapped into a service class without adversely impacting the performance expected of that service class.

The checks made in admission control can vary, depending on the sophistication desired. You at least need to follow some simple and obvious rules of queuing theory; for example, you should not attempt to admit more average traffic on a link than the link capacity. (That is, average link utilization cannot exceed 100%!) Most networks won't let you load that far. In Ascend routers, you are typically restricted to using 95% of the link, with 5% reserved for network control traffic and slack.

The goal of admission control is to ensure that the average link utilization remains high, while the performance requirements of the applications are satisfied. The right link utilization to be used depends on several factors, such as traffic characteristics and the amount of multiplexing. The general approach has been to make an appropriate queuing model and not let the utilization exceed specific values that are adequate to meet the desired performance level at the routers.

For example, consider a router with an outgoing T-1 link with a QoS requirement that 99% of packets receive less than 10ms of delay. Assume that packets are 200 bytes on average with the lengths exponentially distributed. You can use the M/M/1 queue model discussed in Chapter 3 to see that the 99% delay would be 10ms if the link utilization becomes 51%. Therefore, the goal of admission control would be to keep link utilization less than 51%.

Let's extend the model and say that the router has two priority levels with the delay requirements of the higher-priority traffic being 10ms and the delay requirement of the lower-priority traffic being 100ms. An analysis of the queue would show that the constraints of the higher-priority traffic can be met if utilization is less than 51%, and if the overall utilization (lower + higher priority traffic) is less than 95%. Thus, admission control would want to restrict higher-priority traffic to be no more than 51% and the combined traffic to be no more than 95% of the link's bandwidth. Note that 95% of link bandwidth is what you would normally restrict for the case of best-effort traffic anyway. Therefore, admission control may not be needed for those classes of traffic where the performance requirements are relatively less severe.

Admission control tests depend on the assumptions made in the queuing model, such as the distribution of traffic and packet sizes. They can be made more sophisticated than the simple cases described above. However, any type of admission control depends on the router being aware when more traffic is being injected into the network, at least for the traffic that needs better than the default best-effort performance. This implies that the router should be aware of the establishment of the TCP connections that require better performance.

Normal TCP connection establishment is done only between the end points of a connection, and the routers in the middle are unaware of the existence of the TCP connection. Therefore, some method has to be devised to make the intermediate routers aware of the establishment of new connections. Thus, admission control is usually associated with *signaling*, which is the exchange of messages to ensure that the performance requirements of an application are communicated to network elements such as routers and queues.

> **Note**
>
> The concept of *signaling* is borrowed from telephony networks that use signaling to establish a telephone call within the network. A typical signaling exchange would have one side of a connection send a message indicating that a new connection is being established. This message is forwarded among all the routers in the path that perform the relevant admission control tests and validate that it is possible to accommodate the new connection at the router. Although several protocols for signaling have been explored for IP networks, the predominant protocol is RSVP [RSVP], which is described in the next section.

4.4 Integrated Services with RSVP Signaling

The goal of the Integrated Services (IntServ) Working Group in the IETF is to develop a service model and standard protocols for the Internet that support the transport of such real-time application flows as audio and video, as well as more traditional non–real-time application flows, such as file transfers and transaction processing—all within a single network infrastructure. The dominant QoS paradigm that has emerged from the IntServ Working Group is that of resource reservation using a signaling scheme and the definition of two classes of service.

> **Note**
>
> The way the guaranteed and controlled load services are defined within the IntServ Working Group is that they do not necessarily need RSVP or any other signaling protocol for their operation. However, it does appear that RSVP will be the predominant (if not the only) means for defining and configuring IntServ support in routers. In this section, we consider the support requirements for the application of RSVP and IntServ to be interchangeable.

An application that wishes to reserve resources in the network communicates its requirements to the network routers and the communicating partner(s) using the RSVP signaling protocol. (RSVP protocol is described in more detail in Section 4.4.1.) The routers will reserve local resources for this communication. The reservation is maintained for a *flow*, which is a one-way stream of data flowing to a known destination address and port. Routers in the network create and maintain the state of each flow, in order to determine how much bandwidth (and/or other resources) to allocate to each flow.

As the router receives a packet, it determines the RSVP flow to which the packet belongs and processes it accordingly. Packets belonging to different flows are scheduled differently.

In addition to the signaling support for RSVP, each router has to implement an admission-control function. The admission-control function verifies that the performance requirements of existing flows are not violated when new flows are added. In addition to satisfying performance requirements, other kinds of limits on reservations may be required. You may want to permit the reservation of flows only from specific applications or from specific hosts. The rules that determine which applications can reserve bandwidth by using signaling constitute the reservation policies in the network.

In the next few subsections, we look at the operation of the IntServ functions in more detail.

4.4.1 Signaling and RSVP

The signaling protocol that is most likely to be deployed within an IP network is RSVP. This protocol allows a sender and receiver to reserve resources along the path that is used for communication between them.

The reservation model followed by RSVP is based on simplex flows. The flow is identified by the destination IP address, the transport protocol used by the application, and the port number used by the application. For most practical purposes, we can assume that the transport protocol is either TCP or UDP. In the majority of applications, the flow is data being sent from one sender to one receiver. In some special cases, the flow may represent multiple senders sending to multiple receivers on a multicast group address.

> **Note**
>
> Although RSVP has been heavily influenced by the need to support multicast applications, we will present it mostly in the context of a unicast communication—that is, communication between a single sender and a single receiver. This simplifies the presentation and is closer to our goal of applying RSVP to support SLAs in IP networks, because fewer commercially significant multicast flows exist, as compared to unicast flows, in today's IP networks.

Traffic Specification

A sender of data starts the reservation process by sending out PATH messages. The PATH messages are addressed to the destination and follow the normal route in the network to reach the destination. Each of the PATH messages is sent with a special IP option called the Router Alert option. This option causes the PATH messages to be trapped and processed at each intermediate router along the path of the PATH message. The path traversed by the packet is recorded in the PATH message as it progresses between the routers.

The PATH message also carries a specification of the traffic (Tspec) as it is generated by the sender, as well as the identity of the sender (IP address and port number). The *traffic specification* is a statement made by the sender to the network that it will be generating a packet flow requiring the reservation of resources according to the parameters specified. Further, the traffic specification represents a statement to the effect that the application will not generate packets at a rate that exceeds the traffic rate specified by these parameters. The traffic specification consists of the following terms:

- A peak rate in bytes per second: p

- A bucket size in bytes: b

- A bucket rate in bytes per second: r

- A maximum datagram size: M

- A minimum policed unit: m

The traffic specification implies that the application can send packets into the network only at a long-term average rate of r bytes per second. It is allowed to burst for a short period of time at p bytes per second and can send up to b bytes at the peak rate. When the application has sent up to b bytes at the peak rate, it must cut its rate down to the long-term average rate of r.

The official definition of conformance is that in any period of time t, the number of bytes sent by the application should be less than

$$pt + M$$

and also less than

$$b + rt$$

The number of bytes sent is obtained by adding the bytes sent by each IP packet in that interval. However, IP packets that have a length of less than m, the minimum policed unit, are counted off to become m.

Note
The two limits that define conformance are obtained by the total amount of bytes that the application could send in the time if it was sending in at the peak rate, and if it was sending data at the average rate.

Advertisement Specification

In addition to the accumulated path and Tspec, the PATH message also carries a description of performance characteristics of the path along which the message is being sent. This description is called an *advertisement specification (ADspec)* because it advertises the characteristics of the path to the receiver. The sender initializes the ADspec, and each of the intermediate routers updates the ADspec as it receives the PATH message.

Some of the information carried in the ADspec depend on the type of service class. Other information is always carried and includes the following:

- The count of hops that support RSVP along the path.

- Information about any intermediate hops that do not support RSVP. This is set by a router supporting RSVP which is aware of the existence of the intermediate routers that do not support RSVP.

- Minimum Path Bandwidth specifies an upper bound on the rate available for reservation along the path. If a router cannot allow reservations exceeding this value in the ADspec, it reduces the value to the limit that it can support.

- Path latency specifies the accumulated minimum latency along the path, including the propagation delay and the minimum processing time at each router along the way.

- The maximum size of an IP packet that will not undergo fragmentation along the path.

Note

RSVP assumes that source and destination port numbers will be available during packet forwarding. Therefore, it is essential that packets avoid fragmentation by determining the maximum size of a packet that can be sent without fragmentation during the signaling phase.

Reservation Specification

When the receiver obtains the PATH message, it responds to the PATH messages by sending a RESV message. The RESV message travels hop by hop using the reverse path accumulated in the PATH message. Each reservation message carries a flow specification and a filter specification. The flow specification contains a *reservation specification (Rspec),* which is the rate the receiver would like to reserve along its path, as well as a Tspec. Each router examines the Rspec and may modify it before passing it upstream. The modification of the Rspec is mostly needed for combining reservation requests from multiple users and is not likely to be done for a unicast session.

The reservation of resource is initiated by the receiver, whereas the establishment of flow state is initiated by the sender.

Implications of RSVP

What does the reservation in RSVP really mean? Suppose the receiver has requested a reservation of 56Kbps. The sender could send packets at 128Kbps. However, only some 56Kbps among these packets are deemed to be conformant with the reservation. These packets that are conformant will be assured to have the level of performance implied by their service type. The remaining packets are not assured of any performance better than default best-effort.

It must be realized that the use of reservation would actually degrade the performance of the remaining default best-effort service. Reservations give preferential treatment to some fraction of the traffic, which results in improved performance for them. This would cause best-effort traffic to see a degraded performance. The performance of the system averaged over all the packets is dependent only on packet arrival and service rates and remains unchanged because of reservation. It follows that any reservation attempt to improve the performance of a subset of traffic would reduce the performance of the remaining traffic.

As an analogy, assume you are buying a new plane for a route where you expect 500 people to fly daily. You could buy a plane with 500 seats, all in coach class. Each seat would use 0.2% of the seat space in the plane. If you now decide to have 100 executive class seats, each being 50% larger (use 0.3% of the seat space) than the normal coach class, the remaining 400 seats have to become smaller (use 0.175% of seat space). Alternatively, you can reduce the number of coach seats to 350, increasing the probability of bumping passengers. In either case, the coach class passengers would suffer.

The path and reservation messages are repeated at periodic intervals by the sender and the receiver. If a router does not receive the PATH message or RESV message for a specific amount of time, it deletes the reservation and information about the flow. If packets get rerouted along the network, the PATH and RESV messages would automatically follow the new path and thereby establish a new reservation along the new path.

RSVP has been designed to work well with IP multicast groups. In an IP multicast group, there can be multiple senders as well as receivers. Each receiver sends a Rspec that is dependent on how much bandwidth it can receive. For each multicast group, the same RSVP flow (identified by the multicast group address, protocol, and the port number—although the protocol would almost always be UDP and the port number be 0 as a wild-card or multicast flows) can receive several PATH and RESV messages corresponding to the flow. Each sender would generate its own PATH message. Each receiver in the multicast group would generate its own RESV message.

A RESV message can contain multiple Rspecs of different styles:

- One style of Rspec explicitly names the sender (identified by the sender's IP address and port number) for which the reservation applied. This style is called the *Fixed Filter*.

- Another style of reservation (called *Shared Explicit*) enumerates a set of senders.

- A third style (called *Wildcard Filter*) states that the reservation applies to all the senders that are upstream of the router.

These three styles also specify whether the reservation request from a receiver is for a specific sender, a group of senders, or all the senders. An intermediate router combines all the reservation requests and sends a new Rspec to the upstream router.

Consider a router with three outgoing interfaces and assume that receivers have asked for 56Kbps, 128Kbps and 64Kbps respectively, from a specific sender. The router needs to ask only for a reservation of 128Kbps on the upstream link to satisfy the requests of all the receivers on the three links.

The net result of RSVP signaling is to create a number of reservations at each router. Each reservation is identified by a set of source addresses and ports, a destination address, a destination port, and a protocol. If we concentrate on unicast communication with fixed filters (explicitly naming the source), each reservation would be identified by a 5-tuple consisting of a source address, a source port, a protocol, a destination address, and a destination port.

4.4.2   Service Types and Classes

The IntServ approach provides for two types of services that can be offered in an IP network. The first type of service guarantees quantitative upper bounds on the communication delays seen by the application. The second type of service offers no quantitative guarantees but makes a qualitative assurance that the network performance will not be much worse than the performance of the application on an unloaded network. The former is known as the *guaranteed service*, and the latter is known as *controlled load service*.

The guaranteed service is easy to understand from an application's perspective. However, it can be quite wasteful in its use of network resources. The controlled load service does not offer an easily understood service from an application's perspective, but it can achieve better utilization of network resources.

The remaining traffic, which does not need RSVP signaling, constitutes the best-effort traffic that is supposed to be delivered at a lower priority than the guaranteed or controlled load services.

Guaranteed Service

The guaranteed class of service provides bounds on end-to-end delay and assures a minimum throughput assurance to communicating applications. To obtain an RSVP session with a guaranteed service, an application needs to send a PATH message to the network containing its traffic specification (Tspec) and the advertisement specification (ADspec). Along with the usual items in the ADspec, two additional terms are added for guaranteed class of service:

- Accumulated rate-dependent queuing delay along the path: Ctot

- Accumulated rate-independent queuing delay along the path: Dtot

To manage rates at multicast branching points, reshaping may be done at some nodes. The ADspec also carries the queuing delays that have accumulated since the last reshaping point. The accumulated value determines the maximum buffer space that is needed for reshaping at some other point in the network.

Each router offering guaranteed service is required to compute two parameters: C and D. If a flow has a reserved rate of r Bps in the network, then the variable delay of a packet in the flow at the router must be between 0 and D+C/r ms. The term C is the rate-dependent contribution to the queuing delay. The term D is the rate-independent contribution to the queuing delay. The ADspec for guaranteed service carries the accumulated sum of these terms along the path.

As an example, let us consider a PATH message that traverses three nodes in sequence. The first node has determined that it can schedule packets so that its processing delay is less than 1+10/r ms, where r is the local reserved bandwidth (in Mbps). Similarly, the second node has determined that the processing delay is less than 2+20/r ms. The third node has determined that the processing delay is less than 1+30/r ms. The bounds are determined by analyzing the queuing behavior of the different nodes. The rate-independent bounds are a measure of the minimum fixed delay a packet will experience in the node.

As the PATH messages traverse the first, the second, and the third node respectively, the values of Ctot and Dtot are updated. Assume that the utilization of the link at each of the nodes is 50% after the new connection is accepted. When the ADspec is created, the value of Ctot is 10 and the value of Dtot is 1. At the second node, the values in the ADspec are updated; Ctot is increased by 20 and Dtot by 2. The new value of Ctot is 30 and Dtot is 3. At the third node, Ctot is increased by 30 and Dtot by 1; then the final Ctot is 60 and the final Dtot is 4.

> **Note**
>
> In the example, we have scaled Ctot and Dtot to make the numbers smaller for the sake of illustration. In actual RSVP messages, Dtot is carried in microseconds (1,000 times the values we have used in the example), and Ctot is scaled so that dividing it by the rate in Bps yields answers in microseconds.

After the PATH request for a guaranteed service packet flow reaches the destination, the destination can determine the total amount of delay that would be experienced along the path. This can be done by summing up the propagation delay (carried in the ADspec) with the total queuing delay.

For a traffic with a Tspec of (p,b,r,M), you would typically reserve a rate R, which would be between the long-term average rate r and peak rate p. The total queuing delay can be shown to be less than

$$[(b - M)/R \times (p - R)/(p - r)] + (M + Ctot)/R + Dtot$$

You can reduce the delay further by reserving a rate that is greater than the peak rate p. If a rate R exceeding the peak rate is reserved, then the maximum end-to-end variable delay can be shown to be less than

$$(M + Ctot)/R + Dtot$$

Consider the case of the ADspec described above where on a three-length path, the value of Ctot was 60 and the value of Dtot was 4ms. (Again, we use smaller values for the purpose of illustration.) Assume that the Tspec for the flow being specified required a peak rate of 1Mbps, a bucket size of 10,000 bytes, an average rate (bucket size) of 0.5Mbps, and maximum datagram size of 1,000 bytes. Assume further that the propagation delay is 20ms. The end-to-end delay for different bandwidth assignment would be

Reserved Rate	Delay
2.0Mbps	54ms
1.5Mbps	64ms
1.0Mbps	84ms
0.75Mbps	104ms
0.5Mbps	124ms

If the delay desired by the application was greater than 124ms, you could reserve a bandwidth of 0.5Mbps (its average rate). If the delay desired was less than 84ms, it would need a reservation of 1.0Mbps (peak rate). At lower delay requirements, a higher amount of reservation would be needed. As shown in the table, delay requirements and bandwidth in the network can be traded off for each other.

The total delay bound is obtained by combining the variable delay shown above with the propagation delay in the network. Of course, if there is a link failure and the path of the communication changes, the delay bounds change.

A point-to-point guaranteed delay RSVP flow with a target delay would be established in the following manner:

1. The sender would send PATH messages containing a Tspec and an ADspec that would contain the accumulated delay along the path.

2. The receiver would generate a RESV message upon receipt of the PATH message. The receiver knows the target delay for the session and can determine the rate that would be adequate to meet the delay on the basis of the fields in the ADspec. Suppose the rate selected is R. Of course, if the target delay bound is less than Dtot, it cannot be satisfied for any choice of R.

3. The receiver sends a reservation request back to the sender requesting a rate R and a slack parameter. The *slack* is the difference between the target delay and the rate obtained using the reserved delay R. The routers on the path can use the slack to adjust their resource reservations.

The reservation style used for unicast communication is typically fixed filter.

The Controlled Load Service

Any practical network cannot support too many connections with guaranteed delays. Given the constraints on the service guarantees, network utilization will be fairly poor. The *controlled load service* offers an option to improve the network utilization without unnecessarily impacting the network quality.

The idea behind controlled load service is that the actual performance of the network traffic should not be much worse that the performance when the network is unloaded. This means that the end-to-end network delay must not be significantly greater than the minimum latency carried in the ADspec. Also, the loss rates in the network should be small.

Note

Unfortunately, the specification does not specify what the meaning of not "significantly worse performance" is. Implementers and network operators are free to choose their own definition of acceptable performance and customize their admission control policies around it. One interpretation of it could be that the controlled load traffic reservations should not exceed a fixed percentage of the link bandwidth.

No quantitative assurances are made about the end-to-end performance of controlled load service. Qualitatively, the service is not as good as the guaranteed service, but it is better than the best-effort service.

For example, consider a network with three connections established across it: one belonging to the guaranteed delay class, one belonging to the controlled load class, and one belonging to the best-effort class. The guaranteed delay connection is given a delay bound of 100ms. No packet on that connection will have a delay of less than 100ms. A controlled load connection is not given any delay bound, but you would expect the delay to be typically greater than 100ms but less than, say, 200ms. However, no delay bounds are assigned to the delivery of the packets belonging to the best-effort connection. Depending on the provisioning of the network, the best-effort packet may experience delays up to 500ms.

When an application wants to set up the controlled load service on the network, it specifies its Tspec in the PATH message using the standard Tspec format. The Tspec is received by all the routers along the path. The receiver sends a reservation request containing an amount of traffic to be reserved for its flow. The format used to specify the amount of traffic to be reserved is the same as the one used for specifying the traffic characteristics (that is, a Tspec).

For establishing a unicast connection with a specific rate characterization, it is difficult to imagine a situation in which the rate requested by the receiver would not be identical to the rate advertised by the sender. However, different receivers in a multicast group may want to have different reservations, depending on their capabilities.

Best-Effort Service

For completeness, we must also mention the *best-effort service class,* which would need to coexist with the guaranteed and controlled load service class. This is the default class of service provided to applications that did not use signaling to establish a state for themselves in the network.

The only caution regarding best-effort service is that you should exercise care in not degrading the best-effort service too much when deploying controlled or guaranteed services in the network. The fact that this traffic exists and that its requirements are important is often missed in the details of guaranteed and controlled load services.

When multiple types of traffic are in the network, the performance of best-effort traffic depend not only on the load on the network, but also on the type of traffic mix in the network. The percentage of traffic in the mix can significantly influence the performance and delay characteristics of the network traffic. In general, as the percentage of higher-priority traffic increases, the performance seen by the best-effort class of traffic degrades.

4.4.3   Packet Processing

In this section, we describe the operations that need to be performed on IP packets as they are received at a router that supports the IntServ model of service classes. The first step is to determine whether the packet has an associated reservation with it, either for the guaranteed load or the controlled load service.

As mentioned in Section 4.4.1, the reservation is identified by the 5-tuple consisting of the source IP address, the source port, the protocol, the destination address, and the destination port (at least in the case of fixed-filter reservations). Therefore, the packet scheduler has to extract these five fields from the packet header and determine whether a corresponding reservation exists.

After the reservation has been found, you need to determine whether the packet is conformant to the Tspecs. If the packet is conformant, it should be forwarded at the corresponding class of service priority. However, if the packet is not conformant, it is given the default best-effort priority. A nonconforming packet can also be dropped.

Packets that are deemed conformant are scheduled for processing or transmission on the outgoing link. These can be scheduled according to one of the many queuing schemes described in Section 4.3.3.

Neither RSVP signaling nor the IntServ class of service specify any details on admission control, leaving this function strictly up to the local implementation. For guaranteed delay service, admission control would be fairly strict. However, the router can accept any number of connections as long as the constants C and D included in the ADspec of different connections are valid.

4.4.4   Policy Control

The main issue with policy is to try to answer the following questions:

- Who is entitled to signal a reservation request using RSVP?

- Which requests should be honored by a router and which ones should be rejected?

Consider a corporate intranet in which RSVP is deployed. Any application can signal that resources be reserved for it. If no internal charge back is associated with any reservation, no incentive exists to not ask for the maximum possible reservation that you can extract from the network. Obviously, a free-for-all reservation architecture is not likely to perform any better than a best-effort service. It can even perform worse. A user who is relatively sloppy at ending reservations may hog a large amount of bandwidth and never give any of it up.

The policy control module in RSVP decides who should be allowed to make reservations and also limits the amount and duration of a reservation that can be made. When reservation requests are received by the routers, they check the policy control module to ensure that the reservation will be honored.

Some of the routers in the network may not be capable of making policy decisions on their own. In those cases, the routers can obtain policy decisions from an external policy server using a protocol called *COPS (Common Open Policy Service)*.

When signaling for the reservation using the PATH message or RESV message, the end points involved in an RSVP flow can include a policy object as part of the message. This policy object can (among other things) identify the user requesting the reservation, the organization requesting the reservation, or the application requesting the reservation. The policy server can thereby enforce policy decisions at various levels of granularity.

Policy decisions can prevent a person from hogging resources, or they can allow reservations to be made only by specific applications that are considered business-critical.

Note

The problem of resource hogs is painfully apparent in any organization that deploys software with limits on the maximum number of simultaneous users. At the IBM Thomas J. Watson Research Center, we had such a limit on FrameMaker licenses for UNIX workstations. Although a timeout period existed for licenses, it was quite large. One late night, when preparing a document urgently needed next day, I found all licenses in use. Puzzled by the demand for the tool late at night, I checked out the first 10 users who were holding the licenses. Eight of the 10 users had an idle time of more than six hours on their workstations. They had just forgotten to give up their license or to quit their editor when they went home. One of my coworkers had three simultaneous licenses for the editor. It happened that he had several windows open on his screen and could not remember that he had two other instances of the same application when he launched it for the third time. None of the folks were maliciously trying to hold on to the licenses and would have readily given it up had they realized that other people needed it.

Like the hogging of software licenses, hogging of bandwidth reservation in the network is quite likely to occur because of human nature—for example, perfectly decent folks who inadvertently forgot to stop a resource-intensive application before leaving. Although the technical issues with resource reservation have been more or less solved, the operational issues are very much in the dark. These issues make policy control much more important in RSVP-enabled networks.

4.5 Differentiated Services

Differentiated Services (DiffServ) offers an alternative way to support QoS in IP networks. The original push for DiffServ comes from the realization that the signaled approach may not be the best possible one in many environments (see Section 4.6 for more discussion on the comparison of the two approaches).

The DiffServ model dispenses with signaling altogether and relies on the use of network provisioning to offer multiple classes of service in the network. From a pragmatic point of view, it makes for a significantly simpler system than the IntServ approach.

One of the main difficulties involved with RSVP/IntServ is that the routers in the network need to use the 5-tuple to associate packets with network flows. Although the number of network flows in most campus and access routers is manageable, the number of network flows that can occur in a core router could be quite large. Consider the transport of compressed telephone-quality voice (around 7Kbps) connections over a T-3 (45Mbps) line. This results in about 6,000 possible flows. Tracking such a large number of flows in routers poses a significant challenge.

The main idea behind the DiffServ approach is that the information about the QoS of a packet is encoded in a single byte of the IP header and that this is used to provide a limited number of different classes of service in the network. This leads to the DiffServ architecture as described in the following section.

4.5.1 DiffServ Architecture

The model of a DiffServ network is shown in Figure 4.7. The network shows a single administrative domain. The network contains two types of routers: access routers and core routers. The access routers connect the network to different customer networks or other ISP networks. The core networks provide connectivity among the other routers in the same administrative domain and are not connected directly to any customer network.

Note

This model is almost identical to the structure of most ISPs as described in Figure 1.1.

The core routers in the network can handle packets differently depending on the contents of the Type of Service (ToS) byte contained in the IP header. This is essentially reusing the ToS for its original, intended purpose. Instead of the full 8 bits in the ToS byte, only 6 bits are available for service differentiation. The other 2 bits are reserved for future use (with the most likely candidate being explicit congestion notification for TCP). These 6 bits constitute the DiffServ field in the IP header.

Figure 4.7   DiffServ network architecture.

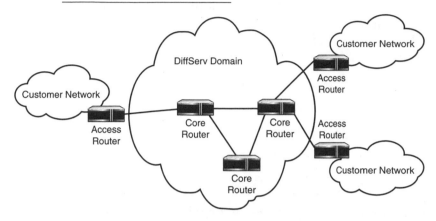

Each of the 32 possible combinations, with the 6 bits of the DiffServ field, signify that the packet should be handled differently by the core routers. Each different type of processing that can be provided to the packet is called a different *Per Hop Behavior (PHB)*. Currently, four types of PHB are specified for use within the DiffServ network. These are the class selector PHBs, expedited forwarding, assured forwarding, and the default set of PHBs. These PHBs are described further in Section 4.5.3.

The access routers in the network have the responsibility of classifying the packets marked for processing by one of the PHBs that are supported within the DiffServ network.

4.5.2 DiffServ Access Routers

The DiffServ access routers perform the following functions on the packets they receive from the customer network:

- Classification

- Rate control

- Metering

- Marking

The classification of packets can be done in one of two manners, depending on the connectivity of the access router. Some of the access routers are connected to customer networks (that is, these customers are not themselves network operators), and some access routers are connected to other network operators (ISPs).

An access router that is connected to a customer network is expected to use six fields in an incoming IP packet to determine the PHB that the packet should receive in the core networks. These six fields are

- IP source address

- IP destination address

- Transport protocol

- DiffServ field in the incoming packet header

- Source ports in the transport headers

- Destination ports in the transport headers

A rule that maps a packet to a PHB does not need to specify all six fields. We refer to these rules as *classification rules*. When a classification rule does not specify any specific value for a field, that specific field's packet header is not used for the purpose of classification.

As an example of a classification rule, a rule can state that all packets with a transport protocol field value of 6 and a source or destination port number of 80 should be assigned to the expedited forwarding PHB. The protocol field value of 6 indicates a TCP connection, and the port number of 80 is usually used by Web servers. This rule is essentially mapping all Web traffic into the expedited forwarding class. By specifying a destination or source IP address along with the port number, you can restrict the rule to Web servers running on specific machines.

Other types of access routers could use just one field in the incoming IP packet to determine the PHB for their network. This field could be the DiffServ field contained in the incoming packet. An access router would simply change the DiffServ Field to some other value that corresponds to a specific PHB at the core routers. This type of classification would be the one expected at the exchange points of other ISPs. The other ISP domain may have been using a different set of PHBs or may use different DiffServ field values to represent the same PHB.

The specific DiffServ field value that corresponds to a PHB is called a *DiffServ code point*. The DiffServ specifications state that code points should be assigned by means of configuration by an ISP operator.

In addition to the classification process, the access routers should change the DiffServ field value so that it corresponds to the correct PHB behavior in the core network. It can also exert rate control or shaping on all the packets that have been determined to be in a specific PHB. Thus, an access router may limit the total number of packets that can be sent into each PHB. Although no traffic specifications have been explicitly standardized for the access router, the format of Tspec as used in IntServ could provide a reasonably decent traffic specification for rate control. If it is found that a packet cannot be mapped into any of the PHBs because a limit is being exceeded, it may either be mapped into a different PHB or discarded.

Statistics can also be calculated and kept at the access router to determine how many packets of each class are being received at each access router.

4.5.3 DiffServ PHBs

The DiffServ PHBs represent the different types of processing that a packet can receive in the network. Four types of PHBs are currently defined in the network:

- Default behavior

- Class selector

- Expedited forwarding (EF)

- Assured forwarding (AF)

A core router only needs to support a subset of all possible PHBs.

The default or best-effort PHB corresponds to the default best-effort packet forwarding in a network. Packets belonging to this PHB could be forwarded in any manner without any restrictions. The recommended code point for best effort PHB is 0x000000.

The class selector PHBs define up to eight classes in the network. These class selector PHBs are required to have a DiffServ field that takes one of the following eight values:

000000	010000	100000	110000
001000	011000	101000	111000

In other words, this PHB uses only the first three bits of the DiffServ field, and the last three bits are zeroed out. The first three bits form a numeric number from 0 to 7. A packet with a higher numeric value in the DiffServ field is supposed to have a better (or equal) relative priority in the network for forwarding than a packet with a lower numeric value. A router need not implement eight different priority levels in the network for supporting the class selector PHBs. It can claim compliance with the standards by supporting only two priority levels, with the eight numeric values mapping to one of the two classes. The DiffServ field of 000000 in the case of class selector PHB is the same as that for default forwarding.

The EF PHB has a rate associated with it. This rate must be configurable by the system administrator. An upper limit as well as a lower limit may be specified for this rate. Packets belonging to the EF PHB must be serviced at a rate that is between the two specified limits. The rate limits must be obeyed independently of the load on the queue from other types of traffic. The recommended code point for EF PHB is 101110.

The AF PHB defines a set of four classes, which have to be assigned individual bandwidth and buffer allocation at each router. The classes are independent of each other. These classes are to be served at the assigned bandwidth on average. Within each class, three loss priorities are defined. The loss priorities may be collapsed into two loss priorities. Packets within the same class with a lower loss probability should be less likely to be discarded than the one with a higher loss probability. The recommended code points for AF are as follows:

	Class 1	Class 2	Class 3	Class 4
Low Drop Precedence	001010	010010	011010	100010
Medium Drop Precedence	001100	010100	011100	100100
High Drop Precedence	001110	010110	011110	100110

4.5.4   PHB Implementation with Packet Schedulers

In this section, we look at some typical packet schedulers and how they can be used to support the PHBs described in Section 4.3.3.

Static Priority Queues

Consider a static priority queue scheduler with two levels of priorities. Such a scheduler serves packets in the higher-priority queue if they are available and only serves the lower-priority queue if the higher-priority queue is empty.

This scheduler can support the class selector PHBs by mapping packets with the DiffServ fields of 100000, 101000, 110000, and 111000 into the higher-priority queue and those with the DiffServ fields of 000000, 001000, 010000, and 011000 into the lower-priority queue. Other mappings are also possible. The DiffServ standards require that packets with the DiffServ fields of 110000 and 111000 should map to the higher-priority queue, and packets with the DiffServ field of 000000 should map to the lower-priority queue. Packets with other DiffServ fields can be mapped to either of the two queues. A network administrator should ensure that the mapping is consistent across all the routers within a single administrative domain.

It cannot support the AF PHB because there are only two levels instead of four. It can support some of the function of the EF PHB by mapping it to the higher-priority level. However, it cannot enforce an upper limit on the rate at which the packets in the higher-priority level can be supported. As a result, a simple two-level priority queue cannot support the EF or AF PHB.

If the static priority queue is augmented with rate controls, it can be used to implement the EF upper rate limit. The rate–controlled, static-priority queuing system can be used to implement EF.

If at least four rate-controlled priority queues exist, they can be used to implement the four AF classes with limits on their maximum rate utilization as well.

If a router wants to support AF as well as EF traffic, it would need to map the packets into separate levels. Mixing EF with another level in AF can cause fairness issues between them and may result in one or more classes not receiving the minimum assured rate.

Weighted Round-Robin

A round-robin scheduler with weights assigned to each of multiple queues would be the closest match to the implementation of the EF and AF PHBs. The round-robin queues could be assigned weights so that they would be able to serve each of the queues in the normal order. Class selector PHBs could be supported, provided packets with the DiffServ field of 110000 and 111000 are mapped to a queue with a larger weight that the queue to which packets with the DiffServ field of 000000 are mapped.

If a router were to implement only the EF and default PHBs, it would need to implement only two queues, which are served round-robin with specific weights assigned to them. If the router were to implement EF, AF, and the default, it would need six queues overall, each with a different assigned weight.

4.5.5 DiffServ Policies

With the availability of any level of differentiation, you have to answer the question: Who or what gets which class of service? The answer to this question constitutes DiffServ policy. To manage the performance of a DiffServ network, you must also obtain the configuration information for all the DiffServ access routers so that the classifiers and rate controllers at DiffServ boundaries can be managed to meet expectations.

Communication in any network is bidirectional, and improving the quality of communication requires improving performance in both directions. Thus, trying to improve the performance of a specific application session requires configuring at least two access routers. Coordinating a consistent configuration of multiple access routers is a nontrivial task.

The goal of policy architecture for DiffServ is to have a consistent configuration of the different access routers in a single administrative domain, under the control of a logically centralized repository, which, in turn, is under the control of a single network administrator for that domain. A simplified example network topology that uses this approach is shown in Figure 4.8. The different access routers obtain policy configuration from a centralized policy server. The policy server is implemented as a directory server and is accessed using LDAP (Lightweight Directory Access Protocol). A management tool populates the server with the policy information after validating that the policies stored in the repository are mutually consistent.

The core routers in the network must also be configured to support the different PHBs in a consistent manner. The core routers can also access the policy server to obtain the mapping from the configured code points to the different scheduling queues that are supported by the routers. (For a more complete description of policy architecture, see Chapter 5, "A General SLA Architecture")

Figure 4.8   Policy model for DiffServ.

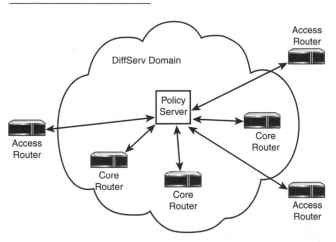

A standard format for representing service policies in the repository is being developed in the Policy Framework Working Group within the IETF [POLICY]. Related standards work in this area is also going on in the Service Level Agreements (or Policy) Working Group of the DMTF [DMTFREF].

4.6   Comparison of Approaches in Different Environments

In this section, we compare the IntServ/RSVP and DiffServ approaches to manage QoS in networks and assess their effectiveness in different environments. Keep in mind that neither signaled reservation nor DiffServ are of much use in networks with a homogeneous traffic mix. By a *homogeneous traffic mix,* we mean a traffic mix where the performance requirements of applications do not differ significantly. If the network mix is predominated by a single application type and all instances of the application are equally important, then neither of the two approaches result in a significant gain. Neither RSVP/IntServ nor DiffServ are capable of improving the average performance of the network. What they provide is preference for selected sets of applications over others. The average performance characteristics of the network do not improve by the deployment of any of the QoS approaches.

In the case of homogeneous traffic, no gains are made by the use of service differentiation over a properly provisioned best-effort network. Most of the packets will be classified into the same category, and any per hop behavior will be reduced to essentially a FIFO behavior. If anything, the extra processing required to classify the packets and to configure the classification policies is likely to introduce additional overhead and complexity.

If you use RSVP/Intserv signaling to reserve connections in a homogeneous traffic case, the results are somewhat different. In a best-effort network, the connections would have experienced a bad performance in those cases where the network links get overloaded. The admission control algorithms ensure that only those connections that can be assured a good performance are going to be established. Thus, the decreased probability of bad performance would be translated into a corresponding increased probability of connection blocking.

It is unclear which of the two is a better option. For most applications, it would be better to have the application be able to communicate at a slightly worse performance. Many applications are able to adjust for some degradation in the network performance by buffering at the end points. It is possible that some applications would be better off getting no service rather than a degraded service, but such applications are hard to think of. Because admission control assumptions used for reserving connections are usually pessimistic, even links that may be considered overloaded using the admission control can quite often result in acceptable performance for applications.

Because of these reasons, it is probably better to simply use a well-designed best-effort network when the traffic on the network is predominantly of one type.

At the same time, most of the networks in practice are likely to carry a mix of traffic. In corporate networks, it is quite common to have business-critical traffic mixed with lower-priority traffic. For example, financial firms often need to distribute stock quotes in a timely manner over their internal networks. This same network also carries Web-surfing traffic from different users as well as email, which can wait a few minutes for delivery. Service differentiation techniques could be used advantageously in such environments.

Similarly, when SLAs have been put into effect for different organizations, the performance levels specified in the SLAs may or may not differ for different customers. If different customers get different performance levels, then QoS techniques can be used effectively to support them. On the other hand, if all that is offered to different customers is a generic SLA that offers the same level of performance to all customers, appropriate network design coupled with network monitoring is the most appropriate approach.

In the following sections, we consider the merits and drawbacks of both RSVP and DiffServ as an approach to provide QoS in a mixed environment.

4.6.1 *Strengths and Weakness of IntServ/RSVP*

As a service differentiation, RSVP/IntServ provides a way to negotiate end-to-end QoS. The service class that is requested could result in guaranteed end-to-end delays or a qualitative controlled load class of service.

As we consider the applicability of RSVP/IntServ to support SLAs in the network, the major strengths of the IntServ/RSVP approach are the following:

- *Assured Quality of Service*: After RSVP is deployed in the network, you can ensure that specific network flows reserve specific amounts of resources in the network. If the RSVP reservation is successful, a connection can obtain an assured level of service from the network.

- *Automatic adjustment to route changes*: Because RSVP messages follow the same route as normal datagrams in the network, they are able to reserve capacity along the right path without making assumptions regarding how routing protocols work. Doing proper capacity planning and allocation using DiffServ or in best-effort networks makes assumptions regarding the routes taken by packets in the network.

Note

One of the strengths of RSVP is its support of multicast communication. However, that may not be very relevant for supporting SLAs in the network.

However, you must also be aware of the limitations of this approach:

- *Scalability.* The use of RSVP flows requires that the routers in the network maintain information about the application flows. This can translate into a large number of flows that need to be tracked at intermediate routers, which can slow down processing considerably. Another aspect related to scalability is that of the signaling load on the network. Because each application flow has to generate periodic PATH and RESV messages that need to be processed by intervening routers, the routers have to process a large number of messages per reserved flow.

- *Reservation latency.* Each reservation is established by an exchange of PATH and RESV messages. The sender is only assured of reservation on the receipt of the first RESV message from the downstream router. These messages take a much slower path in each router's packet processing when compared with the usual packets, which are only forwarded by the routers and extensively processed only at the end points of the connection. This implies that the approach would not work too well for short-lived connections.

  The general approach to deal with the reservation latency is to recommend that communication be started while the reservation is in progress. For connections that are short-lived, the connection would likely be terminated before the reservation completes, rendering the entire effort useless. On the other hand, if we decide to defer communication until the reservation is made, the overall connection latency increases significantly, which would result in a perceived lower network performance.

- *Traffic burstiness.* The signaled approach works best when the data on the connections is relative predictable. The predictability does not necessarily mean that the traffic is generated at a constant rate, but only that the rate be amenable to effective admission-control techniques. Although admission control is orthogonal to reservation protocols, it forms a key component in the overall mechanism to ensure QoS. Most admission control algorithms work best with predictable traffic. Although admission control algorithms for bursty traffic do exist, they do a relatively poor job at efficient utilization of link bandwidth.

- *Coexistence with IP Security protocols.* IntServ relies upon the capability to look at the destination (and source) port numbers to determine the flow to which a packet belongs. When the IP payload is encrypted so that the information in the header protocol is no longer available, no way exists to determine this information any more. Thus, the use of secure communication with IPsec in combination with IntServ is not possible the way the current standards are defined, except by creating RSVP tunnels at the endpoints, carrying the IPsec encrypted payload within the tunnels.

> **Note**
>
> Two prevalent modes of obtaining secure communication exist in IP networks. The first mode uses encryption above the Sockets API to encrypt messages between a client and server. This is the common mechanism using SSL (Secure Sockets Layer) and is commonly used between Web servers and browsers for secure communication. Using SSL information, transport headers remain visible to intermediate nodes.
>
> The other common form is to encrypt packets at the IP Layer between end machines, and/or to create encrypted tunnels between firewalls. In this method, the payload of an IP packet is encrypted. Because the payload of the IP packet includes the TCP and UDP packet headers, the latter are no longer visible to intermediate routers.
>
> This can be done using the IPsec protocol specifications, and it poses problems for RSVP-style reservations.

- *Mismatch with TCP/IP application establishment model*: The RSVP signaling model requires the initiation of the PATH messages by the sender of a flow and the initiation of the RESV messages by the receiver. In most of the client/server applications, the major bulk of data flows from the server to the client, but the communication is initiated by the client. To use RSVP with the client/server mode of communication (for example, in a Web page access using HTTP), the client needs to establish a connection to the server, the server needs to generate a PATH message, and the client needs to generate a RESV message in response to the PATH message. These extra flows are at odds with the most common form of unicast communication. Therefore, the use of RSVP to improve access to a preferred Web site is likely to not work very well.

Despite these limitations, you can use RSVP with some restrictions to support SLAs in the network. Further details on the exploitation of RSVP to support SLAs in networks can be found in Chapter 6, "SLA Support in Different Network Environments."

4.6.2 Strengths and Weaknesses of the DiffServ Approach

The DiffServ approach is much simpler than the IntServ approach. The strengths of the DiffServ approach for supporting and managing SLAs include the following:

- *Simpler architecture*: The architecture used by DiffServ is much simpler than that of IntServ/RSVP approach. Although this simple model does not achieve all the guarantees in an end-to-end manner, it does provide for a simpler and more efficient deployment. An important point about the DiffServ architecture is that is very close to the SLA architecture that we propose in Chapter 6, as well as the ISP network architecture described in Chapter 1.

- *Scalability*: Because the classification of packets into different classes of service is done using the ToS field, routers supporting DiffServ only have to learn about a few limited types of PHBs. This allows for a much more scalable architecture.

- *Coexistence with IPsec*: If the marking of the DiffServ field can be done before packet payloads are encrypted, the DiffServ fields can be used to provide service classification even in the presence of encrypted packet headers. IPsec protocols ignore the ToS field for the purpose of packet integrity checks; therefore, the field can be marked and remarked as appropriate at various points in the network.

At the same time, the DiffServ architecture has the limitation that the QoS it offers is relatively coarse. The different classes are provided assurances about the performance of the aggregate, but no end-to-end QoS is provided for explicitly at the level of a single source to single destination application flow.

4.7 Further Information

We have provided only a very broad overview of TCP/IP Networks. An excellent detailed overview of the architecture can be found in a series of books by Douglas Comer [COMER]. A good general overview of network protocol and architecture can be found in the text by Tannenbaum [TANNEN].

In addition, a few books are written explicitly on the topic of QoS in the network. A good overview of QoS approaches using RSVP is given by Ferguson [FERGUSON]. A book describing DiffServ in detail [KILKKI] is also available.

We have mostly concentrated on IP version 4, which is the one most commonly deployed in current networks. A newer specification of IP, IP version 6, is also available, which simplifies many of the issues with the current version of IP. Both RSVP and DiffServ can be used with IPv6 networks. More information on IPv6 can be found in the books by Thomas[THOMAS] or Loshin [LOSHIN].

4.8 Endnotes

[COMER] Comer, Douglas. *Internetworking with TCP/IP: Principles, Protocols, and Architecture*. Upper Saddle River, NJ: Prentice Hall, 1995.

[DEERING] Deering, S., and R. Hinden. Internet Protocol, Version 6 (IPv6) Specification, Internet RFC 2460, December 1998.

[DMTFREF] Desktop Management Task Force. Technical Committee on Service Level Agreements. Available at http://www.dmtf.org/info/sla.html.

[FERGUSON] Ferguson, Paul, and Geoff Huston. *Quality of Service: Delivering QoS on the Internet and in Corporate Networks.* New York: John Wiley & Sons, 1998.

[HUITEMA] Huitema, C. *Routing in the Internet.* Upper Saddle River, NJ: Prentice Hall, 1995.

[KILKKI] Kilkki, Kalevi. *Differentiated Services.* Indianapolis, IN: Macmillan Technical Publishing, 1999.

[LOSHIN] Loshin, P. *IPV6 Clearly Explained.* San Francisco: Morgan Kaufman, 1999.

[MTUDIS] Mogul, J., and S. Deering. "Path MTU Discovery," Internet RFC 1191, November 1990.

[POLICY] IETF Policy Framework Working Group. Available at `http://www.ietf.org/html.charters/policy-charter.html`.

[POSTEL] Postel, J., ed. "Internet Protocol——DARPA Internet Program Protocol Specification," RFC 791, DARPA, September 1981.

[RPSL] Alaettinoglu, C. et al. "Routing Policy Specification Language (RPSL)," Internet RFC 2280, January 1998.

[TANNEN] Tannenbaum, Andrew S. *Computer Networks.* Upper Saddle River, NJ: Prentice Hall, 1996.

[THOMAS] Thomas, Stephen A. *IPng and the TCP/IP Protocols: Implementing the Next Generation Internet.* New York: John Wiley & Sons, 1996.

[TOPOC] Topolcic, C. "Experimental Internet Stream Protocol, Version 2 (ST-II)," Internet RFC 1190, October 1990.

5

A General SLA Architecture

Thus far in the book, we have discussed the problem of defining service level agreements and reviewed some of the basic concepts associated with TCP/IP networks, network design and quality of service (QoS). In this and the next chapter, we outline an approach that can be used to support SLAs in TCP/IP networks.

SLAs have different meanings depending on the services provided by the network operator. A network operator providing raw IP connectivity offers a different SLA than the CIO of an enterprise IT department. In spite of the differences, many common techniques can be used to support SLAs in a large number of environments. We present these techniques as part of a common SLA architecture.

This architecture defines what functions are required at different parts of the network to support SLAs and where these functions may be located. It also defines how devices supporting these different functions can be configured and managed to support SLAs.

5.1 *Prevalent SLA Types in IP Networks*

At least three types of SLAs can be provided in an IP network. The difference between the SLAs depends on the nature of services provided by the network operator to its customers.

- The first type of SLA is the one that is offered by a provider offering IP connectivity to its customers. Such network providers (UUNET, for example) provide SLAs specifying the reliability and availability of connectivity to the network. We refer to these SLAs as *network connectivity SLAs.*

- The second type of SLA is the one that is offered by a provider offering I/T support to its customers. A common example of such an operator is the executive of an I/T department. The I/T department is in charge of clients as well as servers in the network, and it needs to control end-to-end performance of the different applications. We refer to such SLAs as *application SLAs*.

- A third type of SLA is the one that is offered by providers such as Exodus. These providers offer server-hosting capabilities to their customers. These providers control only the server's end of the network. We refer to such SLAs as *service provider SLAs*.

In the following subsections, we discuss each type of SLA. The discussion of SLAs is done from the perspective of the service provider.

5.1.1 Network Connectivity SLAs

The network connectivity SLA is illustrated in Figure 5.1. The network operator has several access points to the customers. Customer networks are attached to the provider network via access routers that are present at the access points. For each customer, the network operator has defined performance and availability limits in the appropriate SLAs.

For each customer, the SLAs may define performance requirements for the entire network as follows:

- The average delay between any two access routers is less than 200ms (depicted as a cloud in Figure 5.1).

- The average delay between any two access routers is from specific access routers to all other access routers. For example, the average delay from the access router in New York City to any other access router is less than 200ms, but the average delay from the access router at Boston to any other access router is less than 150ms. This is the funnel approach described in Chapter 2, "IP Networks and SLAs."

- The average delay between any two access routers is across specific ingress and egress access routers. For example, the average delay between the access router at the client site in New York City and the data processing center in Jersey City is less than 50ms.

Figure 5.1   Environment for network connectivity SLAs.

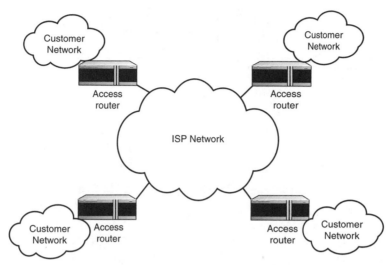

Without loss of generality, we can consider only the last among the three as the generic problem to be solved. For each customer, we need to provide specific communication pipes between pairs of access routers that provide specific performance requirements. The cloud and funnel specifications can be looked upon simply as mechanisms that assist in simplifying the statement of the network performance to the customer.

As we explore the solutions provided by different techniques in Chapter 6, "SLA Support in Different Network Environments," to support the SLA framework, we see that the most common mechanism in most (but not all) networking technologies deals with point-to-point connections. Therefore, if we can support the performance of specific connections between two pair of access points, it would be adequate to meet the SLA requirements specified in the funnel or cloud contexts.

As an example, consider two customers supported by an ISP that has four access points, as shown in Figure 5.2.

The first customer uses the ISP to connect its three sites and is attached at three access points. Let us assume that each access point is connected by a T1 link, so that each customer is sending no more than 1.5Mbps of data into the network. This customer's SLA requires that the maximum network communication delays be less than 100ms between any of its access routers.

Figure 5.2 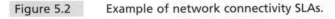 Example of network connectivity SLAs.

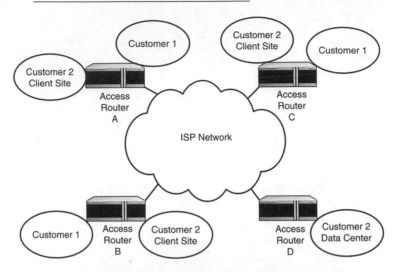

The second customer is attached at all four access points. It runs its data center at one of the sites and is mainly concerned with managing the performance of its client's access to the different data centers. Thus, this customer has a funnel specification with bounds on communication delays between any point and the data center to be less than 1000ms. This problem specification can be looked upon as a requirement to support the performance between the different access routers as described in the following table:

Customer	First Access Router	Second Access Router	Performance Requirement
Customer 1	A	B	100ms
Customer 1	A	C	100ms
Customer 1	B	C	100ms
Customer 2	A	D	1000ms
Customer 2	B	D	1000ms
Customer 2	C	D	1000ms

If the ISP is able to specify the performance requirements as stated above, the SLA requirements of all the customers are met. Thus, the general SLA problem can be studied in terms of satisfying the performance requirements of a network between specified access points.

Technical Reasons for Network Connectivity SLAs

You may wonder whether offering network connectivity SLAs of the type described in the previous section makes sense from a technical perspective. Is it better to have a network operate without SLAs—or with different SLAs for different applications?

We assume that you need to offer network connectivity SLAs of some nature. A cloud SLA is most appropriate when the traffic to and from the different access routers is of the same nature. If the network supports similar types of applications between the different access points, then the cloud SLAs are most appropriate. It is also the simplest one to specify.

In many networking environments, the bulk of communication occurs to or from specific sites; a common example is the case of several geographically dispersed branch offices trying to access a data center for transactions such as credit card processing. Communication is not usually needed among the different branch offices. In these cases, the funnel SLAs that specify the performance requirements to or from the specific data centers are the most appropriate.

The tunnel SLAs are the most appropriate when you want to provide special connectivity between two specific customer sites. This arises in cases where the performance requirements between the two sites is more stringent than the one required for other types of network communication. A customer in financial services may want to back up the information in the data center to a backup site. Communication between these two sites may require a different type of access than from the branch offices to the data center.

The performance bounds in a tunnel SLA would depend on the traffic mix between the sites. If most of the communication between a pair of sites is interactive, that may require a lower average latency than the communication between sites involved in data backup.

Business Reasons for Network Connectivity SLAs

From a business perspective, the easiest SLA to specify, track, and manage is the cloud type of SLA. However, different customers may have different expectations of network delays and throughput from the network operator. Consider a network provider with two customers: one distributing real-time stock quotes over the network and the other using the network for more traditional data transfer. The customer using the network for real-time stock quotes may demand a much more stringent bound on network delays in its SLA as compared to the customer using the network for detailed access to the network.

If different types of network SLAs are offered, their performance characteristics must be distinct enough to be priced differently. It may not be wise to offer two pipes: one with delays less than 100ms and the other with delays less than 80ms, because the difference is too small. On the other hand, it probably is reasonable to offer bounds in delays of 100ms and 1 second, because the difference is large enough to make sense to the customer. The tighter delay bound service also needs to be priced high enough to make sense to the provider.

5.1.2 Application SLAs

For an I/T operator, SLAs are often specified in terms of application performance, not just network connectivity performance. The generic problem of managing application response arises in cases where the provider (quite often the corporate IT manager) controls not just the network, but also the clients and servers which support the applications.

Another case where this generic problem arises is where a business unit manager must build upon the available or negotiated network connectivity service level to support a required application SLA. Because most clients tend to be dedicated single-user machines, the main performance issues arise at servers and at the network. Furthermore, in a corporate environment, the corporate I/T executive can often mandate a minimum client-machine profile in terms of processor speed, memory, and so on to eliminate the client system from becoming the performance bottleneck.

As an example of an application SLA, consider an I/T department that is running transaction servers as well as Web servers for its enterprise. The I/T department wants to prevent the Web traffic from interfering with the performance of the ISP traffic. The response time of a transaction to the user should be less than 1 second, regardless of the amount of Web traffic on the network.

Correlating Application Response Time and Network Performance

A strong correlation exists between the performance of the network and the end-to-end response of the application. For example, consider the transfer time for one Web page of 100KB. A requirement of transmitting it in two seconds requires a network throughput of at least 0.4Mbps. The exact bandwidth would be slightly higher because you need to account for network and transport headers. The simplest IP header adds 20KB for each packet, and the TCP header adds at least 20KB (plus options) for every TCP segment sent out on the network.

The packet size has a strong influence on the amount of bandwidth required. If the average size of transferred packets is 100KB, then the IP header adds 20% to the amount of required bandwidth. On the other hand, if the average packet size is 4KB, additional overhead is only 1%. Most bulk-transfer applications that are serving files attempt to use larger packet sizes.

Figure 5.3 shows the flow of packets in the network that is needed to complete one page transfer. The actions taken at the client and server side to complete the packet transfer are shown on different vertical lines. As shown in Figure 5.3, the response time seen by the user requesting the Web page consists of three components:

- The time it takes for the request to get from the client to the server and for the response from the server to reach the client

- The time it takes for the server to start sending the packets

- The time it takes for the entire file to be transmitted

We have made several simplifying assumptions in Figure 5.3. The transfer of packets has been error-free, and no losses have occurred. We have also assumed that the browser displays the page only after all the packets have been received. In practice, many browsers start to paint the user screen before all the data in the page is received.

Figure 5.3   Application response for simple network transfer.

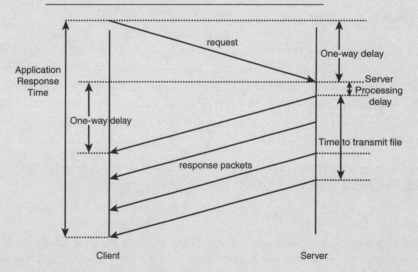

In this case, assuming that the server is not the bottleneck, the dominating factor in meeting an SLA is the time it takes for the file to be transmitted on the network and the delay in reaching the client from the server.

Suppose a network connectivity SLA has a one-way delay of d ms and a throughput of b bytes per second. Then the response time seen by the user for a 100KB page would be

$2d + (100/b)$ ms

Any combination of network delay and throughput that meets the constraint that the response time be less than the required response time of 2 seconds can be used as appropriate to meet the SLA requirements.

Assuming that the one-way delay constraints of the network are known, the service provider can compute the network bandwidth required to satisfy the application level response time requirements (assuming that we can ignore the overhead of transport and network headers). When multiple applications exist for which response time requirements need to be satisfied, similar analysis yields the total network bandwidth required to satisfy the response time for all applications.

Consider, for example, an I/T operator that needs to support applications of three types with the following response time requirements:

Application	Average Request Size	Average Response Size	Response Time Requirements	Average Time Requirements
Transaction	200 bytes	500 bytes	1 second	100
File download	100 bytes	200 Kbytes	10 seconds	1
Web transfer	300 bytes	10 Kbytes	2 seconds	10

Assuming that the network one-way delay is an average of 100ms, the bandwidth required to satisfy the requirements of the three applications is 700Kbps for transaction traffic, 163Kbps for file download, and 445Kbps for Web transfer. Thus, the total bandwidth expected from the network is 615Kbps. If the network could provide an SLA offering a bandwidth of at least 1-2Mbps and a one-way delay of 100ms, the application-level requirements would be fulfilled.

If you could support a funnel-type SLA with the required capacity between the clients and the server, you could meet the application's performance requirements.

Note

Note that, although we have made a simplifying assumption that bandwidth required between the client and the server is symmetric, none of the applications requires it. In other words, you may want to support a more complex SLA in which the bandwidth requirement from the client to the server differs from that of the server to the client.

Scope of Network Connectivity SLAs

Application SLAs are based on the network connectivity SLAs that are available from the network. In the most generic case, you can assume that the network provider supports a set of logical links between the client and server locations with specific network connectivity SLAs. However, these logical links need not extend all the way between the client and server machines. You may want to scope the extent of network connectivity only to parts of the network that are likely to be performance bottlenecks.

An example in which the scope of network connectivity SLAs covers only a subset of the network is shown in Figure 5.4.

Figure 5.4   Scope of network connectivity SLAs.

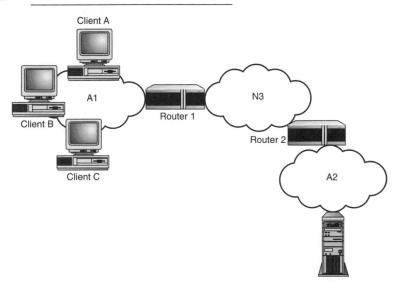

We assume that the portion of the network connecting the clients to Router 1 is uncongested. This assumption can be verified by measuring the utilization of the LAN. In some simple cases, the physical topology of the network dictates that the LAN is uncongested. For example, if the LAN is a Fast Ethernet and the access link to the network from the Access Router 1 is an ISDN link, you would expect that the LAN is uncongested. Therefore, no need exists to manage the performance of the Network A1, which is relatively uncongested.

Similarly, the portion of the network connecting the server to Router 2 is uncongested. Therefore, no need exists to provide support for SLAs in the Network A2. In this case, you need to track and monitor the logical links only on the Network N3 between the two routers. Managing the performance of the network between the two routers shown would be adequate to support application-level SLAs.

The model to approach the application-level SLA could then be reduced to the following two steps:

1. Determine the appropriate network-level SLA on the basis of application-level SLAs.

2. Provide the appropriate network SLAs.

The network SLA would be provided by having multiple logical links from the server to the clients. Each logical link would be associated with specific SLA parameters—for example, link delays or bandwidth requirements. If these SLA parameters are met, the application SLA requirements can also be met.

Reasons for Providing Application SLAs

The compelling reason for supporting application SLAs is that they come close to the type of performance expected by the users of an I/T infrastructure. Users expect specific response time from their applications, and the application SLAs are the most natural for them.

Different applications have different expected performance requirements. A clerk at a supermarket checkout counter may be willing to wait a few seconds for a credit-card approval to come through. On the other hand, a customer calling into a Voice over IP (VoIP) gateway for a phone call may require that packets be processed and converted into voice signal with latency not to exceed a few hundred milliseconds. Different types of applications therefore need different application SLAs to be specified.

From a business viewpoint, application SLAs provide a means by which the performance of the I/T department can be measured and deemed acceptable (or otherwise) by the other departments in the enterprise that are the customers of the I/T infrastructure.

5.1.3 Service Provider SLAs

Service provider SLAs are the ones offered by operators that host and support different types of servers on behalf of their customers. The most common case of these providers are the Web-hosting companies that provide servers to operate the Web sites for individual companies. Examples of such companies are Exodus and IBM Global Services.

The context of a service-provider SLA is illustrated in Figure 5.5. The figure shows a service provider that is connected to the Internet by a T3 line and provides Web-hosting for three businesses. Each of the businesses is assigned a set of Web servers. Access to the T3 line is shared by means of an access router, which may be connected to the servers by means of LANs. These LANs may be shared by all the customers, although it is more common to have separate LANs for each customer server. Separate LANs enable the provider to permit super-user privileges to customers to manage their own servers without being able to access the information on other customer servers. Recent LAN technology (for example, IEEE 802.3P standard) provides support for virtual LANs (VLANs), which allow multiple logical LANs on the same physical hardware.

Figure 5.5   Context for service provider SLAs.

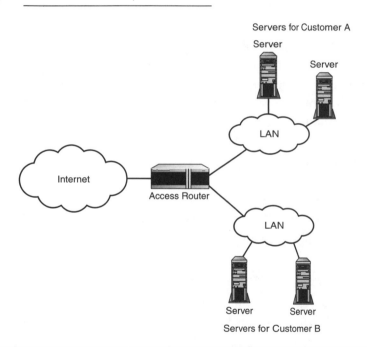

Note

Most Web-server hosting is performed on machines that run one of the many variants of the UNIX operating system. UNIX machines have a privileged super-user account (the root account) that can perform almost any action on the machine, including examining other packets on the same LAN. If two customers have servers on the same LAN, and both have super-user privileges on their own machines, each one can examine packets headed to the other server. Although most of the content on the server is public information, each server may want to protect other information contained in the packets that can be used to obtain information about clients, such as addresses of clients, and so on.

The SLAs offered by these operators deal with the uptime and performance of the servers that are being hosted. These operators are able to control only the server side of the total communication. In most cases, they have no control over the client side of the communication, nor over the performance of the network.

As a result, Service Provider SLAs usually specify the amount of sustained throughput or connection request rates that need to be supported for a specific server. This determines the aggregated number of requests that must be handled by the server with acceptable performance.

A service provider may host multiple customers at the same site and thus is responsible for ensuring that the performance of one customer's server is not adversely affected by requests directed to other customers.

Reasons for Providing Service Provider SLAs

Service provider SLAs can offer varying amounts of capacity to their customers and allow customers to buy specific amounts of server capacity from the provider. The server capacity can be specified in terms of network throughput, the number of connection establishment requests served per minute, or simply the number of servers used to host the customer sites.

In addition to hosting Web servers, service providers may host other types of enterprise servers, such as Lotus Notes servers, that provide mail and groupware services. Several Web servers act as a front end to transaction servers, which are accessed using CGI scripts on the Web front end. Typically, all the servers (transaction servers and Web servers) are provided by the same service provider company.

5.2   The Generic SLA Architecture

We now present an architecture within which solutions to supporting different types of SLAs in the network can be provided. The architecture is shown in Figure 5.6.

This architecture consists of three types of devices:

- *Edge devices*: The boxes that define the boundaries within which SLAs are to be supported. An edge device could be a router or a server. The edge device is often (but not necessarily) an access router (that is, one that spans the administrative boundary between a customer network and an ISP network). The edge device can also be implemented inside the TCP/IP stack in the servers. The edge device defines the edge of the network within which SLAs have to be supported.

- *Policy server complex*: A set of software components hosted on a box, or complex of multiple boxes, that contains the information about the configuration of the different edge devices and also stores the information pertinent to the performance levels specified in the different SLAs that are to be supported in the network.

- *Performance monitor*: A box that is responsible for validating that the SLAs are being satisfied within the network.

Figure 5.6   The SLA architecture.

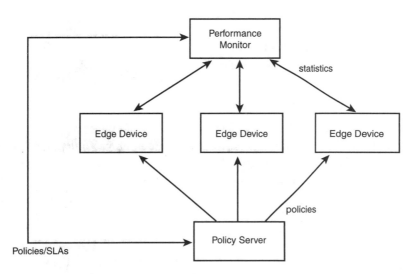

The edge devices, the policy server complex, and the performance monitor are software components rather than physical boxes. They represent the collection of functions that have to be performed in order to automate and validate the support of SLAs in the network.

The SLAs that are identified by the network operator are converted into performance specifications for the connectivity that exists between the different edge devices. The implication of different types of SLAs is to ensure that the flow of packets between a specific pair of edge devices should be within specific performance or reliability limits.

5.2.1 The Edge Device

The *edge device* is responsible for the functions of identifying the packets and determining the level of performance that is to be provided to them. Thus, the edge device would be responsible for identifying packets that belong to specific customers or specific applications.

The edge device needs to take specific actions to ensure that the SLA requirements are satisfied for each of the packets. To support network connectivity SLAs, for example, the edge device identifies the logical tunnel to which the packet belongs and places the packet on the appropriate logical tunnel. The logical tunnel may be provided by different mechanisms in the network—for example, the use of RSVP to establish reserved bandwidth pipes, the use of Differentiated Services (DiffServ) to support specific rates in the network, or the use of a frame relay or ATM tunnel to the appropriate egress edge device. Each of these mechanisms is described in more detail in the next chapter.

Because the edge device is the endpoint of network SLAs, it is also responsible for collecting statistics about the performance of the network between these two points. The statistics may be kept for an actual tunnel, or it may be just a logical tunnel. These statistics are used by the performance monitor to validate conformance with SLAs.

5.2.2 The Policy Server Complex

To meet the SLA objectives, the edge devices need to be configured to treat packets in an appropriate fashion. Each of the edge devices can be configured individually. However, separate configuration of different edge devices can lead to possible inconsistencies in their configuration. It is easier and more scalable to validate the consistency of the different edge device configurations in a centralized location and to distribute them to the different edge devices in an automated fashion.

The *policy server complex* is the software component (or group of software components) that contains the configuration information about all the edge devices in the system. In addition to the configuration details, the policy server can also contain a management system that includes the details of the specific SLAs expected of the logical links between the different access routers, as well as the administrative interface for creating and modifying SLAs.

As an example of the possible inconsistencies that can arise in the configuration of different edge devices, consider an operator that offers network connectivity SLAs to its business customers. These customers connect to the operator's access routers (the edge device, in this case) at several cities where the network operator has a point of presence (POP). The network operator exploits the DiffServ support in the network and needs to mark the packets of each of the different customers with different ToS fields in the IP header. All packets of the same customer need to be marked identically in the network.

If the configuration of each of the access routers is not coordinated, it is likely that packets belonging to the same customer may be marked differently at different access routers and fail to get the desired priority treatment in the network. On the other hand, if the configuration is coordinated through a policy server or another centralized tool, the chances of incorrect configuration are less likely.

The policy server need not restrict itself to maintaining configuration information that is only relevant to the edge devices. It can also be used to configure other devices in the network (for example, core routers).

Any number of protocols can be used to transmit the configuration information from the policy server to the edge devices. One common approach is to store the network policies in a directory server. A *directory server* is a repository that contains information about the different users in an enterprise. The same repository can be used to contain policies regarding the configuration of different edge devices.

Other schemes can be used to transport policies from the repository to the edge devices. It is possible for automated programs to take the configuration information and convert it into native commands understood by the routers. For example, most routers from Cisco networks can be configured using a command line interface (CLI). Policy-management software can be used to read the policies from the central repository and configure the routers using CLI.

Policy Architecture in IP Networks

A *policy* is a directive to the network as to how it should behave. It could contain simple mandates such as that one type of application is considered more significant for a business than another type of application, or that a specific type of file be encrypted before it is transmitted on the network.

The policies active in the network are defined by the administrator via a management tool that translates the high-level policies into a format that could be interpreted by the network elements. An example of such a management tool is the CiscoAssure QoS Manager [CISASS] .

The translated format is essentially the abstracted configuration parameters for different network elements. The network elements then operate in accordance with the policy to provide the desired QoS or security in the network.

The network elements that enforce the policy are called the *policy enforcement points,* or *PEPs.* The PEPs for QoS/SLA policies are end hosts and access routers, whereas the PEPs for security policies are firewalls and end hosts. In the context of the SLAs, the PEPs are the edge devices that take appropriate actions depending on the SLA specifications in the policy server. The PEPs may communicate directly with the policy repository or may do so using an intermediary.

The intermediary is called a *Policy Decision Point (PDP).* A PDP can be a physically separate box, or it can be a software module that is colocated with the PEP. Physically separate PDPs support PEPs that are not able to communicate directly with the policy repository or that

continues

may not want to take on the added complexity of dealing with policies. A physically separate PDP is also useful when you need to do a last minute translation of policy formats (to replace all domain names in a policy with the corresponding IP addresses, for example). The architecture to support network policies is illustrated in Figure 5.7. A separate PDP is also required if a dynamic network state must be maintained on behalf of multiple PEPs and if that state must be consulted before a policy decision is made—as in the case of RSVP when used to support an application such as video conferencing.

Note

The configuration parameters are called *abstracted* at the policy server because they may need to be translated further into device-specific configuration parameters at the PEP. For example, the directive to put a packet into a high-priority queue at the policy server may be translated as queue number 0 at the PEP.

Figure 5.7   Policy architecture in IP networks.

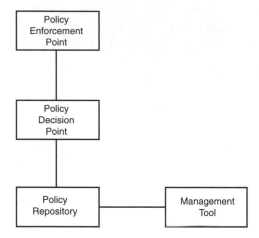

5.2.3 The Performance Monitor

The network monitor is the component that monitors the performance of the network between pairs of edge devices and verifies that these are within the bounds specified by the SLA requirements. The network monitor gathers the statistics collected by the different edge devices and examines them to ensure that the desired SLAs are being satisfied.

The network monitor can keep track of the utilization of the different devices in the network and determine which of the components have failed. These functions are usually provided as part of standard network-management packages. Although the functions to monitor the compliance with SLAs are not commonly found within network management tools, they can easily be provided as additional functions.

> **Note**
>
> In Chapter 7, "Network Monitoring and SLA Verification," we look in more detail at how the performance monitor could be implemented and the different ways in which networking performance information can be collected.

5.2.4 *Overall Operation of the SLA Architecture*

The support of SLAs in the network within the framework described above occurs in the following steps:

1. The network is designed and provisioned to satisfy SLAs.

2. The configuration of different edge devices to satisfy the SLAs is determined and stored at the policy server.

3. The edge devices are configured as per information in the policy server.

4. Edge devices classify packets into different classes and collect statistics regarding their performance.

5. The network monitor collects performance data from the edge devices and verifies that SLAs are being satisfied.

As long as the SLA parameters are being satisfied, you can rest easy. However, if SLA parameters are not being satisfied, the network monitor needs to take some action. Some of the possible actions that can be taken are the following:

- Alert a network administrator that the SLAs are being violated. The alert may take the form of an email to the administrator or other alternative means, such as sending a message to the administrator's pager.

- Reconfigure the different edge devices and routers in the middle of the network so that the appropriate network responses are being satisfied.

> **Note**
>
> The method for reconfiguration depends on how the architecture is implemented. We take a closer look at the different implementations of the architecture in the next chapter.

5.2.5 Levels of SLA Support

The support of SLAs can be done at different levels; each level requires additional functionality and processing within the network. These levels of SLA support apply to any of the three SLA types described previously.

The first level of SLA support consists of only two steps:

1. Define the SLA terms and conditions.

2. Measure the performance of the network or applications and validate that the SLAs are being satisfied.

This level of SLA support requires little change in the operation and maintenance of a network, applications, or servers. It does require that the network performance be monitored and measured continuously. Some of the techniques for network monitoring are described in Chapter 7. The only other aspect required for SLA support at this level is that care be taken in network design and information that the SLA requirements are indeed feasible.

The second level of SLA support can be done by introducing edge devices in the network that operate over a best-effort core. The edge devices control access to the best-effort network and determine which applications get access to the network resources. The steps required at the second level of SLA support are the following:

1. Define the SLA terms and conditions.

2. Determine the policies required at the edge devices in the network and configure these devices.

3. Monitor the performance of the different service levels to ensure that SLA terms and conditions are being satisfied.

The third level of SLA support involves exploiting the support for QoS within the network. This exploitation can enable a more cost-effective way of supporting SLAs with varying performance and availability requirements. At this next level of SLA support, you need to perform the following steps:

1. Define the SLA terms and conditions.

2. Determine the configuration required for different QoS components (edge devices/core routers) in the network, and configure these devices.

3. Monitor the performance of the different service levels to ensure that SLA terms and conditions are being satisfied.

The third level of SLA support assumes that the network supports some form of QoS support (DiffServ or IntServ).

A final level in which the network can readjust the configuration of the different devices to adapt to possible or potential SLA violations can also be assumed. However, this area has not been explored fully and needs to be researched more before it can become a viable option.

5.3   The Architecture Applied to Different Types of SLAs

We explore how the generic architecture presented in Section 5.3 can be used to support different types of network SLAs. Specifically, we examine how the concept of the edge devices, the policy server, and the network monitor can be used to support network connectivity SLAs, application SLAs, and service provider SLAs.

5.3.1   Architecture Applied to Network Connectivity SLAs

Figure 5.8 illustrates how the architecture can be used to support network connectivity SLAs. The edge devices software component is implemented as part of the access router that is used to connect the provider's network to the customer's network. The policy server and the performance monitor are software functions that are placed somewhere in the provider's network.

Logical tunnels are established between pairs of edge devices. These logical tunnels are used to keep statistics about the traffic between each of the edge devices and the performance of the network between these devices. Depending on the mechanisms available in the network, the logical tunnel may be a physical tunnel (for example, a Frame-Relay or ATM pipe) connecting different edge devices. A more detailed discussion of how specific mechanisms can be exploited for SLA support is available in the next chapter.

Figure 5.8 Architecture applied to network connectivity SLAs.

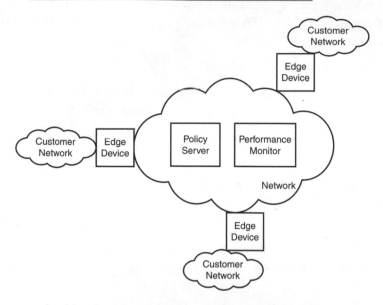

As packets are received by the edge device, one or more of the following functions may be performed:

- The packet is classified as its SLA requirements determined.

- Packet statistics (for example, the number of bytes and packets) are seen by each customer.

- The logical link or tunnel for the packet is determined.

- The packet's ToS field is changed to exploit DiffServ support in the network.

- The packet is put onto a logical or physical link in the network.

The policy server is used to define the rules that determine which packets are mapped onto specific logical tunnels. The selection of the logical tunnels is done by a combination of the destination of the packet as well as the SLA requirements of the customer or application sending the packet.

The performance monitor obtains the packet statistics collected by each of the edge devices and combines the information received from them to determine whether the SLAs are being satisfied.

5.3.2 *Architecture Applied to Application SLAs*

The support for application SLAs in the generic architecture is shown in Figure 5.9. We assume that the SLA is being provided by an I/T operator who controls the client and server LAN connectivity. The I/T operator builds the application SLAs on top of network connectivity SLAs that are supplied to the I/T operator by a network provider. The application SLAs are provided for communication between the clients and the servers and are shown as the arrow within the dashed circle in Figure 5.9. The network connectivity SLAs are supported between the access routers and shown as the arrow within the network in Figure 5.9.

Figure 5.9   Architecture applied to application SLAs.

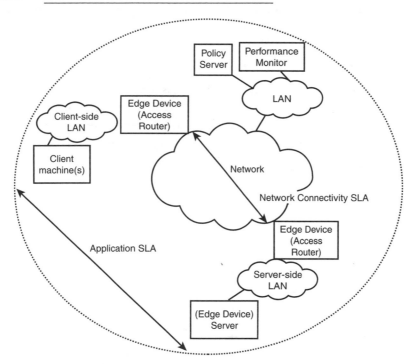

The edge device function is present at the servers and the access routers in the network. These access routers are within the control of the I/T operator and regulate the transmission of the packets from the LANs to the network.

The edge devices at the server or the access router are responsible for determining how to map each packet into the appropriate class of traffic that is available from the network.

Information regarding the end-to-end performance is collected by the edge devices present at the servers. This information about the end-to-end performance can be reported to the performance monitor, which could be located anywhere in the network. The performance monitor can also collect performance information from the clients, depending on the type of application. Some applications—for example, the TN3270 clients—keep track of the application-level response time. However, keeping track of the network performance in an application-independent generic manner could be done by exploiting edge devices at the access routers or at the servers.

The policy server can also be located anywhere in the network. In Figure 5.9, we have shown both the policy server and the performance monitor as parts of a different LAN.

Further details on how application-level SLAs can be supported exploiting different types of network SLAs are provided in the next chapter.

5.3.3 *Architecture Applied to Service Provider SLAs*

The architecture as applied to service provider SLAs is similar in nature to the case of application SLAs. However, because the service provider typically controls only the server-side connectivity to the network, the operations at different edge devices are different. The architecture as applied to service provider SLAs is shown in Figure 5.10.

Figure 5.10   Architecture applied to service provider SLAs.

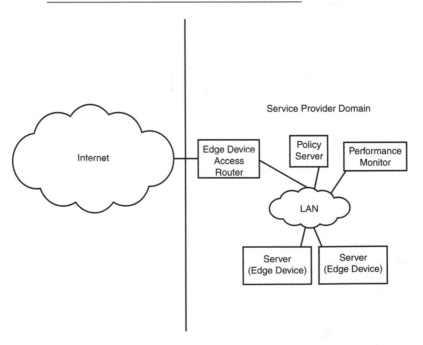

The architecture for the generic service provider would be done using an edge device at the access router and edge devices at each of the servers belonging to the different customers. The edge device at the access router determines how to share the bandwidth of the access link among different customers. The edge devices at the servers include information identifying their network support and collect statistics about the network performance.

Multiple ways exist by which the edge devices can support service provider SLAs. One of the ways is for the edge device in the server to mark the ToS bytes in the IP packets from the server in different ways. The edge device at the access router looks at the ToS byte to determine how much bandwidth on the access link to assign to each of the different customers. Other modes of operation, such as one in which edge devices are present only at the server or only at the routers, can also be used. Each of these modes is described in more detail in the next chapter.

The policy server and performance monitor are typically co-located at the service provider LAN.

5.4   *Further Information*

Many ways of implementing the SLA architecture and supporting the different types of SLAs are possible. We discuss these ways in the next chapter.

We have provided a very high-level view of policies in the IP network and show how they can be applied to supporting SLAs. The scope of policies in the networks is much broader than SLAs and includes aspects such as security, address allocation, and authentication. The IETF is working on a generic framework for defining network policies [POLICY]. For the more specific case of QoS support using RSVP, a policy transport protocol [BOYLE] is also available.

Many vendor products support the functions of policy management and edge-box functions as we have described. Policy management tools are available from companies such as Cisco [CISASS], Allot [ALLOT] and Orchestream [ORCH]. The edge-box functionality is supported by IBM routers, S/390 mainframe servers, and AIX servers.

5.5   *Endnotes*

[ALLOT] Allot Communications. "Policy Based Networking." White paper, available at `http://www.allot.com/products/policymgmt.pdf`.

[CISASS] Cisco Systems. "CiscoAssure Policy Networking End-to-End Quality of Service." White paper, available at `http://www.cisco.com/warp/public/734/capn/caqos_wp.htm`.

[BOYLE] J. Boyle, et al. "The COPS (Common Open Policy Service) Protocol." Internet draft. Available via the IETF RSVP Admission Policy working group page at `http://www.ietf.org/html.charters/rap-charter.html`.

[ORCH] Orchestream Provider 1.0 Product. 1999. Information available at `http://www.orchestream.com/pages/framesets/products.html`.

[POLICY] The IETF Policy Framework Working Group. 1999. `http://www.ietf.org/html.charters/policy-charter.html`.

6

SLA Support in Different Network Environments

In Chapter 5, "A General SLA Architecture," we introduced three types of SLAs and a generic architecture that can support all those types. In this chapter, we look at more specific implementations of each type of SLA.

For each type of SLA and the assumed environment, we look at how the software components of policy server, performance monitor, and the edge devices can interact to support the desired service levels.

6.1 Network Connectivity SLAs

For the network connectivity SLAs, consider a network operator that offers IP network connectivity to its customers via access routers. The network model for the network connectivity SLAs is shown in Figure 6.1. An edge-device function is implemented at each of the access routers. These edge-device–enabled access routers are interconnected by the core network of the operator.

> **Note**
>
> The *edge device* is a software function implemented inside an access router or end host. An access router supports additional functions than that of the edge device needed for SLA support. For convenience of notation in the rest of the chapter, we will simply use *access routers* or *end hosts* instead of the longer *edge-device–enabled access routers*.

Figure 6.1 Network model for network connectivity SLAs.

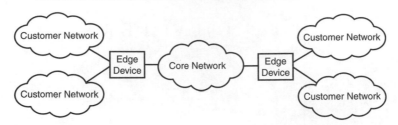

The techniques to support SLAs depend on the features available at the core network of the operator. The following environments are considered:

- The core of the network consists of high-speed, best-effort routers; no QoS support is available at the core of the network.

- The core of the network contains IP routers that are capable of supporting the DiffServ mode of network operation.

- The core of the network contains IP routers that are capable of supporting the IntServ/RSVP mode of operation to establish reserved pipes in the network.

- The core of the network consists of several point-to-point connections using Frame Relay or ATM. The access routers are responsible for encapsulating and transmitting IP packets into Frame Relay or ATM links.

Within any of these environments, you could offer varying levels of support for SLAs. The simplest option would be to offer a single SLA to all customers. The network provider would define a generic SLA that would be offered to all its customers. The generic SLA would specify bounds on performance and availability that would be satisfied by the network. Such a bound could be determined by monitoring the performance of the network in operation or be predicted on the basis of expected network load and the topology of the network.

Although this approach is attractive because of its simplicity and ease of implementation, it can only be successfully used when the network provider is in the position to dictate the terms of the SLA to its customers. When the terms of the SLA are dictated by the customer rather than the network operator, different SLAs may need to be offered to different customers.

Consider a hypothetical network provider called Virtual Networks, which offers network connectivity to customers in New York City. The network operator has leased T1 and T3 lines from the local telephone carrier (Bell Atlantic) and has access routers placed in the basement of several buildings in the city. The network operator can offer connectivity to its customers who are located in the building by running a LAN between the customer's office and the access router, as shown in Figure 6.2.

Figure 6.2   Building access scheme for Virtual Networks.

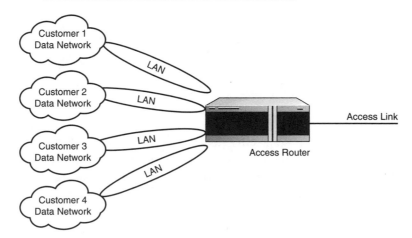

Most of its customers are small businesses with a single office location, and they use the operator to gain access to the Internet. However, some of the larger customers have offices at multiple locations in the city, and they use the network operator to connect the different sites into a virtual private network. The largest customer has 10 sites in the city and wants to have the maximum delay in the network to never exceed 400ms and a network down-time of no more than 30 minutes in any 24-hour period. The second largest customer with eight sites (five of these are co-located with the sites of the largest customer) in the network requires the maximum delay in the network to never exceed 500ms and a net-work downtime of no more than 20 minutes in any 24-hour period.

Because the delay and availability requirements of the two customers do not differ signifi-cantly, the network operator would be better off designing a network that can have a downtime of no more than 20 minutes and a maximum delay of no more than 400ms. Although this gives better-than-expected performance to each of the customers in some way, it results in a network that is much simpler to manage and operate.

If the requirements of the different customers are quite diverse, such a single SLA may not be appropriate for all the customers. A better option for the network operator is to offer a few different levels of services. Each service level can be used to support customers whose SLA requirements are reasonably close to the service level. The SLA for each customer must be satisfied by the service level available for that category. In the rest of this section, we assume that the network provider is supporting a small number of service levels in the network, each with specific limits on the performance to be seen by customers or applications belonging to that service level.

The different levels of service can be characterized by any combinations of the various performance metrics described in Chapter 2, "IP Networks and SLAs." Each of the different environments offers different trade-offs in the cost of providing the multiple levels of service.

6.1.1   Best-Effort Core Networks

The simplest case of network connectivity is an IP network where all the routers (access routers as well as the core routers) use traditional best-effort IP routers. Within this environment, you need to support different service levels to the customers.

If the core is best-effort, the network operator has several possible service schemes, including

- Support only one single-service level and offer it to all the customers.

- Support multiple service levels where each service level is supported by a separate physical network.

- Support multiple service levels where each service level is allowed access to a limited amount of bandwidth at the access routers.

Single Service Level Support

If the network operator goes with the first option and supports only a single service level, the following steps need to be taken to ensure that the SLAs for all customers are being satisfied:

- Each SLA is offered so that its performance and availability requirements are less stringent than that of the supported service level.

- The performance of the network is monitored continuously to ensure that the network is meeting the desired service level.

In this option, the only component of the SLA architecture that is needed is the performance monitor. The performance monitor is described further in Chapter 7, "Network Monitoring and SLA Verification." Some additional functions may be needed in the access routers to collect statistics.

Separate Network for Each Service Level

When different service levels are implemented as different networks, the structure of the operator's network appears as shown in Figure 6.3. Packets belonging to different service levels are directed to different networks. This function is also known as *alternate routing*. With this approach, the core network is effectively split into two core subnetworks.

Figure 6.3   Parallel physical subnetworks for SLA support.

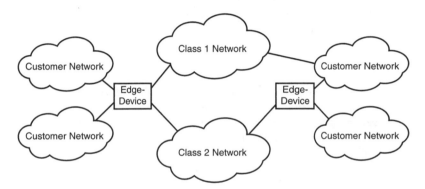

The responsibility for identifying the correct service level to which a packet belongs and routing it to the corresponding core subnetwork belongs to the access router (edge device). The edge device can classify packets into the different service levels on the basis of any of the combinations of IP and TCP/UDP headers. Some of the fields that can be included in this combination are the source and destination IP addresses and the protocol field in the IP header, and the source and destination port numbers in the transport header.

The exact fields that are needed to support SLAs depend on the granularity at which SLAs are defined. Consider the case where different performance requirements are offered at the granularity of a customer organization; that is, all traffic from a single customer organization is offered the same performance bounds. In this case, the classification can be done simply on the basis of the source IP addresses of the packets. You can alternatively do the classification on the basis of the adapter on which an incoming packet is received. When each customer organization is mapped into a different service level, it is as if each has a separate intranet of its own. They simply happen to share the same access router.

An alternative approach would be to assign different service levels to different applications. Each core subnetwork is used to carry a different set of applications. In this case, the classification of packets would be done using a combination of the IP source and destination addresses and the TCP or UDP port numbers used by the applications.

For example, consider the case of an enterprise that used to operate an SNA network and has decided to migrate over to an IP-based network. The legacy SNA applications are encapsulated in IP using the *Data-Link Switching Protocol (DLSw)*. The SLAs for SNA applications typically require a much higher availability. To prevent interference among the DLSw traffic and other IP traffic, one of the core networks is used to carry DLSw traffic, and the second core subnetwork is used to carry all other IP traffic. DLSw uses TCP as the transport protocol and typically uses the port numbers 2065 and 2067. The access routers determine the packets that use TCP (the protocol field in the IP header is 6) on ports 2065 or 2067 as source or destination port numbers, and then direct them to specific core subnetworks.

Note

The identification of applications using only port numbers is best done when applications are run on standard, well-known ports or on ports that are used universally within the network. In this case, the port numbers can be used to identify applications. If an application is run on a server at a different port number than the standard one, you have to introduce additional rules specifying the server and the nonstandard port to identify the application. If port numbers are not managed properly, the number of rules required to identify an application can become large.

As another example, assume that the two networks are used to carry voice traffic and data traffic separately in the network. Assume, too, that the voice traffic is generated by using specific Voice over IP (VoIP) gateways, as shown in Figure 6.4. The traffic between the VoIP gateways is predominantly voice and is routed on the voice network. The IP addresses in packet headers can be used to distinguish the voice traffic in contrast to data traffic.

Note

Although conventional voice traffic is carried over a separate switched network, VoIP is gaining ground and expected to grow in usage.

Figure 6.4   SLAs for parallel voice and data networks.

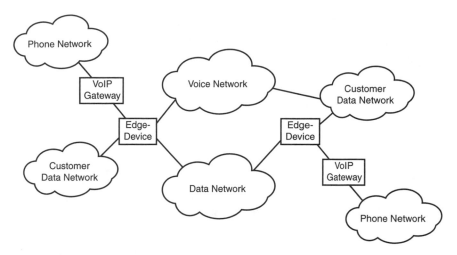

Running different networks for different service levels has several advantages from an SLA support perspective. Traffic in each service level is insulated from each other. Thus, the idiosyncrasies of one type of traffic do not interfere with the other types of traffic. For example, voice packets typically happen to be small (less than 100 bytes) and require low jitter in the network. Data packets could potentially be large (a transfer size of 4,096 bytes for file transfer is typical). These large packets can cause a significant amount of jitter in the congested nodes. Imagine a voice packet stuck behind a few of the bulk transfer packets at a queue in the network. Separating the two types of packets into different networks insulates them from each other. This is assuming that the separation point (the edge device) is itself not congested and the interference between the two types of packets at the edge device is negligible.

The same arguments hold true for networks that are used to support two different customers' organizations. If a customer requires low delays, its packets can be routed on a subnetwork consisting of faster links. If a customer requires higher availability, you can design a subnetwork that is a more dense mesh of lower-speed links. Other customers can be routed on networks with different characteristics.

Although running parallel networks simplifies the task of providing different SLAs, it is a relatively expensive solution. It is much cheaper to be able to combine the different networks into a single network.

The roles of the different components in the SLA architecture are as follows in the context of parallel networks:

- The policy server complex records the rules that define which packets belong to which service levels. These rules, in turn, determine the subnetwork to which each type of packet should be routed. This information is distributed to the edge device(s).

- The edge device is responsible for classifying the packets and routing them on to the appropriate subnetwork.

- The network monitor is responsible for monitoring the performance of each of the subnetworks and validating that it is within the desired SLA bounds.

Resource Allocation at Access Routers

A type of network connectivity SLA that can be offered to customers without running parallel subnetworks deals only with the allocation of bandwidth at the access link to different customer organizations.

For example, consider the case of the hypothetical network operator Virtual Networks, which needs to support several companies in a building. Each of the office LANs in the building is connected to a customer site router (typically placed in the basement of the building). The office LANs may have dedicated LANs connecting them to the customer site access router (the edge device). The customer site access router has a leased high-speed line to the rest of the network. Assume that each of the companies in the building desires a T1 access (1.5Mbps) to the network. Virtual Networks has the option of running separate T1 lines from the building into its point of presence. However, if several customers are in the building, it may be much more cost efficient for them to concentrate all the customers into the access router and to run a higher capacity (for example, a T3) line from the building. The decision as to whether multiple T1 or a single T3 is a better solution depends on the number of active customers, as well as the tariffs charged by the telecommunications operator that supplies the line connectivity. Usually, beyond five or six T1 links, it is beneficial to switch over to a T3 link.

The sharing of a common link can be obtained by means of rate control. The easiest way to obtain rate control is by exploiting the physical characteristics of the link connecting the customer sites to the backbone router. For example, a configuration shown in Figure 6.5 can be used to provide T1 access to the customers, which are then simply multiplexed onto the T3 access link out of the building.

Figure 6.5   Supporting SLAs with bandwidth allocations.

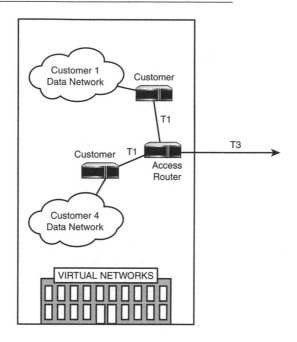

Using the physical infrastructure to control the rate of traffic has several advantages. It insulates the customers from each other, and the rates at which packets are sent are limited to the physical link capacity in both directions (to and from the customer LAN). However, it is difficult to change the amount of bandwidth assigned to any customer with this approach. If a customer does want a rate that is a fraction of the physical link speed, then he or she is out of luck.

Note

An interesting question is how the customer can determine the amount of bandwidth needed for its usage. See the sidebar "Estimating Bandwidth Requirements" for a discussion of a way to do so.

A more flexible approach to rate control can be obtained by using either the token-bucket or the timestamp mechanism described in Chapter 4, "Service Differentiation and Quality of Service in IP Networks." With this scheme, the access to the customer site access router from customer routers consists of a LAN. The rate-control mechanism needs to be applied both to the packets coming from the customer, as well as to packets destined to the customer.

A T3 link in a configuration, as shown in Figure 6.5, can support about 28 customers with T1 connectivity.

An ISP may have less than 28 customers in the building. Philosophies differ as to how the excess capacity ought to be treated. One school of thought is that the customers should be allowed to use the spare capacity in the network because it does not cause any additional cost. If the excess is used to over-engineer the access to the network, it makes it easier to satisfy the SLA performance bounds. Another school of thought is that the customers should be provided only with a T1 access, even if excess capacity is in the network. Otherwise, customers would get used to and expect a throughput, which is better than what they have contracted for. When other customers are added, the effective throughput of an existing customer is decreased and may cause dissatisfaction. In this case, you need to restrict the access of customers to what they have paid for, even when excess capacity is available in the network.

When the rate used by each of the customers is restricted, you can combine it with the routing topology of the network to determine the maximum load that can be experienced at any router. By controlling the total amount of load at any router, the performance of the network can be controlled so as to conform with the SLAs offered to the customers.

One of the following two methods can be used to support SLAs with bandwidth allocation using the different architectural components. The first method is to simply monitor customer usage:

- The policy server establishes the rules that define how much bandwidth is allocated to each of the customers. This information is distributed to the edge device(s).

- The network monitor is responsible for monitoring the amount of bandwidth used by each of the customers and validating that it is within the desired SLA bounds.

- If a customer is found using more bandwidth than the SLA parameters, he or she is notified of the excess usage. An extra charge may be associated with the use of excess bandwidth.

The second method is to assign a strict limit on the bandwidth that can be used by any customer:

- The policy server establishes the rules that define how much bandwidth is to be allocated to each of the customers. This information is distributed to the edge device(s).

- The edge device is responsible for controlling the rate used by each of the customers.

This bandwidth could be somewhat over the limit specified in the SLA (for example, 110% of the rate specified in the SLA). In case a customer monitors the bandwidth, the excess allocation would increase the probability that the value measured is above the customer's expectations from the SLA.

Estimating Bandwidth Requirements

How does a customer estimate the amount of bandwidth to purchase from a network operator for its needs? If an organization is establishing a new network, it is essentially an educated guess. However, the amount of bandwidth needed in an operational network can be estimated to a somewhat better degree of accuracy.

The model of the customer we assumed is shown in Figure 6.6. It shows a customer LAN connected to the access link through an access router. We want to determine the best possible capacity of the access link needed to satisfy the applications on the network.

We can monitor the amount of bandwidth usage on a real network and determine whether the capacity of the access link is adequate for the needs of the customer LAN. The bandwidth usage can be estimated by monitoring the traffic leaving and entering the LAN through the access router—that is, measuring the bandwidth at the measurement point shown in Figure 6.6. We would expect that the measured bandwidth usage shows variations over long time periods, as well as over short time periods.

To determine the access link capacity that is needed, you would typically consider the busiest period of the day and use that to determine the bandwidth needs of the customer. The duration of the busiest period would be in the order of a small number of hours. A common duration is that of one hour; that is, the busiest hour is used for determining the bandwidth needs.

During the busy period, the bandwidth would show variations. Two important metrics are the *peak bandwidth* that is used over a small interval (for example, the duration of a minute) during the busy period and the *mean bandwidth* used during the entire busy period.

The access link capacity is configured somewhere between the measured mean bandwidth and the measured peak bandwidth. If the access link capacity is less than the measured mean bandwidth, packets can experience large queuing delays and significant packet losses at the access router.

On the other hand, using an access link capacity in excess of the peak bandwidth is wasteful. Given that line costs are the dominant costs in the operation of a network, you want to have the lowest possible capacity that results in an acceptable performance. The amount of bandwidth that yields an acceptable performance is known as the *equivalent capacity* or *effective bandwidth*.

continues

Figure 6.6   Network model for bandwidth estimation.

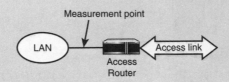

For some types of traffic patterns in the network, the equivalent capacity can be computed from the mean bandwidth, the peak bandwidth, the length of bursts of peak bandwidth usage, and the acceptable loss probability. Mathematical expressions giving the equivalent bandwidth in terms of these parameters for some types of traffic can be found in the paper by Guerin, et al. [GUERIN].

6.1.2 Differentiated Services Core Networks

When the core network is capable of supporting Differentiated Services, it is possible to implement different levels of service by mapping each service level into a different PHB (Per Hop Behavior) supported by the network. In many ways, it is like having a separate subnetwork for each PHB in the core network. However, the separate subnetworks are logical rather than physical.

The model of supporting different service levels using DiffServ is as shown in Figure 6.7. The figure shows two PHBs supported at each link in the network. Assume that one of these PHBs is a higher-priority forwarding class (with the DiffServ field of 110000) and the other one is the default forwarding class (with the DiffServ field of 000000). The physical network is essentially divided into two logical networks sharing the same physical lines. The bandwidth along the physical links is allocated among the different PHBs in a manner that is determined by the network operator.

For this example, let us assume that the allocation of bandwidth along the two priority classes shown is done so that 40% of each link's capacity is reserved for the higher-priority class, and the other 60% is used for default forwarding. You can treat the two subnetworks as logically different subnetworks with the capacities divided in the ratio of 4:6. However, some differences exist from the physically separate networks described in the section "Remote Control of Bandwidth" that you must be careful about:

- The separate networks can interfere with each other's packets, as far as delays and delay jitter are concerned. If one subnetwork has large data packets and the other subnetwork has small packets, the delay jitter due to packet differences would be visible to the subnetwork with small packets.

Because we have assumed a priority scheduling, the performance of the lower-priority traffic would be impacted strongly by the higher-priority traffic. The impact of lower-priority traffic on the higher-priority traffic would be relatively small. However, because packet transmission is usually nonpreemptive, a higher-priority packet can get queued behind a large low-priority packet. Even with priority queuing, one cannot assume that the impact of lower-priority traffic on higher priority traffic is zero.

- If little or no traffic exists on one of the subnetworks, the other subnetwork can obtain larger throughput and fewer delays than expected on the basis of the SLAs. In a physical partition, that is not the case.

Figure 6.7   SLA support using Differentiated Services.

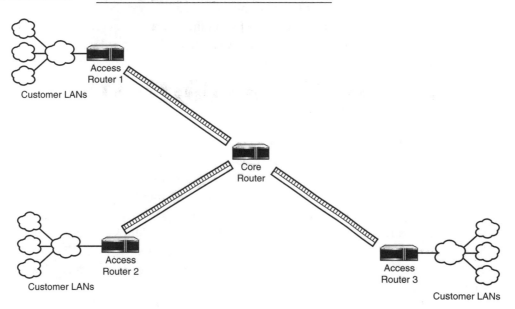

To ensure that the DiffServ network meets the desired SLAs, each of the components in the SLA architecture must perform specific functions. These functions are described in the following sections.

Policy Management in DiffServ Networks

Two functions need to be performed to satisfy the SLA requirements of the various customers using the DiffServ network environment described in the previous section.

- Determine the portion of the links that needs to be assigned to each of the different service levels in the network. This information needs to be determined for the core routers, as well as the access routers (edge devices) in the network.

- Distribute the configuration information about how link bandwidth is to be shared among different PHBs to the core routers, as well as the access routers in the network.

The determination of the amount of bandwidth to be used needs to take into account the performance requirements of all the customers belonging in a specific service level. This requires that performance analysis tools analogous to the ones described in Chapter 3, "Network Design and SLA Support," should be used. However, the performance analysis in this context is somewhat more complex because multiple classes of service are available in the network. The sidebar "Performance Analysis of Multiclass Queues" gives some information on how such an analysis might be done.

Consider the case of the network shown in Figure 6.7. Assume that two customers are at each of the three access router sites. The first customer is sending some delay-sensitive stock quotes from the LAN at Access Router 1 to the LANs at Access Routers 2 and 3. The amount of the delay-sensitive data does not exceed 0.4Mbps in each direction. The second customer operates a data center at the site of Access Router 3 and has client sites at the other two access routers. It also requires a bandwidth of 0.4Mbps between the clients and the data center. The network operator has decided to use class-based PHBs with a higher priority traffic for stock quotes for the first customer and the best-effort PHB for the other customer.

Table 6.1 shows the resulting allocation of traffic bandwidth on the three links because of the previous allocation. The access routers have been abbreviated to AR in the table.

Table 6.1   Allocation of Bandwidth to Different PHBs

Link	Amount of Priority Traffic	Amount of Best-Effort Traffic	Percentage of Priority Traffic
AR1-Core	0.8Mbps	0.4Mbps	67
AR2-Core	0.4Mbps	0.4Mbps	50
AR3-Core	0.4Mbps	0.8Mbps	33

As shown in Table 6.1, the ratio of the total bandwidth used by the priority traffic on each of the links is different. In a DiffServ network, you may need to allocate different shares of the bandwidth to different PHBs at different links.

Because the total bandwidth requirements on each of the links is less than 1.5Mbps, the network operator can use T1 links to satisfy the demand.

On the link between Access Router 2 and the core router, the capacity needed is only 0.8Mbps even though 1.5Mbps is available. The network operator has the option of splitting the capacity equally between the two PHBs or of restricting each to use only 0.4Mbps each.

If the network operator wants to ensure that the SLAs offered to Customer 2 are not violated, it must ensure that Customer 1 is not sending more than the contracted amount of priority traffic in the network. Thus, it needs to put in rate controls at each of the access routers. The rate control limits that need to be put into place at each of the access routers are as shown in Table 6.2.

Table 6.2	Rate Limits Required at Access Router	
Access Router	**Rate Limit on Priority Traffic**	**Rate Limit on Best-Effort Traffic**
AR 1	0.8Mbps	0.4Mbps
AR 2	0.4Mbps	0.4Mbps
AR 3	0.4Mbps	0.8Mbps

Thus, SLA requirements of customers can be translated into the configuration values for core routers, links, and access routers in the DiffServ network. For the real-world examples, which use a larger number of PHBs as well as several customer SLAs, policy-management tools are needed to automate this process.

After the appropriate configurations are determined, they need to be transported to the corresponding edge devices or core routers. Two of the common ways in which it can be achieved are as follows:

- The configurations are stored into a repository (the policy server) in the network, which typically is an LDAP accessible directory. Core routers and access routers can access the directory to obtain their configuration information.

- The policy management tool that determined the configuration of the different access routers sends the configuration directly to the core routers and the access routers.

After the configuration information is known to the edge devices and the core of the network, the edge device can take appropriate actions to classify and process the packets.

Edge Device in DiffServ Networks

The edge device in a DiffServ network plays a key role in supporting the SLAs offered to the customer. It needs to perform the following functions to this effect:

- Upon receiving a packet, examine the fields in the packet header to determine the service level of a packet.

- Determine the rate limits associated with the specific service level and enforce the rate limits.

- Determine the right PHB to be used for the service level and change the Type of Service field in the IP header to the right code point for the PHB.

- Keep counters measuring the number of bytes and packets belonging to each service level and collect any information needed for estimating the network performance.

The definition of service levels, how each service level is mapped onto a specific DiffServ header field code point, and how rate limits are associated with each service level are provided by the policy server complex. The policy server complex also determines the action to be taken on an IP packet when rate limits are exceeded. The packet can either be delayed until it is conformant with the rate limit, or it can be discarded. If the packet is delayed, it occupies buffers at the edge device. Limits on how many buffers can be occupied by packets belonging to a specific service level are also determined by the policy server complex.

The core devices in the DiffServ network need to implement the appropriate queuing behavior that results in the delivery of the requisite SLA. This is in accordance with the behavior of a core router supporting DiffServ, as described in Chapter 4.

Performance Monitor in DiffServ Networks

The performance monitor in the DiffServ network is responsible for keeping track of the network performance. One twist in the DiffServ network performance monitoring is that each of the different network PHBs have different delay and loss characteristics in the network. This implies that some of the performance monitoring tools to be described in Chapter 7, "Network Monitoring and SLA Verification," will need to be enhanced to support the different service levels in DiffServ networks.

In addition to keeping track of the performance of the network, the monitor also needs to track changes in the routing topology of the core DiffServ network. The configuration of the core routers in the DiffServ network depends on the routing topology of the network; that is, it depends on the path taken by the packets between a pair of access routers. If the path changes because of routing updates, these rate allocations may need to be recomputed. The performance monitor has to keep track of these changes and notify the policy manager to recompute the rates when such changes occur.

A concern with failure scenarios is that some of the flows that can meet their SLAs with the original network configuration may not be able to meet the same SLA requirements after reconfiguration. Policy rules dictate how these flows ought to be treated. Optimum techniques for managing performance in the case of failures in IP networks are open research issues.

Performance Analysis of Multiclass Queues

A core router or access router in a DiffServ network needs to service packets that are marked differently; this also means that these packets have to be treated differently. Packets that belong to different PHBs will have different queuing behaviors in the DiffServ network, with the queues being formatted while packets are contending for processing by the routers or for transmission on a link. This gives rise to a queue with more than one class of packets.

Multiple classes of packets can be handled in many ways. Two common cases of multiclass queues are the *priority queue* and the *weighted round-robin queue*. In a priority queue, all packets belonging to class 0 will be served first; packets belonging to class 1 will be served only if there are no packets from class 0 to be served, and so on. A packet from a lower-priority class will be served only if no packets of higher priority are present at the queue. Most networks implement *nonpreemptive queuing*—that is, ongoing transmissions of lower-priority packets are not aborted if a high-priority packet arrives at the queue.

In a weighted round-robin queue, weights are assigned to each of the classes. Packets are processed in a round-robin manner, moving from one class to another. The weight assigned to the class determines how many packets will be served from each class when its turn comes.

The analysis of the performance of a multiclass queue is a fairly complex problem. The answer depends on the arrival pattern of traffic, the service time distribution, and the queuing scheme (FIFO, priority, round-robin, and so on). Closed-form solutions are known only for a few simple cases. Approximations are often used to solve the problem to a reasonable degree of accuracy. Some of the common approximation techniques for analyzing queues are described in the book by Aggrawal [AGGRA]. However, closed-form solutions for estimating some queue characteristics, such as mean queuing delays, are known for several types of traffic for both priority and round-robin queues [KLEIN] [TAKAGI].

continues

For example, consider the queuing delays for a class with N priority queues with the service time being a constant of $1/\mu$ and the arrival rates being $l1, l2, l3, \ldots$ in the different queues. Suppose that 1 is the highest-priority queue, and N is the lowest-priority queue. Then the mean queuing delay of a packet in the jth queue can be shown to be [WOLFF]:

$$\frac{\sum\limits_{i=1}^{i=N} \lambda_i}{2\left(\mu - \sum\limits_{i=1}^{i=j-1} \lambda_i\right)\left(\mu - \sum\limits_{i=1}^{i=j} \lambda_i\right)}$$

Thus, consider the simple case where there are three priority queues with $\lambda1=\lambda2=\lambda3=10$ and $\mu=50$ Assuming that rates are specified in packets per seconds, a packet is serviced in 20ms, and a packet of each class arrives at the queue every 100ms. In this case, the mean queuing delay of the packets in the first class is 30/(2*50*40) seconds or 7.5ms. The mean queuing delay of packets in the second class is 30/(2*40*30) seconds or 12.5ms. The mean queuing delay of packets in the third queue would be 30/(2*30*20) seconds or 25ms. If we add in the service time of 20ms for each packet, the average time spent at the queue for each class of service would be 27.5ms, 32.5ms and 45 ms, respectively.

Similar solutions for other types of priority queues and round-robin queues can be found in texts of queuing theory such as those by Kleinrock [KLEIN] or Takagi [TAKAGI].

6.1.3 Integrated Services Core Networks

The use of Integrated Services (IntServ) with RSVP signaling protocol in the network provides an alternative way to support SLAs in the network and provide several service levels. As described in Chapter 4, IntServ/RSVP enables the creation of reserved pipes in an IP network that can have guarantees on delay or that can reserve a specific amount of bandwidth in the network.

The model for supporting SLAs using RSVP pipes is shown in Figure 6.8. Customers connect to the network provider through the access routers that act as edge devices. The edge devices establish several reserved bandwidth pipes among themselves to support packets belonging to different service levels. As packets are received by the access router, they are placed on one of the reserved bandwidth pipes for transport through the core network. Although the figure shows RSVP pipes as bidirectional arrows, each RSVP flow is simplex, and two RSVP flows in opposite directions needed to be established to get a bidirectional pipe.

Figure 6.8   SLA support using Integrated Services/RSVP.

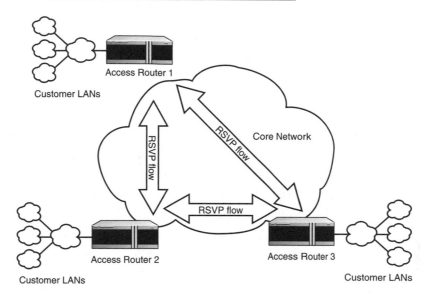

This particular use of RSVP pipes is not what the protocol was originally designed for. RSVP was designed to provide end-to-end reserved bandwidth pipes between applications. If the core routers do support RSVP, reserved bandwidth pipes can be established between access routers using the same software and protocols.

The reserved bandwidth pipes are created between pairs of access routers. Each of the bandwidth pipes aggregates several application flows and transports them on a single reserved pipe. This aggregation can significantly reduce the number of pipes that need to be seen by the core routers.

The Edge Device in RSVP Core Networks

The edge device has to perform the following functions on the receipt of any packet:

1. Examine the fields in the packet header to determine the service level of a packet.

2. Determine the right RSVP pipe for the transport of the packet and use that to transport the packet.

3. Keep counters measuring the number of bytes and packets belonging to each service level and collect any information needed for estimating the network performance.

The transport of packets using a reserved pipe requires that the packet be encapsulated in an external IP header. We'll take a closer look at why this is necessary.

The core routers in the network keep track of each established RSVP flow in the network. An RSVP flow is typically characterized by the source IP address, the destination IP address, and the destination protocol number. In the case of reserved bandwidth pipes established between pairs of access routers, the core routers would only give preferred processing to packets that contain the source or destination IP address of the access routers of the pipe.

When packets are sent by the customer network, they typically include the source and destination addresses of the final machine, which does not match the ones used to establish the reservation. Thus, to gain access to the set of reserved resources, a packet needs to be created that contains an IP header from the ingress access router to the egress access router and the correct port number in the transport header. The original IP packet is encapsulated into this larger packet at the ingress access device and decapsulated at the egress access device.

Because an IP header is a minimum of 20 bytes and a UDP header is another 8 bytes, the use of RSVP tunnels in the manner defined above requires an overhead of 28 bytes per packet.

Policy Manager and Policy Server in RSVP Pipes

Because the RSVP protocol is designed to work around network failures and with any routing scheme, the main issue with policy management in RSVP is to determine the amount of bandwidth that would be needed by each service level in the network. The estimation of the required bandwidth can be done as described in the sidebar on estimating bandwidth requirements earlier in this chapter.

Because RSVP messages are transmitted as periodic keep-alives (refreshes), network routing changes can lead to the RSVP tunnels being reestablished along different paths. In these cases, some of the reservations may conflict with each other. One of the tasks of the policy manager in core RSVP networks is to determine which of the reservations takes priority in the case of a conflict.

RSVP allows the signaling messages to carry a policy object that can contain information regarding the identity of the requestor and a priority for the reservation request. This policy object can be used to resolve conflicts among competing requests. Policies can also be used to set aside specific bandwidth for some users or applications or to ensure that reservations would succeed for pipes between specific pairs of access routers. Because the policy object resolution can be fairly complex, there is a provision that routers can consult an external decision point for resolving these policy questions. The protocol used between the router and the decision point is *Common Open Policy Service (COPS)*.

The decision point may, in turn, look upon policies that are configured and placed into a repository by the policy management tool. Another option is for the policy management tool to deliver the policies directly to the policy decision point and the access routers. The different interacting entities and the protocols used by them for RSVP policy control are shown in Figure 6.9.

As shown in the figure, access routers and core routers interact with each other using RSVP to establish the reserved pipes. They can communicate with the policy decision point (COPS server) using the COPS protocol. The COPS server makes decisions on the basis of policies configured by the policy management tool. The policy management tool generates policies as to how much bandwidth should be requested by each access router and which requests should be given higher priority. One of the ways in which the management tool can communicate the policies to access routers and the decision points is by storing it in the repository (which is likely to be an LDAP directory). However, some policy management products use a proprietary protocol to communicate the policies from the management tool to the decision point.

Figure 6.9   Policy components and protocols for IntServ/RSVP.

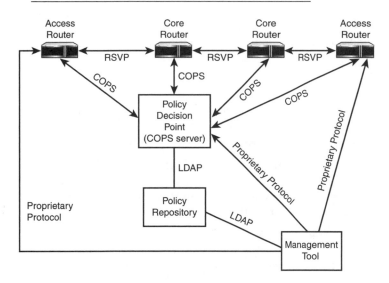

The performance monitor in the core network needs to validate that the performance of the RSVP pipes indeed satisfies the performance requirements. However, assuming that the reservation protocols and policies are implemented properly, the establishment of reserved pipes should ensure that the pipes do indeed meet the intended performance requirements, and the monitoring acts only as a secondary confirmation.

IntServ/RSVP Versus DiffServ for Network Connectivity SLAs

IntServ/RSVP and DiffServ are competing approaches to supporting network connectivity SLAs. Each approach has its merits and drawbacks. The advantages of using aggregated RSVP pipes in the manner described above for SLA support are

- The policy management software needs only to concern itself about the bandwidth/performance requirements of the communication between the pair of access routers. It need not worry about the possible interactions with the topology of the network.

- The RSVP reserved pipes automatically keep track of changes in network routes and adjust to them. This eliminates the need for the policy management tool to continuously track the changes to the routing tables in the network. The RSVP protocol has built-in mechanisms to accommodate dynamic route changes.

- The signaling mechanisms of RSVP allow the amount of reservation to be changed dynamically by an edge device. The edge devices can operate in a semi-autonomous fashion after they know how much bandwidth to request on each of the reserved pipes.

These advantages have to be compared against the drawbacks of the RSVP approach, namely:

- An overhead of 28 bytes needs to be paid for every packet that needs nondefault service. Because average packet sizes in IP networks tend to be relatively small (around 200 bytes), this overhead is relatively expensive.

- The complexity of specifying policies using RSVP to resolve conflicts is higher than the equivalent specification using DiffServ. In DiffServ, policies are configurations of the different routers. With RSVP/IntServ, you need to consider the different failure modes of the network and how to resolve policy conflicts among them.

- Although the scaling problems associated with RSVP are reduced significantly because of aggregation at access routers, you still may need to manage and establish a large number of RSVP tunnels. For the larger network providers, where the number of access routers is large, the use of RSVP may not be feasible.

- RSVP is constrained to follow the default routing path in the network. If not enough resources are available along the shortest path, no provision is made within the protocol to reroute the connection along another path that has more resources.

Because of these limitations, it is likely that the use of RSVP pipes for SLA support may be only of academic interest.

6.1.4 Frame Relay/ATM Core Networks

To support different service levels in the network, the goal of the network operator is to effectively obtain separate logical networks for each of the different service levels.

At the same time, the operator wants to avoid the cost of paying for duplicate line costs associated with the physical links. You can obtain this goal by building the core network, which is a connection-oriented network capable of supporting reserved bandwidth pipes.

The two most common technologies that are used for building a connection switched networks are *Frame Relay* and *ATM (Asynchronous Transfer Mode)*. Both offer connection-oriented communication and support reservation rates; however, quite a number of differences exist in the way these networks operate.

The model of the network when SLAs are supported using a Frame Relay or an ATM network is as shown in Figure 6.10. The only routers in this model are the access routers that provide IP connectivity to the customer network. As soon as the packets are received from the customer, the appropriate Frame Relay or ATM connection to forward it to the egress access router is determined, and the packet is placed on that connection.

Figure 6.10   SLA support using Frame Relay/ATM core network.

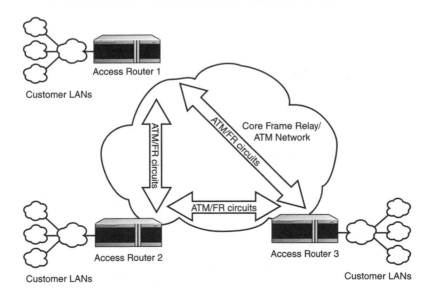

To build the core network, a network operator can purchase Frame Relay or ATM connectivity from the telecommunication operator in the area. When Frame Relay or ATM connections are purchased from a telecomm provider, the effect is the same as running different physical networks for different service levels. The costs and benefits of the approach are identical to those discussed in the section "Separate Network for Each Service Level." The cost savings are dependent on the price and the policies under which the Frame Relay or ATM connections are available from the telecommunication operator.

An alternative approach is for the network operator to obtain direct-line connectivity (T1, T3, or higher speed lines) from a telecomm provider and operate the Frame Relay or ATM networks on top of these lines. This allows the operator to multiplex multiple Frame Relay or ATM connections over the same physical set of links and may result in a lower cost of operation. To determine whether this is indeed the cheaper of the two options, this cost savings must be compared to the additional cost of maintaining a staff to manage and run the Frame Relay or ATM networks.

> **Note**
>
> Note the similarities between Figures 6.8 and 6.10. In both cases, traffic is carried on virtual circuits (VCs) established between access routers. In the case of Frame Relay or ATM, the VCs are explicitly created using another protocol underneath the IP layer. In the case of RSVP pipes, IP packets are being carried in tunnels or circuits created on an IP network using RSVP.

Frame Relay Overview

Frame Relay is a networking protocol that provides a connection-oriented communication with a committed information rate (CIR). All information in Frame Relay is carried in data units called *frames*. Each Frame Relay network supports a maximum frame size of 1600 bytes, but it can occasionally be up to 4KB. The structure of a frame is as shown in Figure 6.11.

Each frame begins and ends with a special bit pattern, 0x7e, shown as the *flag*. It is followed by a Frame Relay *header,* which is followed by the *payload (user data)* of the frame. This is followed by a *checksum* to validate the integrity of the frame.

Figure 6.11 Structure of Frame Relay frames.

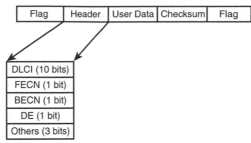

Fields in header (not in order)

The fields and the lengths of the fields of the Frame Relay header are also shown in Figure 6.11. This is a simplified representation of the frame header, which breaks some of these fields across the two bytes. The *data link connection identifier (DLCI)* is a local label for the Frame Relay connection. If you combine the originating Frame Relay box in the network and the DLCI used at the originating box, the Frame Relay connection can be uniquely identified. The DLCI label is 10 bits long and can be changed as the frame traverses the network.

Frame Relay connections are usually preset in advance by configuring the switches in the network, and they are known as *permanent virtual circuits (PVCs)*. Frame Relay also permits the establishment of dynamic connections using a signaling protocol; such connections are called *switched virtual connections (SVCs)*.

Each Frame Relay connection is assigned a CIR in the network. The originating point of Frame Relay is required to ensure that frames are not sent in a connection exceeding the CIR. If a frame is found to be exceeding the CIR, it can be marked as eligible for discard by intermediate switches. The *DE (Discard Eligible) bit* is used to indicate that a frame has exceeded the CIR. This can be done using the rate-control schemes described in Chapter 4. The other two interesting bits used in Frame Relay indicate congestion at intermediate Frame Relay switches. A switch that encounters congestion locally would set the *FECN (Forward Explicit Congestion Notification) bit.* Congestion is usually detected by having the number of frames queued at the switch cross specific thresholds. The FECN bit tells the receiver end of a Frame Relay connection that the sender is pushing too much data into the connection.

The *BECN (Backward Explicit Congestion Notification) bit* is placed on packets traveling on the same Frame Relay connection toward the originating point of a node that is sending too much data. A Frame Relay end point receiving the BECN bit knows it is pumping too much data in the network and should cut back on it.

When congestion is detected in the networks, Frame Relay end points typically cut back their transmission rate to the CIR level in the network. All Frame Relay boxes support a *local management interface (LMI),* which is a protocol that can be used to configure and manage the box.

Frame Relay is typically used to encapsulate and transport IP data across wide area links. The standard mechanism to transport IP (and other protocols) over Frame Relay is defined by RFC 2427 [BROWN].

If an IP packet is too long to fit into a frame, it can be fragmented into multiple packets that fit into a frame. The Frame Relay protocol is simple and works extremely well. However, because of its large frame size, it is not well-suited for applications that require low delay or delay jitters, such as carrying voice traffic.

Frame Relay is commercially available with a variety of CIR values ranging from 56Kbps to 10Mbps.

ATM Overview

ATM or the *Asynchronous Transfer Mode* can be described as a cell-relay protocol. Like Frame relay, ATM provides a connection oriented network which switches small cells that are 53 bytes long. Of the 53 bytes, 5 bytes are used for the ATM header and 48 bytes are used to carry the payload. ATM service can be obtained from various telecomm providers at speeds up to OC-48 (2.5 Gbps).

The connections in ATM are structured in a two-level hierarchy. The finest granularity connection in ATM is known as a *virtual circuit (VC).* Multiple VCs that share the same path are bundled together into a virtual path.

The interface between the provider of an ATM network and its customers is called the *UNI (User Network Interface).* The interface between different switches in an ATM network is the *NNI (Network-Network Interface).*

The 5-byte cell header of an ATM cell consists of five fields:

- *The Virtual Path Identifier (VPI)*: This field is 12 bits long in cells at NNI, and 8 bits long at UNI. This identifies the virtual path to which the cell belongs.

- *The Virtual Circuit Identifier (VCI)*: is a 16 bit label that identifies the connection to which a cell belongs.

- *The Payload Time Indicator (PTI)*: Indicates the type of cell and whether it contains user data or network maintenance or administrative data.

- *Connection Loss Priority (CLP)*: Serves the same function as DE in Frame Relay networks.

- *Header Error Check (HEC)*: A checksum to ensure the integrity of the packet header.

The 4 bits missing from the VPI field at the UNI form a *Generic Flow Control (GFC) field*. It is effectively useless.

ATM is a fully functional networking layer like IP, and it has analogous transport layers that correspond to TCP or UDP. The transport layers in ATM are called *ATM adaptation layers*. The most common among the adaptation layers is AAL5, which is the standard used for transmission of data (including IP packets) over ATM. ATM standards are defined by the ATM Forum [ATMF].

When it was originally conceived, ATM was to be the grand, unifying protocol that would provide support for all types of traffic over an integrated network structure. However, its most dominant use involves providing connectivity for IP networks.

An ATM connection (VC) can provide one of the following four types of services:

- *Constant Bit Rate (CBR)*: Connections belonging to this category have a fixed peak cell rate (PCR) at which cells can be placed into the connection and transmitted. These cells are delivered to the network

- *Variable Bit Rate (VBR)*: Connections belonging to this category can send in data at an average sustained cell rate (SCR) with bursts allowed up to a PCR. VBR can be classified as real-time or non–real-time. The real-time connection typically has an upper bound on the cell delays and delay variation that the ATM network can provide. Thus, VBR-nrt has larger buffers with possibly greater delay and lower loss than VBR-rt.

- *Available Bit Rate (ABR)*: Connections belonging to this category are assured a minimum cell rate (MCR) but also provide feedback by the network if they can send in cells at a higher rate. This rate can change during the lifetime of the network, depending on the amount of the load on the network.

- *Unspecified Bit Rate (UBR)*: Provides a best-effort delivery with no assurances about rates or guarantees. An ABR connection with a minimum cell rate of 0 is a UBR connection.

ATM offers QoS support for CBR, VBR, and ABR traffic. Connections can ask for bounds on performance metrics, such as cell loss rates, cell transfer delays, cell delay variation, and so on.

On a higher level, the techniques used by ATM to provide QoS are similar to those used by IntServ/RSVP, although there is quite a significant difference in the details. Both QoS approaches are based on the notion of reserved pipes (VCs in ATM, flows in RSVP), rate control (token bucket in RSVP, a timestamp-based approach called GCRA—generic cell rate algorithm—in ATM), and admission control. The type of services offered by the two differ (controlled load or guaranteed bandwidth in RSVP in contrast to the four categories provided by ATM).

One of the significant differences in the QoS approach taken by the ATM and RSVP has to do with the routing of reserved pipes. RSVP flows take the default path that the network routing protocols assigns to them. ATM protocols precompute a path with available bandwidth before establishing the connection. Thus, if enough resources are not available on a path for a reserved pipe, ATM can reroute the virtual circuit along another path. However, RSVP cannot do so.

Note

Multiple techniques have been devised for transport of TCP/IP over ATM. An overview of these techniques can be found in the texts by Stallings [STALL] and Kercheval [KERCH].

The SLA Architecture for Frame Relay/ATM Networks

When we use Frame Relay or ATM pipes to support IP SLAs, the basic approach used is the same. We connect all the access routers by point-to-point Frame Relay or ATM lines. Each service level gets its own set of dedicated lines. The parallel networks for each service level can be designed separately to provide a specific network performance and availability performance.

The functions of the different components in the SLA architecture in this case are as follows:

- The policy server complex contains the rules that determine the service level to be assigned to each of the IP packets.

- The edge devices determine the service level to which a packet belongs and determine the right Frame-Relay/ATM connection to which it should be mapped. The edge device then forwards the packets onto the right Frame-Relay/ATM pipe.

- The policy monitor monitors the performance of the different service levels and validates that the performance of the network is within the SLA requirements.

To design the separate Frame Relay networks or ATM networks to connect the different access routers (edge devices), it is not necessary to create connections between all the possible pairs of edge boxes. Instead, network design tools should be used to determine a logical network that can be used to obtain the desired connectivity without needing a full mesh. Within this logical network, access routers connect to customer LANs and core routers only forward packets, they do not connect to the customer LANs. This is the same as a standard IP network except that the links between the different routers are made up of Frame Relay or ATM circuits.

6.2 Application SLAs

For the application-level SLAs, consider an I/T operator that is required to offer application-level SLAs. We examine the following different environments:

- The network operated by the I/T operator delivers only best-effort services at a maximum available rate.

- The network operated by the I/T operator promises different levels of network services and supports a different maximum bandwidth for each level. A special case would be when the network supports reservation of resources. These different service levels may be offered using any one of the schemes discussed for network connectivity SLAs.

Within each of these environments, the I/T operator that has provided application SLAs needs to support the different SLA requirements of the various applications.

Both of the cases mentioned previously assume it is the network that is the bottleneck and is having performance problems. Under this assumption, the method to support application SLAs is to find a way that a preferred set of applications gets a bigger share of the limited resource—namely, network bandwidth. A third case is where the server processing power may be the performance bottleneck rather than the network bandwidth. The management of processing resources at the server is discussed in Section 6.2.3.

6.2.1 Application SLAs on a Best-Effort Network

When the network is a bottleneck and different applications have to be offered different SLAs, you can enforce rate control on the basis of different applications at the edges of the network. In effect, the I/T operator is using resource allocation at the edge in the manner described in the section "Resource Allocation at Access Routers."

The model of the network needed to support application SLAs is as shown in Figure 6.12. Because the network only supports best-effort traffic, different service levels can be defined only by the amount of network bandwidth used at each level. Each application is mapped into one of the service levels, and each service level is restricted to use only a specific portion of the network bandwidth. The mapping of applications to different service levels is done at the edges of the network by an edge device.

Figure 6.12   Model for application SLAs in best-effort networks.

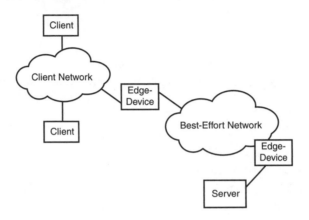

When rate allocation is to be done at an access router, the application's performance depends on its interactions with the TCP congestion control algorithm. TCP's throughput is very sensitive to the dropping of packets in the network, and its congestion control algorithms reduce the instantaneous sending rate of a connection when a packet is lost in the network. Therefore, rate control must be done by delaying packets (a shaping operation) rather than dropping packets.

To illustrate the difference between shaping and dropping, consider the case of an application that is constrained to use only 1Mbps, even though it is connected on a high-speed LAN (for example, a 16Mbps token ring). The rate control can be enforced by a token bucket scheme or a timestamp-driven scheme that will drop the packets when the rate of 1Mbps is exceeded. Measurements in our laboratory showed that the TCP connections end up getting an application throughput between 50Kbps and 300Kbps depending on the scheme used to drop packets. However, if packets are delayed at the access router and sent out in the network at the rate of 1Mbps, the application throughput is closer to the network rate. These results are consistent with independent simulations performed by other researchers [MISHRA].

The lower application throughput in the case of dropping is due to several factors:

- The behavior of TCP congestion control schemes

- The retransmission of dropped packets

- The overhead of TCP segments and IP headers

Because of a combination of these factors, rate control in networks should be done by means of rate shaping and not packet dropping at the access router.

An alternative to explicit shaping is *random early discard (RED)* of packets. With the RED scheme [FLOYD], gateways keep track of their average queue size. The queue size is statistically sampled, and when it exceeds a specific threshold, some of the newly arriving packets are probabilistically selected and discarded until the queue size falls below the threshold. The probability of discard increases as the measured average queue size increases. RED (or a variant) is implemented in most routers. Although RED is a very effective mechanism for avoiding congestion at queues, it is hard to determine the amount of bandwidth allocated to specific applications using RED.

The access routers that implement rate shaping can be placed at both the client and the server end of the core network. However, it is also possible to do the shaping at only the access router at the server site, as well as to do the shaping in the server itself. The support within servers for rate shaping and how server-based shaping can be used to provide for application SLA at remote clients is discussed in the following sections.

Packet Shaping and Policy Functions in Servers

The IBM mainframe (System 390) and AIX server platforms have implemented support for policy-enabled QoS in their TCP/IP stack since their release in 1999. The architectural model used by the IBM server platforms to implement policy support is as shown in Figure 6.13.

The *policy agent* is a user-level application that is capable of reading policy rules from a local configuration file, or from an LDAP repository, and interpreting them. In this example, the policy agent incorporates the PDP function described earlier. The LDAP repository is part of the policy-server complex. The management tool is used to populate the policy server with the QoS policies as to which applications belong to which service levels and how much rate is to be used by each service level. Rate controls can be specified on a per connection basis or on the basis of an aggregate service level.

Figure 6.13   Policy components within servers.

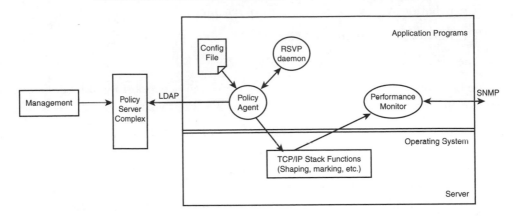

The policy agent can configure device parameters that enable the marking of packets to exploit the DiffServ capabilities of the network, if any exist. To accomplish this, the policy agent must first acquire and interpret the DiffServ QoS policies, and thus acts as a PDP. Similarly, the policy agent can act as a policy decision point for RSVP requests that arrive at the RSVP daemon or for reservation requests that originate from the RSVP daemon. The *RSVP daemon* is the process responsible for handling and generating RSVP connection control messages (PATH and RESV messages).

In a best-effort network, the servers can control the amount of bandwidth that is to be used by the applications belonging to any service level. This control in servers can be applied at the TCP layer rather than at the IP layer. The sidebar "Edge Device Functions in Server Versus Routers" later in this section compares the issues associated with performing various functions at the TCP layer rather than at the IP layer.

In addition to the policy agent, the IBM servers also support a performance monitor. The statistics are also collected on a per service level basis. These statistics are reported via a SNMP MIB (see Chapter 7 for a discussion of SNMP protocol). The information reported includes the average round-trip time for connection (or all connections in a same service level), the number of retransmissions, the throughput on the connections, and so on. These metrics can be compared against SLA performance bounds to validate compliance with SLAs.

The statistics measured by the performance monitor still deal only with network information and do not include the processing by the application. However, in many cases, the lifetime of a connection provides an approximate value for the user response time of the connection. This approximate measurement can be obtained in a generic manner without modifying applications.

Chapter 7 discusses techniques related to how the actual response time of applications can also be monitored to ensure compliance with the SLAs.

Edge Device Functions in Servers Versus Routers

The functions associated with an edge device, such as marking each packet's ToS byte for DiffServ, determination of the service level of a packet, rate control, and so on can be implemented at servers as well as at routers. Although the functions are identical, a significant impact is made in the efficiency of such functions when implemented at the servers in contrast to the routers.

A server implements these functions at the connection level; that is, it determines the correct service level when the connection is first initialized. At the connection establishment time, the structures for rate control can be initialized, and the right ToS marking for packets can be determined. This information is stored in the connection entry for the specific TCP connection. When a packet is to be sent out on the network, it can be marked correctly by looking up the information stored in the connection entry. A router, on the other hand, needs to make these decisions on every packet arrival. On every packet, you need to search among the classification rules to determine the right service level for the packet.

Another advantage for the servers is that they can determine the appropriate QoS metrics before network security protocols such as IPsec cover information about the port numbers. Although routers cannot easily handle the case of encrypted port numbers, servers have no problems in this regard. Most operating systems have information about the process that owns a connection or the program that invoked the process owning the connection. This permits marking and classification of data even for applications which do not use well-known port numbers.

The performance monitor at a server can obtain information about the performance of the TCP connections or about its lifetime. These features are not easily done at routers.

Because of these advantages of providing edge device functions in servers, we expect the servers to play a key role in the exploitation of QoS mechanisms within enterprise networks as well as in support of SLAs.

Remote Control of Bandwidth

When the core network supports only best-effort services, different service levels can be provided by sharing the bandwidth at a bottleneck link in proportion to the importance of different applications. This situation is shown in Figure 6.14 (refer to A), where multiple clients and servers are sharing a bottleneck link in the middle of the network.

Figure 6.14   Allocation of bandwidth on bottleneck link.

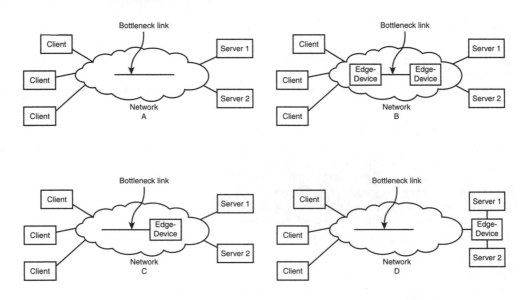

The obvious way to manage the bandwidth of the bottleneck link would be to have an edge device function at both ends of the link. The edge devices would regulate access to the link's bandwidth and allocate them in some proportions of the different applications. This configuration is shown in Figure 6.14 (refer to B).

In some cases, the edge device function may not be needed at both ends of the bottleneck link. For example, if the bulk of data transfer is in one direction of the link (for example, from the server to the client), only an edge device placed at the server's end of the link, as shown in Figure 6.14 (refer to C), would suffice for an effective control of bandwidth on the bottleneck link. The assumption is that there is no congestion in the path from the client to the server.

In other cases, the edge device need not even be located close to the bottleneck link. The edge device can be located at another point in the network but still manage to effectively control the bandwidth at the bottleneck link, as shown in Figure 6.14 (refer to D).

Consider a customer-support application where SLAs are supported by means of edge device functions placed in the server. The application consists of an online call-processing center and help desk, which is connected to the Internet. Clients installing software components on their machines can use Internet telephony to contact the help desk for problem resolution. The clients also need to be connected to the help desk so that the help-desk clerk can help the client in diagnosing problems with the computer system. The configuration in this case is shown in Figure 6.15.

Figure 6.15   Remote bandwidth management in customer help desk.

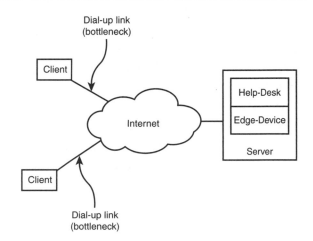

Most client machines dial in to the network using modems operating at 28.8Kbps. This dial-in link is typically the bottleneck link. The help-desk operator wants to ensure that voice packets get an assured rate of at least 10Kbps out of the 28.8Kbps possible. The other major communication is to receive the rest of the bandwidth. The major flow of data is from the server to the clients.

Instead of putting the support for edge devices in the client machines, rate control is done remotely for packets flowing from the server to the client. In these cases, 10Kbps are reserved for voice packets, and the other programs can use the remaining 18.8Kbps. The use of a weighted round-robin discipline ensures that all the capacity can be used by one type of packet when there are no packets of the other type.

The decision not to put in the edge device at the client is done for reasons related to logistics. Because native rate-control functions are not available on the client platforms, installing the edge device function on numerous client machines is not feasible. However, installing this function at the server side can be accomplished much more easily.

Because most of the traffic being sent to the client originats at the help desk, simply controlling the rate of outbound packets at the help-desk server allows distribution of bandwidth among the different sets of applications at the dial-in link. Thus, application SLAs are supported and bandwidth is allocated for a remote link at the server.

6.2.2 Application SLAs Using Network Service Levels

When the network is supporting different service levels, the management of application SLAs is somewhat simplified. The key aspect of exploiting network SLAs is that different applications can be mapped onto network pipes of varying bandwidths and delay characteristics.

Consider the case of a network that provides two service levels using DiffServ, with the capability to send up to 1Mbps of EF PHB traffic and the capability to send up to 4Mbps of default best-effort PHB traffic. You can then map applications desiring a better response time into the first service level and those requiring higher throughput into the second service level.

Following the discussion in the sidebar "Edge Device Functions in Servers Versus Routers," the mapping of the application packets into network service levels can be done by means of any of the following combinations of edge device placement:

- A pair of edge devices on the client and server access points to the network

- An edge device at the server access point to the network

- An edge device in the server TCP/IP stack

Any of these combinations can provide better performance to a preferred set of applications.

Regardless of the combination of edge devices used, the policy server determines their configuration and contain rules to ensure that the desired application-level SLAs are satisfied.

If the core network provides support for establishing reservations for applications using RSVP signaling, reserved pipes can be used to support application-level SLAs. Under this operating environment, the application that needs to obtain a specific share of network bandwidth needs to establish a reservation in the network using RSVP. The reservation is subject to policy control in the network. Policy control specifies which connections in the network are allowed to make reservations and how much should be reserved for each connection.

We assume that the server implements the policy components shown in Figure 6.13. The flow of messages are shown in Figure 6.16. Figure 6.16 (refer to A) shows how policy control is exercised for requests originating from the client. To establish a reservation, an application makes a request to the RSVP daemon to send out a PATH message. Before sending out the PATH message, the daemon checks with the policy agent to validate that the reservation should indeed be allowed for the communicating client and application. Figure 6.16 (refer to B) shows how policy control is exercised for RESV messages. The RSVP daemon generates RESV messages in response to the PATH messages sent to it. Before responding to the RESV message, the RSVP daemon would check the permissions and amount of resources for the flow from the policy agent.

Figure 6.16   Policy enforcement at servers.

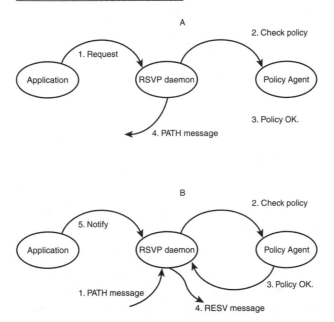

> **Note**
>
> The only caveat about using reservation is that it works best for applications that have a relatively long-lived communication with the clients; it does not work very well if the connections are short-lived. Reservation is not the right approach for applications such as Web servers, but it is quite acceptable for applications such as serving video or audio clips to the clients, or for assuring that backup of enterprise databases proceeds at a specific rate.

6.2.3 Server Workload Management

Although the discussion above has focused on allocating bandwidth to a different set of applications in the network, we have avoided the scenario where the server itself is a bottleneck. In this case, we need to allocate the server processing capability among the multiple applications, in accordance with the I/T operator's defined policies.

The capability to assign different priorities to executing processes is available in some form in most operating systems. Generally, the assignment of processes or applications to a priority level is done automatically by the operating system on the basis of their processor utilization, and so on. However, some level of user control is also permitted. UNIX systems permit the option to execute some processes at a priority different from the default one via the nice command. Any user can use nice to lower the priority of the processes. The super-user can use nice to increase the priority of any process.

Such priority mechanisms provide a crude way to share processing resources among the different applications. In contrast, the IBM OS/390 operating system on mainframes provides a relatively sophisticated system to manage the workload at a server.

The *Work Load Management (WLM) function* in OS/390 allows the system administrator to specify the business objectives for specific applications. The system administrator can set the goals for each application, which can be specified in terms of a relative importance and a performance goal. An example of a performance goal is the target response time for completion of an application. Another type of performance goal specifies how often the task must be executed. This goal, which the OS/390 calls *velocity,* is defined for long-lived processes that need to be run periodically. For any application, the goals may be defined differently over different time periods during which the application is active.

After the administrator has specified the performance goals, the system uses these to divide each of the processes into internal service classes. The service classes are associated with specific performance, and the system tracks the performance of each service class to see if it is meeting its goals. At each 10-second interval, the allocation of system resources (processor, disk I/O) to each of the service classes is updated on the basis of how close the class is to meeting its service goals.

A more detailed description of WLM describing its use in a cluster of OS/390 processors is found in the paper by Aman, et al. [AMAN]. WLM is one of few commercial systems that offers a complex level of support for meeting a task's requirements. However, many experimental operating systems provide support for different types of QoS.

6.3   Service Provider SLAs

The support of SLAs for the service provider is similar to that of the I/T operator (application SLAs), except that the service provider has control only over the server side of the connection. Thus, the SLAs provided by the service provider usually deal with the rate of connections that can be supported by the server (server capacity) or with the total amount of outgoing bandwidth that can be used by the server.

6.3.1   Service Provider Environment

The environment in which a service provider needs to support a single customer or a single class of customers is shown in Figure 6.17. The service provider connects to the Internet through an access line of fixed capacity.

The most common type of servers outsourced for support and operations consists of Web servers. However, it is also quite common to find other types of applications servers being hosted. Typical types of applications servers that are hosted are Web servers, electronic-commerce transaction servers, mail servers, groupware servers, directory servers, and so on.

A simplified configuration of a hosted site is shown in Figure 6.17. It shows the service provider accessing the Internet through one access router, which is connected to a bank of servers. Again, we will make the simplifying assumption that each of the servers belongs to a different customer and is to be given a distinct service level. The configuration where multiple replicas are hosted for the same customer is described in the following section.

In practice, this configuration is likely to include more than one access router to improve the reliability of the site. To obtain scalable performance, you may also have a load balancer that distributes requests to multiple replicas of the same server. Similarly, if the servers are not intended to be available for general-purpose access on the Internet, a firewall will be needed to enforce access restrictions.

The two most important factors composing service provider SLAs are the total amount of access bandwidth and the server capacity (the rate of connections that the site can support) allocated to a customer.

Figure 6.17 Simplified model of service provider environment.

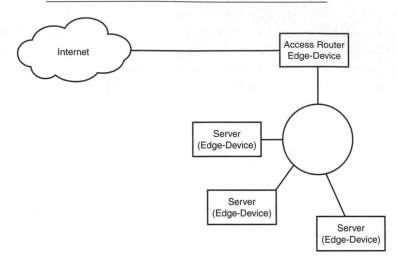

Bandwidth SLAs for Service Providers

The main aspect of dealing with SLAs for service providers involves the proportion of the network bandwidth that is to be allocated to each of the service levels. In most cases, the bandwidth is the amount of traffic generated by the servers, rather than the traffic coming into the servers. The allocation of access link bandwidth can be done in one of the following ways:

- The access router maintains separate queues for each of the service levels. Most access routers can be configured to support a limited number of queues and use weighted round-robin queuing discipline to service the queues. The queuing discipline enables the sharing of access link bandwidth in the specified manner in cases of high load. If a customer is not using its allocated capacity, the remainder is shared among the active customers. The drawback to this approach is that most access routers permit a relatively limited number of queues (four or eight) that can be created in this manner. If a service provider is supporting many customers, this approach is likely to be inadequate. The other drawback of rate control at the access router is that the behavior of the TCP connections in the presence of packet drops at the access router results in erratic application performance.

- Allocate rates to different servers, each of which implements packet shaping and rate control at the server. This shaping can be done at the TCP connection level, and therefore is more efficient at meeting the desired throughput on a per connection basis. The advantage of the approach is that unnecessary packet losses (and resulting TCP cut down of rate) is avoided. Server-based rate control tends to produce more predictable application performance than network-based rate control. However, the partitioning of bandwidth among different customers means that excess capacity may be assigned to a customer who is not using it, but no other customer is able to use that bandwidth. This also requires that the server's TCP/IP stack supports packet shaping and rate control. Not all commercial servers provide this support.

The partitions of bandwidth among different servers can be made more dynamic by using the performance monitor. The performance monitor measures the amount of capacity used by each of the servers, and then reallocates the partitions at a slow timescale. This repartitioning can be done every few minutes.

A number of companies offer bandwidth management and regulation products that can be placed between the access router and the servers to manage the bandwidth, as shown in Figure 6.18. Some of these products are PacketShaper from Packeteer (`http://www.packeteer.com`), FloodGate from Checkpoint (`http://www.checkpoint.com`), and the AC 200/300 boxes from Allot (`http://www.allot.com`). They provide support for a larger number of queues to manage the bandwidth; the increased number of queues are not offered by existing routers. Some of them also manipulate transport header fields to obtain the same level of application performance that can be obtained at a server. Transport header manipulation is described in the next subsection.

Figure 6.18   Intermediate bandwidth management boxes.

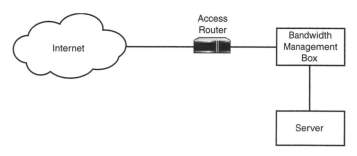

Case Study: *Providing Web-Hosting Facilities to Customers*

To illustrate the management of bandwidth SLAs, we consider the history of a hypothetical company, vHosts Incorporated, which provides Web-hosting facilities to its customers. When vHosts was incorporated, it had three customers: eAuction Corp, eBuy Corp, and eCards Corp. eAuction provided a site to auction curio items over the Web; eBuy was an online store selling toys and books over the Web; and eCards provided online greeting cards. vHosts had a T3 link connecting it to the Internet. It connected all customers via a dedicated token ring operating at 16Mbps. It sold connectivity at the maximum rate of 5Mbps to eAuction and 15Mbps to eBuy and eCards. The same rate constraints apply for traffic coming in from the Internet, as well as to traffic going out to the Internet. vHosts wanted to ensure that it was satisfying the SLA requirements of each of the customers.

vHosts satisfied its SLAs by configuring its access to enforce rate constraints for traffic to or from the Internet. At the access router, it set up a weighted round-robin system with four queues, one for each of the customers, and assigned them weights in the ratio of 1:3:3. The link bandwidth of 45Mbps was shared in the desired ratio among each of the customers. It expected each customer to obtain throughput about 28% higher than the contracted SLA.

Because of recommendations from existing customers, a new company, eExperiment, decided to use vHosts for its Web site as well. It only wanted to purchase 5Mbps of bandwidth from vHosts. True to its name, eExperiment decided to run a simple experiment to measure compliance with its SLA. Before going online publicly, it measured the throughput obtained by a Web client during the busiest hour when the other servers were very active. vHosts had configured its router to have four queue servers with round-robin weights of 1:3:3:1 to support eExperiments. The access router implemented rate control and dropped packets exceeding the rate constraints. To its dismay, eExperiment found that it could barely reach the throughput of 1Mbps compared to the contracted 5Mbps. The impact of dropped packets on TCP throughput was significant.

Dismayed by the unfavorable results, vHosts decided to move rate control back to the servers. Using a server whose stack supported rate control, it ensured that each of the servers was only sending out the contracted amount of bandwidth, although each server was connected via a token ring that could enable each of them to send up to 16Mbps at peak. The server stack enforced rate control by delaying packets rather than dropping them. vHosts then asked eExperiments to repeat its test, and the company was happy to get close to the 5Mbps it expected. However, with this solution, vHosts found that its capacity was statically allocated among the different token rings. It knew that eBuy did not often use its full 15Mbps capacity, whereas eAuction sometimes needed up to 10Mbps because of a popular item being auctioned. However, vHosts are not able to divert the excess bandwidth away to eAuction as it could when it used an access router to regulate the bandwidth.

vHosts migrated to an access router that supported packet shaping rather than packet dropping. Now all four customers were happy. eExperiment's experiment showed that it was able to get close to 5Mbps. Excess bandwidth could be shared, and all SLAs were being satisfied.

Due to excellent recommendations by customers, vHosts found that it now had 10 customers, and all of its current customers were demanding 10Mbps. vHosts upgraded to a 155Mbps link to the Internet. However, the access router permitted only four queues to be defined for round-robin service. vHosts therefore had to fall back to putting rate control at the servers, even though the sharing of excess bandwidth was no longer possible. Each of its 10 servers was allowed to pump out 10Mbps of data, at most, to the Internet. However, that allowed 55Mbps of unused bandwidth on the access link.

To enable dynamic sharing of bandwidth, vHosts introduced a performance monitor to track the usage of bandwidth by each server and to adjust the rate limits accordingly. Rate usage information was collected every minute and rate adjustments were made in the same timescale. The average bandwidth used over the last five minutes was used to allocate the excess bandwidth to the different customers for the next minute. Suppose a server generated traffic of 8Mbps in the last five minutes, and the total traffic generated by all the servers was 80Mbps in that time period. The proportionate share of this server was $55 \times 8/80$, or 5.5Mbps. The rate limit was then set to be the SLA amount 10Mbps + 5.5Mbps, or 15.5Mbps.

vHosts was aware that this adjustment mechanism did not ensure 100% dynamic sharing of network, but felt it was an adequate solution to satisfy its SLAs and to share the excess bandwidth.

Rate Control Using TCP Header Manipulation

To understand how transport header manipulation can help in rate allocation services, we'll examine how TCP regulates packet transmission in the network. The TCP protocol requires that the receiver acknowledge the bytes that it has received. The number of bytes that have been sent but not acknowledged by the other side is the amount of data in flight. TCP also keeps track of the round-trip delays experienced by the packets on a connection. These round trip delays are tracked by a timestamp option that is carried in the TCP header for packets and acknowledgments.

The amount of data in flight is controlled by two main factors:

- *Size of receiver's buffers*: Both sides of a TCP connection inform each other about the amount of data that it can receive without overflowing its buffers. The sender ensures that the data in flight never exceeds the value advertised by the receiver.

- *Congestion in the network*: The sender tries to maximize the amount of data in flight (up to the limit requested by the receiver) as long as it does not cause an overload at any of the intermediate nodes in the network. The amount of data in flight is increased when packets can be successfully transmitted, and reduced when TCP detects that there has been a loss of packets in the network.

The maximum amount of data that can be received, as well as the acknowledgment of packets, is calculated by using byte sequence numbers, which depend on the number of bytes received since the inception of the connection. (The *sequence number* is the number of bytes received if TCP always started with a sequence number of 0. The starting sequence number is usually randomly selected.)

The round-trip in TCP is computed by including the time when a segment was transmitted as one of the TCP options. The acknowledgments carry the same timestamp back to the sender. The sender uses the difference to compute the round-trip time for the connection. This round-trip time is used to determine the timeout periods for the connection.

The amount of bandwidth received by a connection is determined by the amount of data in flight, as well as the round-trip time of packets. An intermediate box (such as the bandwidth management box in Figure 6.18) can offer different service levels to different connections by manipulating TCP headers in one of the following ways:

- *Modifying the size of the receiver's advertised buffer*: An edge device can reduce the amount of window buffers for applications that are to receive a lower throughput. It can also increase the size of the receiver's advertised buffer (although caution must be exercised in doing so) for preferred applications, provided the characteristics of the end hosts are taken into account and buffer overflow at the receiver is avoided. Because a smaller number of packets are outstanding in the network, the rate received by the connection is reduced accordingly. By increasing the number of outstanding packets in the network, you can increase the rate—provided the buffers at the receiver are not overrun.

- *Modifying the byte-sequence number of acknowledged packets.* Because the byte sequence numbers of acknowledged packets are the key determinant of the amount of data in flight, reducing this information can cause applications to reduce the amount of data in flight and thereby cause the bandwidth available to the set of applications to be reduced. The bandwidth management box can subsequently generate acknowledgments with larger byte-sequence numbers (up to the sequence number acknowledged by the final receiver) at a constrained rate, so as to force the flow of data to occur in a much smoother fashion. Instead of sending a large packet of 1,024 bytes in the network, this method can ensure that four packets of 256 bytes (excluding TCP/IP headers) are sent.

- *Modifying the timestamp in acknowledgments.* By manipulating the timestamp information in the packet header, the end hosts can be fooled into believing that the round-trip time is larger than the real value. This can be exploited to eliminate the unnecessary timeouts that can occur when the byte-sequence numbers of acknowledged packets are reduced.

Playing with the acknowledgment byte-sequence numbers and timestamps can definitely increase the share of bandwidth for one class of packets at the expense of another class of packets. However, the scheme suffers from a few disadvantages, namely:

- Looking into the transport header fields and modifying them requires a significant amount of state information to be kept at the edge device.

- If encryption is used to protect the contents of a packet, the transport header information may not be available. It should be kept in mind that this problem arises only when IPsec is used to encrypt packet headers. Encryption at the transport layer using SSL (the secure sockets layer) does not hide the TCP headers and can still be manipulated.

Despite these disadvantages, manipulation of TCP headers can be successfully used in some cases to provide different levels of bandwidth sharing among some applications. From a technical perspective, it would be much cleaner and more efficient if rate control was a function supported in the servers.

SLAs Regarding Server Capacity

In addition to SLAs defining different bounds on the rates to be used by different customers, the service provider can define SLAs in terms of server capacity. The *server capacity* can be expressed in terms of the number of replicated servers that are provided to a specific customer by the service provider.

When multiple replicas of the server are supported, the structure of each of the servers looks like the one shown in Figure 6.19. A *front-end dispatcher* is responsible for distributing the requests to multiple replicas of the server. The front-end dispatcher receives packets from the access router and distributes them to one of the replicas of the server. On the reverse path, the replica may send packets back to the dispatcher. In some dispatching architectures, the packets on the reverse path need not flow through the dispatcher. They can be sent to the Internet using an auxiliary router, as shown in Figure 6.19.

Figure 6.19   Front-end dispatcher.

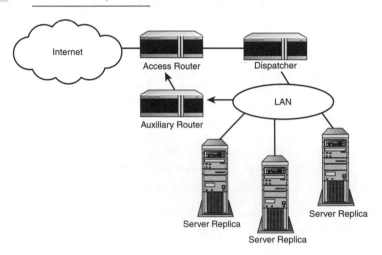

The simplest front-end dispatcher can be implemented as an application-level proxy for the server. The proxy receives clients' requests and forwards them to one of the servers. Because the proxy does not do any of the application functions but is simply relaying packets back and forth, a single proxy can support many server replicas. Requests are simply distributed to the servers. The replies also have to flow back through the proxy. The *proxy* is a single point of failure and can easily become a bottleneck itself. To improve availability, the proxies can be implemented on specialized embedded platforms that can restart faster than the general-purpose servers.

Another way in which proxy performance can be improved is by splicing two TCP connections together. Because the proxy does not do anything except relay packets back and forth, the proxy only needs to do application-level processing for part of the connection. After the connection is established, the proxy device can transport the packets back to the original client, doing the minimum possible processing on the packets so that it appears that the packets are flowing on the same connection that was established by the client to the proxy. The proxy needs to change the TCP and IP headers in the packets to make this transition. The IP layer addresses have to be changed to make them appear to come from the proxy. The TCP headers need to be manipulated because the initial byte sequence numbers negotiated on the two TCP connections (the one from the client to the proxy and the one from proxy to server) would typically be different. Changing the fields also requires checksum entries in the headers to be updated. Further details on splicing can be found in the paper by Bhagwat and Maltz [BHAG].

Other front-end boxes attempt to eliminate the overhead of proxying by simply directing IP packets to different servers. The connect requests from the clients can easily be identified by the front end because the connection packet has a special flag in it. The front-end box selects a server to which the connect request will be directed and creates the minimum state required to redirect the subsequent packets on the connection to the same server. This state requires storing only the client IP address and TCP port number with the server that was selected. The normal packets are forwarded to the server selected with the connect packet. On the reverse path, the IP address of the source is changed to make it appear as if it is coming from the front-end box.

Several variants on such front-end dispatchers are available commercially. They include features that will allow all the servers to share the same IP address so that address translation is not necessary on the reverse path, and the reverse packets do not even need to go through the front end; such features allow selection of specific servers on the basis of current load on the network or on higher-layer information contained in the packets. Dispatching is also available as a feature on some routers.

Some of the dispatching products available include the LocalDirector from Cisco, the eNetwork Dispatcher from IBM, the IB4000/IB7000 products from ipivot (`http://www.ipivot.com`) and WLBS (Microsoft Windows NT Load Balancing Service) from Microsoft.

> ### Note
> Although application-level proxying can work for replicating any application, splicing or front-end dispatching with IP packets only works with TCP-based applications. This may not be a real issue in commercial systems where the predominant traffic is TCP-based, but it is something you should be aware of.

In such an environment, SLAs regarding server capacity typically deal with supporting a specific level of connection requests or on the number of servers that need to be dedicated to a specific customer. If the SLA specifically requires a number of servers, they can be easily provided by configuration.

Quite often, the SLA requires that a specific connection rate be supported, leaving the choice of the number of servers up to the service provider. The support of such an SLA requires that the number of requests directed at each customer should be monitored to see whether the number of machines dedicated to a customer are adequate to meet its performance. If it is insufficient, additional servers need to be devoted to the customer. Otherwise, you might be able to reuse some of the servers available from the customer (provided it does not go below the minimum required by the SLA).

Note

We are assuming a model where all servers are performing similar functions, such as serving Web pages. In many environments, servers of different types may be deployed; for example, Web servers may act as front ends for transaction servers or directory servers. In these cases, the number of servers cannot be simply added, and the difference among servers must be accounted for.

In a service provider environment where different customers are hosted on different LANs, such a configuration requires reconfiguring the physical connectivity of the server farm. However, in an environment where the different servers are on the same LAN, the servers can be dynamically reassigned to different customers. The same can be done if servers are supported on virtual LANs (VLANs) and the VLAN product permits dynamic reconfiguration to add or remove specific servers from the VLAN dynamically.

The reconfiguration scheme in these cases works as follows:

1. The front-end dispatchers (edge devices) keep track of the servers that are assigned to them. They also collect statistics on the connection requests allocated to them.

2. The performance monitor collects information on the load for each server of the expected rate allocated to each server periodically.

3. The performance monitor determines the number of new servers for each customer to best meet the capacity required by the SLAs. The simplest allocation is to allocate the servers in proportion to the rate of requests measured for each customer.

4. The front-end dispatchers and servers are reconfigured, with the front-end dispatcher given a new set of servers and the servers configured to support the new customer.

The capability to reconfigure server forms dynamically is important for service providers in the Internet, where the number of requests to a site is quite erratic.

In contrast to customers with multiple servers that need a front-end dispatcher, multiple small customers need to be hosted on the same physical server. The network interfaces on such a shared server would typically have multiple IP addresses, and the server would accept any packet destined to any of these addresses. An application such as a Web server is aware of the IP address that was used to access the server, and it takes that into account in its operations. An example of such an application is the Apache [APACHE] Web server, which is capable of acting as multiple virtual servers. A single instance of Apache can serve different home pages for different customers, depending on the IP address used to access the server.

For the purpose of SLAs, each of the different virtual servers should be treated as a different application. Because many operating systems do not allow different levels to be assigned to the same application, you should combine the virtual servers belonging to customers with similar SLA requirements into a single application instance and avoid trying to combine virtual servers with widely diverse SLA requirements.

6.4 Further Information

A brief overview of RSVP and Differentiated Services is provided in Chapter 4, and references for further information are also provided. An overview of Frame Relay can be found in the book by Smith [SMITH]. Several books are available on ATM. An overview of the current ATM network and its interoperation with TCP/IP can be found in the books by Stallings [STALL], Kercheval [KERCH] and Amoss [AMOSS]. The official site for ATM information is the ATM Forum [ATMF].

6.5 Endnotes

[AGGRA] Aggrawal, S. C. *MetaModeling—A Study of Approximations in Queuing Models.* Cambridge, MA: MIT Press, 1985.

[AMAN] Aman, J., et al. "Adaptive Algorithms for Managing a Distributed Data Processing Workload." *IBM Systems Journal* 36, no. 2 (1997).

[AMOSS] Amoss, John, and D. Minoli. *IP Applications with ATM.* New York: McGraw-Hill, 1998.

[APACHE] The Apache Project Web Site. Available at `http://www.apache.org`.

[ATMF] The ATM Forum. Available at `http://www.atmforum.com`.

[BHAG] Bhagwat, P., and D. Maltz. "TCP/IP Splicing for Application Layer Proxy Performance." *IBM T. J. Watson Research Report* no. RC21139, (March 17, 1998).

[BROWN] Brown, C., and A. Malis. "Multiprotocol Interconnect over Frame Relay." Internet RFC 2427 (October 1998).

[FLOYD] Floyd, S., and V. Jacobson "Random Early Detection Gateways for Congestion Avoidance." *IEEE/ACM Transactions on Networking*, no. 4 (August 1993): 397-413.

[GUERIN] Guerin, R., H. Ahmadi, and M. Naghshineh. "Equivalent Bandwidth and Its Application to Bandwidth Allocation in High-Speed Networks." *IEEE Journal on Selected Areas in Communications* 9, no. 7 (September 1991): 968-981.

[KERCH] Kercheval, Berry. *TCP/IP over ATM, A No-Nonsense Internetworking Guide*. Upper Saddle River, NJ: Prentice Hall, 1998.

[KLEIN] Kleinrock, L. *Queuing Systems: Theory Volume-II*. New York: John Wiley & Sons, 1975.

[MISHRA] Mishra, P. P. "Effect of Leaky Bucket Policing on TCP over ATM Performance." Proceedings of ICC '96, Dallas, Texas, June 1996.

[STALL] Stallings, William. *High Speed Networks: TCP/IP and ATM Design Principles*. Upper Saddle River, NJ: Prentice Hall, 1997.

[TAKAGI] Takagi, H. *Queuing Analysis: Vacation and Priority Systems*. Vol. 1. North Holland: Elsevier Science, 1991.

[WOLFF] Wolff, R. *Stochastic Modeling and the Theory of Queues*. Upper Saddle River, NJ: Prentice Hall, 1989, pp. 441-442.

Network Monitoring and SLA Verification

Monitoring is an integral component to supporting any type of SLA. The monitoring of network and application performance provides evidence that the SLA is being adhered to by the network operator or service provider. Network monitoring also provides crucial information that can be used for network redesign and capacity planning.

A customer can also monitor the performance of a network or an application to ensure that the level of service contracted for is being received . Although the tools and techniques available to the customer for the purpose of SLA validation differ from those available to the provider, many principles related to measurement of network performance remain the same.

The monitoring of network performance comes within the general area of network management. In Section 7.1, we present an overview of systems and network management. Section 7.2 describes how a network operator can monitor the performance of its network to ensure that network connectivity SLAs are being satisfied. Section 7.3 discusses how an I/T operator can validate that its application SLAs are being satisfied. Section 7.4 discusses the type of monitoring that is appropriate for validating service provider SLAs. Finally, Section 7.5 discusses some related topics, such as the tools and techniques that a customer can use to validate that its SLAs are being satisfied, the monitoring of performance in a multilevel network, and what a general-purpose SLA monitor should have.

7.1 Network Management Basics

The prevailing network management tools are based on SNMP. It is a protocol supported by all the major vendors of IP-based equipment. The version of SNMP currently deployed is SNMP version 2, which was standardized in 1993. A version 3 is in development, which is aimed at improving the security features of SNMP version 2. However, most of the discussion in this section remains true in all versions of SNMP.

The network model assumed by SNMP is shown in Figure 7.1. All nodes (routers, servers) in the network run an application called the *SNMP agent*. The agent listens on port 161 and waits for requests from an SNMP manager. The *manager* is a process that is running on a host in the network and is used to obtain management information. The machine on which the manager runs is called the *management station*. The manager and agent communicate to each other using the SNMP protocol. A network may have more than one network management station.

Figure 7.1   Network model for SNMP.

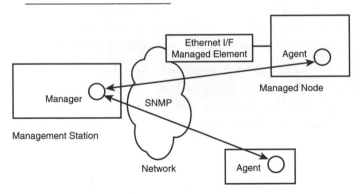

The SNMP manager exchanges management information with the SNMP agents. The management information depends on the type of elements being managed. To manage an Ethernet interface, you need to know about its MAC address, its IP address, the size of the maximum transmission unit, and so on. Statistics collected about the interface include items such as a count of packets sent on the interface or a count of errors in the transmission on that interface. The information you need to manage an open TCP connection includes the IP address and port numbers of both points of the connection and the state of the connection.

7.1.1 *Management Information Base*

The basic type of management information is called an *object*. Loosely speaking, an object describes an attribute variable or a set of attributes that would be useful for the purpose of network management. These objects are collected into a *Management Information Base (MIB)*. Thus, all information needed to manage an Ethernet interface forms a MIB for an Ethernet interface. Each type of SNMP agent supports a specific group of MIBs, depending on the types of network elements for which it is providing management information.

MIBs are defined using a language called *ASN.1*, or the *Abstract Syntax Notation*. ASN.1 defines how to store and transport generic information. The IETF standards require a modified version of ASN.1 to define the MIBs and are defined as the *SMI (Structure of Management Information)* specification for MIB data. SMI eliminates some portions of ASN.1 and introduces a few definitions that make the job of defining MIBs easier. The object description for each attribute variable typically consists of a unique name for the attribute, its syntax (whether it is an integer or a string, and so on), and how it is encoded for transporting over the network. The unique name for the object/MIB is determined in a hierarchical manner.

A set of standard MIBs are defined that must be supported for specific types of managed objects; for example, an SNMP agent that supports the management of an Ethernet interface must support a standard MIB for an Ethernet interface. The list of standard MIB definitions can be found in Internet RFCs. The original MIB-II was defined in 1991 [MIB2], and its definitions have subsequently been updated with revisions in the type of information related to IP [IPMIB], TCP [TCPMIB], and UDP [UDPMIB]. The MIBs that are relevant to SLA monitoring are discussed in Section 7.2.

Adding new types of items for network management is relatively easy. You have to define the new MIB by using the SMI notation. Most network management tools (such as OpenView from Hewlett-Packard) can read the SMI specification and parse it to understand the composition of the MIB. The tool can then obtain or manipulate the MIB through any SNMP agent. The agent has to understand the semantics of the MIB and ensure that the right actions get done.

MIB-based management is fairly flexible, and it works well in practice.

7.1.2 SNMP Protocol

The SNMP manager can obtain the current value of all the objects that are defined in the MIB by querying the SNMP agent on an SNMP-management node. It can also change those values. Manipulation of the MIB contents by the SNMP manager is the bulk of the SNMP protocol. Usually, an SNMP manager polls all the SNMP agents at a slow rate to retrieve (or modify) the MIBs. However, agents also have the capability to send an asynchronous message (called a *trap*) to a configured list of managers. The trap is sent when the manager needs to look at something urgently. On the receipt of a trap, the manager obtains the MIBs from the agent generating the trap. This mode of operation is called *trap-directed polling*.

The SNMP protocol in itself is fairly simple. The main types of messages supported by it are

- `get-request`: Allows a manager to read an attribute from the agent.

- `get-next-request`: Allows a manager to read the next attribute from the agent.

- `get-bulk-request`: Allows a manager to read a group of attributes in one operation.

- `set-request`: Allows a manager to change the value of an object.

- `trap`: Contains a message from the agent to the manager.

Each of these messages has an associated response message. An `inform-request` message can also let a manager inform another manager about the set of local MIBs that it is managing.

Version 2 added the option to get attributes in bulk. Version 2 also added a test and increment operation that allows multiple SNMP managers to increment an attribute atomically, and it added some security features.

7.2 Network Connectivity SLA Monitoring

When monitoring network connectivity, you want to know specific information about the performance of the network between two access routers (edge devices). The performance metrics you want to measure include the following:

- *Availability*: How often is the connectivity available between the two access routers.

- *Traffic*: How much bandwidth is in use between the two access routers.

- *Latency*: What is the delay (one-way or two-way) that is observed between the two access routers.

An overview of the different techniques that can be used to obtain the above information is described in the following subsections.

7.2.1 SLA Information from Standard SNMP MIBs

All networking vendors support the standard MIB definitions for network interfaces as defined as part of MIB-II [MIB2]. Most of these definitions measure the information as seen from the point of view of a single interface. The following information can be determined for all interfaces:

- The current interface status (up or down)

- The time since the interface has been up or down

- The number of bytes and packets that were received at or transmitted from the interface

- The number of packets discarded or received in error at the interface

- The length of the output queue at an interface

At each system, the standard MIBs also keep track of how many IP packets were received at the system (from all the interfaces), the number forwarded, or the number discarded because of any type of errors.

By looking at the statistics of the interface and the system, you would be able to determine which of the interfaces in the network receive the maximum traffic, as well as which of the places in the network have a large output queue. This can help identify potential bottlenecks in the queue.

> **Note**
>
> The queue size defined in the standard MIB is the instantaneous queue size, which can be quite erratic. To get a more stable estimate of the queue length, you need to average it over a few measurements.

Unfortunately, the information available in the standard MIBs is not adequate to ensure whether network connectivity SLAs are being met. However, a network operator can monitor the amount of traffic on the incoming interface of an access router to ensure that it is only receiving traffic within the desired SLA specifications from a customer.

7.2.2 Remote Monitoring of IP Networks

Remote monitoring (RMON) is an architecture that can be used to monitor network performance and characteristics at different points in the network from a single console. The RMON architecture consists of one or more RMON managers and several RMON-compliant probe points that are placed in the network. The *RMON manager* is an SNMP manager that collects management information from the probe points. The *probe point* is an SNMP agent that supports an RMON MIB.

The first version of RMON [RMON] allowed the network operator to view the network as a collection of different LAN segments. The RMON probe supported the collection of the following types of information:

- *Segment statistics*: A count of packets, bytes, broadcast packets, multicast packets, dropped packets, and so forth on the LAN segment.

- *Host specific*: Statistics collected on packets to or from a specific host on the LAN segment.

- *Traffic matrix*: Statistics obtained on traffic and errors between a pair of hosts on the same LAN.

The RMON MIBs enabled some flexibility in how the information could be measured and kept. Within the MIB definitions, it was possible to keep a history of packet statistics, as well as to keep information only for a configurable number of the most active hosts on the LAN segment. You could also instruct the probe to send alarms when specific thresholds were exceeded or to collect data only for packets that met some specific bit patterns. You could define patterns to filter out information that was relevant for performance characteristics.

RMON MIB was defined as consisting of nine groups, each group enabling the collection of specific types of information or for specifying the filters, conditions, or alarms for collecting the statistics. However, the measurements collected by RMON consisted only of the performance of specific LAN segments. No way exists to correlate the performance of different LAN segments. The first version of RMON did not look at any statistics beyond that of MAC (Ethernet/token ring) packets. Ethernet statistics were defined in the original RMON specification [RMON] and token ring statistics were defined shortly thereafter [RMONTR].

A second version of RMON [RMON2] added more functionality to the RMON probe. The RMON2 specifications added 11 more groups of statistics collection. These groups provided a flexible way for the manager to define filtering rules to capture packet and byte statistics. The filters in RMON2 can be defined to select packets on the basis of their IP addresses and not just MAC addresses. This enables you to monitor the traffic in a LAN segment that may be destined to a remote server. Similarly, you could observe traffic that may be flowing to specific applications anywhere in the network.

Using RMON, you can get the amount of bandwidth that is in use on each network segment. RMON enables a network manager to identify which segment is most active, and which segment may need updates as well as which of the wide area links (the ones connected to active segments) may need to be upgraded. You can also collect statistics about the different servers in the network and determine which of the servers are the busiest and therefore may need to be supplemented or upgraded. Similarly, you can determine which applications are the heaviest users of the network.

Information collected using RMON can indicate the bottleneck LAN segments in the enterprise and can provide useful information for examining trends in the network, including information required for capacity planning. However, it is not adequate to keep track of the delays or latency in the network. The RMON probes require the capability to see all the traffic on the LAN segment. This is easily done in traditional LANs, such as Ethernets or token rings, but may not be possible in switched LANs such as Fast Ethernets.

7.2.3 Monitoring Flows

Both the basic SNMP MIB and the initial RMON collected traffic statistics such as packet counts or byte counts at a single interface or LAN segment in the network. Because this information was of limited use, an effort was made to measure statistics about flows in the network. A *flow* is a subset of traffic in the network. The subset could be defined in a number of ways; for example, you could define a flow as the traffic between a source and a destination IP address or as all UDP packets in the network.

The capability to measure flows could yield useful information about the distribution of traffic in the network. For example, if we could measure the amount of traffic that is flowing between a pair of access routers, we would be able to use this information to validate how much traffic is being received at an access router. Flows can also identify the applications and servers that generate significant traffic in the network.

Two important flow-related network monitoring schemes are the following:

- Cisco NetFlow architecture, which is significant because it is available in almost all Cisco routers.

- The standardized way to measure traffic flows, which is being defined in IETF.

Both of these approaches measure the characteristics of a flow at a given point in the network. This enables you to get information such as packet and byte count, but it does not provide any information about the delays or loss characteristics of the network between any two points.

Cisco NetFlow Architecture

The Cisco NetFlow architecture defines a network flow as a one-way stream of packets between specified source and destination addresses. The flow can be further selected on the basis of the transport protocol, the input interface, and the IP ToS byte. The inclusion of ToS byte enables NetFlow to distinguish between packets that would belong to different DiffServ traffic classes.

The NetFlow architecture defined by Cisco consists of two entities:

- A flow collector, which is a management application

- The router, which collects the flow information

The flow collector can configure specific filters as to which of the flows are to be collected at the router. The router collects the statistics on each of the configured flows and reports them back to the flow collection. The flow collector and the router communicate via a private protocol (not standard SNMP).

The statistics collected by NetFlow consist of the count of packets and the count of bytes that were seen for the flow. These counts allow you to determine the amount of traffic that is flowing between (to or from) a server or a subnet. In the context of a network connectivity SLA, NetFlow allows the network operator to monitor the amount of traffic that is flowing among all the virtual links on the network. This information is useful for monitoring traffic distribution to the network and capacity planning. It can also identify information about the applications (port numbers) and servers that are the main source or destination of traffic.

IETF Real-Time Flow Monitoring

Despite the inability to determine network delays, monitoring flows in the network provides useful information about network performance and characterization. Within the IETF, a standardization effort is underway that would provide a standardized way for network managers to look at flow information. Although the SNMP-based MIB might be a more inefficient protocol than proprietary ones such as NetFlow, the capability to have interoperable products is desirable for many reasons.

The MIB for capturing flow-related statistics was defined within the IETF [METERMIB] and is being refined within the RTFM (Real-Time Flow Monitoring) [RTFM] working group within the IETF. The MIB allows capturing point information about flows, which includes the amount of packets and bytes seen in both directions of a flow.

Like NetFlow, RTFM-based approaches can provide useful information about traffic at specific points in the network but do not readily yield information about network delays or loss rates.

7.2.4 Monitoring SLA Compliance Using ping/traceroute

One very common approach that can be used (and often is used) within networks to determine delays and loss rate is the use of the *ping program*. This program sends an ICMP echo message to the specified target, which replies to the ICMP echo. After the echo message is received, the sender can measure the round-trip delay from the destination. When a number of ping messages are sent in the network, the number of lost ping packets can also be estimated. This also yields information about the availability of network connectivity.

The use of ping to determine network delays and loss rates gives the most basic method to validate the conformance to SLAs. The method is available on most platforms and is fairly representative. However, monitoring the performance of the network using ping between all the access routers can lead to a significant amount of overhead in the network.

For example, suppose you are trying to verify an SLA that says that 99.9% of packets will make it through. To do a sample that is significant, you may have to send 30,000 pings into the network, which is not an insignificant extra load on the network.

In addition to ping, another network tool that is very handy to use is *traceroute*. This returns the path that is followed by an IP packet in the network. The manner in which traceroute determines the path is relatively heavy-handed. It keeps on sending a fixed number of ICMP packets (usually three) with an increasing Time-To-Live field in the IP header. An ICMP error message is generated on the expiration of the TTL field in the resulting IP packet, identifying the router at increasing distances from the source of the network. The traceroute also provides an estimate of the network delays from each router. However, the statistical validity of data from just three delay measurements is relatively limited. Furthermore, different routers in the network handle ICMP packets at different priorities. The router-processing delay in traceroute can be a significant portion of the delay. As a result, if you run traceroute on a path of three hops, you may find that the delay reported over two hops is higher than the delay reported over three hops.

The use of both ping and traceroute to monitor SLA compliance must be managed carefully. Otherwise, the tools themselves may generate too much load on the network.

> **Note**
>
> Another word of caution when interpreting results from pings and traceroutes: Many routers process ICMP messages at a different priority level than normal packets. Thus, the delays measured by ping and traceroutes may be somewhat larger than the ones experienced by normal TCP/UDP packets.

7.2.5 *Monitoring Performance Using Network Time Protocol*

Instead of using pings/traceroutes to monitor the performance of the network, an alternative way exists in which the delays of the network can be estimated without excessive overhead. This approach exploits the fact that protocols, to synchronize time among different routers, provide enough information to determine round-trip delays among the different routers.

In general, each router in the network has its own local clock. Because the clocks of the different routers would soon become out of sync with each other, a protocol is needed to synchronize them with each other. NTP is the predominant Internet protocol that obtains this synchronization.

Some servers in the Internet maintain very accurate times on the basis of Global Positioning Satellite (GPS) signals or very accurate atomic clocks. These servers are known as the *primary NTP servers*. A number of secondary servers synchronize their clocks with the primary servers. The other machines running NTP form a spanning tree with the primary servers as the root. The accuracy of time decreases as you proceed away from the primary servers. The primary servers are also known as *stratum 1 servers*, the secondary servers as *stratum 2 servers*, and the remaining ones are at increasing numbers of the stratum depending on the spanning-tree topology.

Two NTP machines can exchange time information in a variety of ways. Typically, a machine in a higher stratum would exchange NTP messages with a machine in a lower stratum using a client/server mode, where the time information of the lower stratum is considered more authoritative. Hosts in the same stratum can also exchange messages with each other to synchronize time with each other.

NTP hosts exchange synchronization messages with other NTP hosts in the same stratum and with one or more NTP servers in the lower stratum. The exchange of messages is designed to produce three products for each pair of communicating hosts, all of which are relative to a selected reference clock:

- *The clock offset*: Represents the amount to adjust the local clock to bring it into correspondence with the reference clock

- *The round-trip delay*: Provides an estimate of the round-trip delay between a pair of hosts

- *Dispersion*: Represents the maximum error of the local clock relative to the reference clock

The time delays obtained using NTP are quite accurate—within a few milliseconds. The delay values measured are smoothed as a result of multiple measurements and tend to show less fluctuation than the delay as seen by ping messages.

> **Note**
>
> Both NTP and ping can measure time delays for best-effort networks. Although it may be possible to extend NTP to measure the delays in the network in multiclass networks, such as DiffServ networks, I am not aware of any effort in this direction.

Further details on NTP can be found in an Internet RFC [NTPRFC] and on the Web at the home page of David Mills [NTPWEB], who has played a key role in defining NTP. The page also contains a list of primary and secondary NTP servers on the Internet.

7.2.6 Statistical Probing

Instead of using NTP to measure delays, you can build a system to monitor the delays and loss rates between access routers by periodically exchanging *probe messages* between the access routers. These probe messages need not be ping or NTP, but could be developed as a simple UDP or TCP application. When a source sends a probe to the destination, the destination sends a response to the probe back to the sender. The round-trip delays in the network could easily be measured as well as the loss rates, depending on the number of probes that are sent but not received.

Probes can also be used to measure one-way delay in networks. Packets sent from a source to the destination do not always have the same path as those on the reverse path from the destination to the source. Thus, a one-way delay measurement yields more accurate information than measuring round-trips. If one-way delays are being obtained using a sending time measured at the source and a receiving time measured at the destination, the results could be erroneous if the clocks at the sender and the destination are not synchronized with each other.

The probe messages need to be generated at a slow interval so as not to overwhelm the network. Similarly, the probe messages can be generated at different service levels in the network in order to monitor the performance of each class of network traffic separately.

An experiment being done on the Internet uses statistical probing to measure one-way delays using GPS synchronized clocks. The representation of delays is also being standardized within the IP Performance Metrics (IPPM) working group of IETF. This work was described in Chapter 2, "IP Networks and SLAs."

A statistical probing scheme can be used to simultaneously measure network delays and traffic volume between access routers [BEIGI] to monitor compliance with network connectivity SLAs. The model of network connectivity SLA is as shown in Figure 5.1. One of the difficulties in monitoring traffic volume between access routers is that the ingress access router does not know which egress access router would be used by an IP packet. To work around this, the proposed scheme generates a probe packet to the destination of a randomly selected packet arriving from the customer network of Figure 5.1. Probe packets are generated to be a certain fraction of customer packets and follow the same path as that of the normal IP packets. When the probe packet reaches an egress access router, it is removed from the data stream. A response probe packet is sent back to the originating access router, along with the identity of the egress access router. Each access router determines how the probe packets generated by it are dispersed in the network. To determine the traffic volume between Routers A and B, the total amount of traffic at A (which is kept by all routers as part of SNMPV2 standard MIB information) is multiplied by the percentage of probe packets that were sent to B. The probe packets also contain timestamps so that round-trip delays between the access routers can be measured.

7.3 Application SLA Monitoring

The monitoring of application SLAs requires that the response time of different applications be logged and compared to SLA targets. The best possible case for application SLA monitoring would be if the applications themselves reported the response time in some manner that can be logged and tracked by a performance monitor.

Some of the applications are indeed thus well-behaved and provide the response-time information; for example, tn3270e, a terminal emulator for mainframes, does report the time taken for each screen refresh. However, such applications are the exception rather than the norm in the TCP/IP world.

A standard exists for reporting the application response times. If applications wrote to this API, it would be possible for most enterprise management tools to keep track of an application's SLA conformance. Most enterprise management tools, such as Tivoli TME-10, are capable of monitoring application service levels using Application Response Management (ARM) information. The catch, of course, is that the applications must be coded with the ARM API. Unfortunately, most applications are not coded to this specification. We describe the structure of a typical systems management in the next section, followed by a description of ARM. Subsequently, several other techniques that can obtain an estimate of application response time without modifying applications are described.

7.3.1 Systems Management

In many large enterprises, the tasks of network management and managing clients/servers is split among different organizational units. Network management is usually done by a description of means of network management tools such as HP OpenView [OPENVIEW] or IBM NetView [BENNETT]. Systems management is typically done using a different set of system management tools, the dominant vendors in that arena being Tivoli or Computer Associates. Systems management places less reliance on SNMP and provides its own mechanisms to manage clients/servers.

To illustrate how system management works, we take a closer look at how enterprise servers would be managed using Tivoli tools. The entire enterprise is divided into many management regions (see Figure 7.2), with each region having a management server and multiple managed nodes. Each managed node runs a TME-10 agent. The TME-10 agent is responsible for communicating with the management server. The agent would configure the local node (PC or server) with the configuration information provided by the management server. Similarly, it could collect statistics from a local node and report them back to the management server. Management servers in two regions can be linked so that a single console can be used to manage all the machines in the region.

Both the agent and the management server are written using a common set of utility functions. The utilities provide the functions that can be used by the agent and the server to communicate, and it is called the *TME framework*. The TME framework also contains support for database access, user interfaces, and so on. On top of the common set of utilities, specific extensions are available for functions such as monitoring, software distribution, or user administration. A set of functions is also available to plug-in extensions from other companies or users.

Figure 7.2   Tivoli management regions.

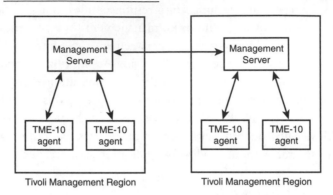

A version of TME-10 agent that does not support the full version of TM10 software is also available. These agents, called *PC agents,* are restricted to a subset of the functions of the full TME agents. The TME-10 architecture is described in more detail in an IBM Redbook [TME] as well as in a book written by Lendermann [TME10]. The TME framework does not rely upon SNMP for communication between the management server and the agents. It is based on Common Object Request Broker Architecture (CORBA) [POPE]. CORBA is a standard for developing distributed applications. It is supported on most PCs and servers but is not quite that common on network routers.

Other system management tool vendors also offer a similar management architecture and a toolkit for developing system management applications. Notable among these is the TNG framework from Computer Associates [TNG].

System management tools such as ones from Tivoli and Computer Associates can be used to monitor application response times and service-level compliance.

7.3.2   *Application Response Measurement*

To obtain an estimate of application response, it is helpful if applications report the time it took for them to complete specific transactions. This information can be used to determine whether SLAs are being satisfied. The ARM API described in this section can be used for that goal.

Application Response Measurement (ARM) is a standard developed primarily by Tivoli Systems and Hewlett-Packard. ARM version 1.0 was created by the two companies, but ARM version 2.0 has been standardized by the Open Group [ARMOPEN], a consortium of companies that standardizes on APIs, with the primary focus on UNIX systems. It is intended to enable enterprise applications to provide instrumentation information about themselves. Applications that have ARMed themselves can be analyzed for their availability and response time by any management tool that understands the ARM specifications.

The ARM API consists of the following calls:

- arm_init: This is invoked at the beginning of an application; it initializes the ARM environment and establishes the identity of the application.

- arm_getid: This routine is called to associate a unique identifier with each transaction in the application. The definition of a transaction is left up to an application. A *transaction* is a distinct action within an application, such as the downloading of a Web page, the refreshing of a screen in a terminal emulator, or the completion of a database search.

- arm_start: This routine is called to mark the starting time of a transaction.

- arm_stop: This routine is called to mark the completion of a transaction.

- arm_update: This routine is called to provide any updates (if needed) for the application during its progress, such as to signal that a specific number of records have been processed. This need not be called by all applications.

- arm_end: This cleans up the ARM environment for an application.

ARM allows the capability to link nested transactions. When both the client and server use ARM, you can track the cause and location of any delays in the network. ARM is described in more detail in the Open Group specifications [ARMOPEN], which is also available over the Web.

Note

We only wish that more Internet applications were written using the ARM API. This would allow a better tracking of application SLAs.

Further information on ARM can be obtained through the working group pages of the Computer Measurement Group [ARMCMG]. A good introduction to the API is provided in an article by Mark Johnson [ARMAPI].

7.3.3 Active Monitoring

One way to monitor the performance of a specific application is by having a monitoring client that generates dummy requests at specific intervals and maintains a history of the time taken to complete the request, as well as whether the application was up and available at that time. The probing of applications is quite similar in concept to ping, which sends probes to check whether a server is operational. Whereas ping can only ensure that there is IP connectivity to a server, a monitoring client can ensure that the application itself is operational at the server.

A few vendor products offer such monitoring capabilities for a set of business applications. Some of these products are listed at the Web site of this book. Active monitoring by a monitoring client requires development of a application-specific client. Care must be taken to ensure that the monitoring client makes requests that do not cause any side effects at the server. Similarly, the load generated by the dummy requests must be carefully controlled to ensure that performance monitoring does not overwhelm the server.

The requests generated by the active monitoring client must be randomized to ensure that no synchronization occurs with the network characteristics of the server. In the absence of such a randomization, you may get a misleading estimate of the application performance. (See Section 7.5.4 for a discussion of the synchronization issue.)

Note

Synchronization may occur in more subtle ways—for example, the sharing of the resources by the performance monitor with the other clients running on the same machine. To avoid this, the monitoring should preferably be done using a machine dedicated for this purpose.

7.3.4 Passive Application Response Monitoring

Active application response monitoring has the disadvantage of generating more load on the server. If the server is the suspected bottleneck point, you might be tempted to turn the monitoring off and get the most out of the server for *real usage*. The push to squeeze the last ounce out of the server's performance is also used as an argument against using APIs such as ARM, which cause extra processing at the server.

With proper configuration, the overhead generated by either ARM or active application monitoring can be kept to be less than 5% of load on the server.

However, it is also possible to monitor the performance of applications without modifying them to conform to the ARM API, or active monitoring. This *passive monitoring* can be done by recording the packets on the network and analyzing their payload. By parsing the payload of the data, you are often able to identify the transactions in the network and to determine the amount of time it took to perform one transaction.

Using tcpdump for Performance Monitoring

On most UNIX systems, a program called *tcpdump* can be used to examine the packets that are seen by the network card. Most Ethernet cards and some token ring cards can be placed into a promiscuous mode. In the promiscuous mode, the card receives not only IP packets addressed specifically to the card, but any packets that may be sent on the LAN segment. After this data is captured, the contents of the packets can be examined to validate SLA compliance. On the Windows platform, equivalent network analyzer software is available from various vendors that provides equivalent capability.

> **Note**
>
> Be aware that security and privacy risks are associated with passive monitoring. A person monitoring the network can see any packets on the network and can obtain information he or she is not entitled to—for example, the contents of email messages or copies of a colleague's annual performance review.

Most versions of tcpdump can output data in a variety of formats and allow the specification of filters so that only data from or to specific servers is captured. The TCP options can be examined to determine when a connection begins and when it terminates. The packet containing the beginning of a TCP connection contains a special flag called the *SYN flag*, and the packet containing the request to terminate the connection contains a special flag called *FIN*. These options mark the total lifetime of a connection. Each packet can also be marked with the time it was seen on the network.

If you parse the contents of the transport header, you can obtain the values of round-trip delays from the options TCP uses to compute its own round-trip times. Parsing further into the contents of the packet, you can determine the time when an application transaction starts and when an application transaction terminates. This has to be done by understanding the structure and format of the application packets. Each application has its own format for where a transaction begins and ends. With the assistance of the analysis software, you can determine the time to complete taken by individual transactions.

It must be pointed out that the analysis of application performance in this manner is an offline procedure. Analyzing the contents of the packet in this manner requires a significant amount of processing power and memory. To monitor SLA compliance, you can start collecting packet traces for some random time in the network (for example, during the busy hour). The packet traces and the responses can then be analyzed to ensure that they comply with SLA requirements. However, it is difficult to use this technique to monitor the response of a transaction currently in progress. Also, the tcpdump machine must be able to see all the packets on the LAN. Although this is not an issue on traditional ethernet or token-ring LANs, such a capability may not exist in next-generation switched LANs.

Depending on the placement of the tcpdump machine, the analysis will provide the response time as seen by the client or the time taken by the server to satisfy the request. In Figure 7.3, a tcpdump machine can be placed at the client network (A) or at the server network (B). When it is placed near the client network, it produces a value close to the response time seen by the client. When it is placed near the server network, it produces a value closer to the time taken by the server to complete the transaction.

Figure 7.3 Location of tcpdump machines.

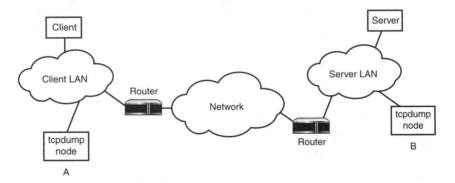

TCP Session Performance Analysis

Although the passive analysis of network packets cannot yield online application performance, an approximation is available to keep track of the online performance of the application at the server. This can be done if the TCP/IP stack in the server (or the clients) keeps track of the statistics related to the performance of the network.

At least one server, the IBM S/390, is capable of collecting and reporting the statistics that are seen by each TCP connection. The statistics reported by the stack include the round-trip delay on the connection, the effective throughput of the connection, the number of retransmissions, and so on. The statistics can be collected on a per-connection basis.

It is also possible to collect the information on the basis of an aggregate set of policies that are defined for the TCP/IP stack.

The structure of a S/390 system with a performance-monitoring application for the stack is shown in Figure 7.4. The policy agent is responsible for obtaining the policies from a repository in the network (or a local configuration file) and installing them in the stack. The performance monitor retrieves the performance information associated with each of the currently open TCP connections. The information can be aggregated into a single performance measure for all the connections that match the same policy defined at the server.

Figure 7.4   Stack performance monitor in OS/390.

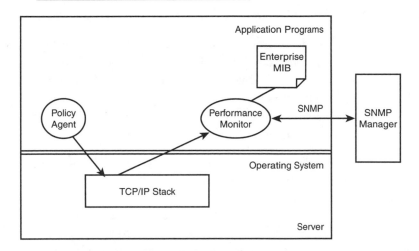

The performance monitor in S/390 is an SNMP agent that can be controlled and managed by any SNMP manager. The MIB supported by the performance manager is an extension made by IBM. Such types of MIBs are often referred to as *enterprise MIBs*. Other server platforms may support similar enterprise MIBs for performance monitoring of the TCP/IP stack. The SNMP manager can collect the performance information and determine whether SLAs are being satisfied. Keep in mind that the response time and other metrics reported by the TCP/IP performance monitor are related to the performance as seen by the TCP layer of communication and are not the eventual performance of the application.

7.4 Service Provider SLA Monitoring

In the case of a service provider, SLA guarantees are specified in terms of one or more of the following parameters:

- The bandwidth going out on the service provider access link

- The number of servers assigned for the customer

- The total number of connection establishment rate at all the servers assigned to the customer

- The response time of a transaction (not counting the network delays over which the provider has no control)

The bandwidth used by each of the different customers or service levels can be measured by analyzing the flows at the access link. If information about different flows is collected at the access link, the amount of bandwidth used by each of the customers can be determined. Similarly, if each customer is assigned to a different server, you can examine the standard IP MIBs to determine the amount of bytes or packets that are flowing out of every server and determine the amount used by each of the customers.

The number of servers assigned to each customer is a slowly changing variable that will usually be changed only by operator intervention. The operator then needs to keep track of the servers assigned to each customer. In many cases, multiple customers share a single server. The common way to support such a sharing is to assign each of the customers a different IP address and to configure the server's interface to accept packets for all the IP addresses. In this case, bandwidth tracking at the access link could be done in a straightforward manner because the IP address distinguishes the traffic for different customers. If the different customers use the same IP address and are dependent on application-level information to distinguish between requests for two customers, the bandwidth accounting needs to be combined with application log analysis to determine the amount of bandwidth used by each of the customers.

The schemes for application-response monitoring using tcpdump, TCP/IP stack measurements, or active network monitoring can be used to determine the response time of applications. These monitors would need to be present on the service provider network rather than on the client network. Additionally, an analysis of server logs or the use of a proxy capable of performance monitoring can assist the service provider, as explained in the following subsections.

7.4.1 Application Log Analysis

Many applications maintain a log of their activities that can be analyzed to determine the performance characteristics of an application. The type of information that can be captured in the log is application specific. As a random sample, we present some of the applications and the type of logs they support:

- The mail program (sendmail) on most UNIX systems generates a log that consists of a record of mail messages received by the mail server, including the information of the user who sent the message, the time the message was received, the host from where the message came, the delay in processing the message, the size of the mail message, the status of processing by the message, and so on.

- Apache [APACHE], one of the most popular Web servers on the Internet, can be configured to produce a log that contains the IP address of the connecting client, the date of the request, the request line from the client, the status of the response (whether it was successful), and the number of bytes transferred in the response.

- The IBM DB2 database has a database system monitor that maintains data about its operation, its performance, and the applications using it. This data is maintained as the database manager runs and can provide important performance and troubleshooting information, such as the number of applications connected to a database, their status, which SQL statements each application is executing, a list of locks held by an application, and any deadlock conditions. The amount of information available to the monitor can be adjusted using a variety of options. Because collecting some of this data introduces overhead on the operation of DB2, monitor switches are available to control which information is collected.

Many other applications maintain a log of their activities in various formats. Several also come with tools to analyze and process their own log files. Log analysis tools for Web servers are quite common, and a listing can be found at Yahoo! [WEBLOG]. The effectiveness of log analysis is determined mainly by the availability of the tools for this purpose.

7.4.2 Proxy-Based Monitoring

In many cases, the service provider deploys a proxy as a front end to its application systems. An important use of the proxy is to provide a Web front end to legacy systems. The front end is a Web server that presents an easy-to-use interface to the legacy system. The legacy system itself is accessed using CGI-bin scripts. This configuration is shown in Figure 7.5.

Figure 7.5 Proxy configuration in the service provider network.

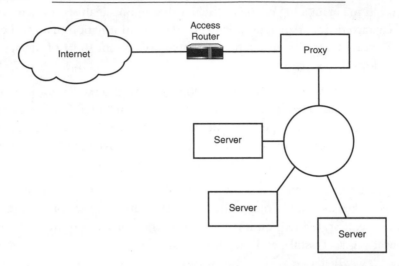

When a front-end proxy is used, it is possible to instrument the proxy to provide the information that is relevant for the monitoring of the response time of a transaction. The proxy can easily record the beginning and the end of a request from the server and log this information. If the performance diagnostics are available from a log file in the proxy, the service provider needs only to look at the output log.

In many cases, these proxies are customizable by the service provider. Most Web servers provide a flexible architecture for such customization. The Apache Web server can be composed of several modules, each of which are called when the proxy is accessed. The module functions can be invoked before, as well as after, the request is processed. In such Web-based front ends, it is relatively simple to add a module that can keep track of the time spent processing each request.

The service provider can also use passive monitoring and programs such as tcpdump to analyze the performance of the proxies. Similarly, if the proxy is running on a platform that supports enterprise MIBs reporting performance statistics, these statistics can be used to gather information regarding application performance. The proxy is a single point of failure, and this aspect, as well as possible countermeasures, are discussed in Chapter 6, "SLA Support in Different Network Environments."

7.5   Related Topics

In this section of the chapter, we look at some issues that are related to SLA monitoring but not covered elsewhere in the chapter.

7.5.1   Customer Validation of SLAs

The schemes and methods described in Sections 7.1 through 7.4 apply mainly to the service provider; that is, the service provider can use those tools to monitor that it is complying with SLA performance and availability objectives.

Some of these tools can be used by the customer to validate that the service provider is complying with its SLAs. For example, statistical probing or ping can be used by the customer to track the performance of the network the operator is providing. Similarly, NTP can be run between two sites in a customer network to determine the round-trip delay between the two machines in the network. The protocol measures the delays between two machines in the customer network rather than the delays between the access router. However, the measurements should suffice to validate whether SLAs are being satisfied. For application SLAs or service provider SLAs, the customer can use active monitoring to determine that its application servers are performing as desired.

From a more practical perspective, the network operator typically generates reports (monthly or daily) on the performance of the network or service. These reports can be made available to the customer or published on the intranet. In most circumstances, the report is adequate to satisfy the customer that the SLAs are being met, and explicit validation by the customer will be done only when the customer doubts the veracity of the reports. If the customer and the provider are not willing to trust each other's reports, one possible approach is to have a third party act as an auditor of SLA compliance.

7.5.2   Multiclass Network Monitoring

All the performance-monitoring schemes mentioned earlier in the chapter implicitly assume that a single performance level exists to which the network or application must conform. However, multiple levels of service can be offered to different customers in the network. Although you can easily compare the measured performance to the different levels, you must be careful to determine which of the performance monitoring methods work in the case of multiclass networks.

Among the various schemes presented in the Section 7.2, only a few can be used to monitor the performance of a network with multiple levels of service, such as a DiffServ network with support for different PHBs. NTP, which provides the most accurate measure of network delays, only reports the performance data for the specific PHB it is using to exchange the synchronization message. The performance of data in other PHBs must be monitored using some different means. Similarly, ping contains ICMP packets that belong to only one class of traffic. These tools were designed to work over a single class best-effort IP network.

When statistics probing is used to generate probes to monitor network performance, you can construct the probes to be carried into the different service levels supported by the network. Similarly, performance data captured using network analyzers and probes such as RMON must be capable of capturing the ToS byte in the IP headers so that data about different types of networks can be collected. Both NetFlow and RTFM support the capability to define flows using the ToS byte and should be able to work properly with DiffServ networks.

For application SLAs and service provider SLAs, you must similarly account for bandwidth used by traffic belonging to different service levels.

7.5.3   The Generic SLA Monitor

The structure and type of performance-monitoring tools deployed in the network determines the structure of the generic SLA monitor. For network connectivity SLAs, the SLA monitor is an SNMP manager collecting information about the performance characteristics of the network and correlating information available from the different types of MIBs. The performance monitor many also use non–SNMP-based mechanisms to retrieve information that is typically not published as a MIB, such as NTP delay data. The monitor then compares the measured performance against the SLA goals and validates that the requisite performance targets have been satisfied.

For application SLAs, SNMP may not be needed at all. Most systems administration in larger enterprises is done using server management tools from vendors such as Tivoli or Computer Associates. These tools have the capability to collect performance statistics from the applications, such as ARM-enabled applications, statistics about the servers regarding their performance, or the performance of the TCP/IP stacks. These management consoles are capable of comparing performance metrics to the desired SLA objectives and displaying them.

The service provider SLA can be SNMP-based for keeping track of bandwidth, and it can use other non-SNMP techniques to keep track of performance statistics, such as those resulting from the analysis of the application log files.

7.5.4 *The Accuracy of Measurement*

All the network performance metrics that we are concerned with are random variables. The delay in the network, the traffic measured at a point, or the number of lost packets yield different results on every repetition of the measurement. From the set of multiple random points, we need to determine the value of network delays, traffic usage, and/or network availability.

To monitor any of the performance metrics, such as network delay, we repeat the measurements at some periods and then determine the average value for the measurement. The average value that we have determined is the estimate of the average network delay. Depending on the number of times our measurements have been repeated, this value may or may not be a good measurement of the network delay. Therefore, you need to have a way to specify how good the measurement is.

The most common way to specify the goodness of the measured value is the confidence interval. A *confidence interval* is a range of values that has a specified probability of containing the performance metric being estimated. The most common confidence intervals are the 95% and 99% confidence intervals. For example, suppose we are measuring the mean network delay, and the results are reported as saying that the 95% confidence interval is 100ms to 120ms. What this means is that the mean network delay is between 100ms–120ms with 99% confidence, and only a 1% chance (probability of 0.01) exists that the mean delay is outside this range, lower than 100ms or higher than 120ms.

Confidence intervals can be computed on the basis of the number of measurements and the type of data being measured—that is, whether we are measuring the mean delay, the variation in delay, or the maximum delay. The formulas determining the confidence interval for a set of measurements can be found in most books on statistics and probability, as well as in texts over the Web (such as [LANE]). In general, the larger the number of measurements, the smaller the confidence intervals.

Another issue to watch for in the measurement of computer networks is related to network synchronization. When using techniques such as statistical probing, active response monitoring, or pings to measure computer performance, you must try to avoid synchronization that may occur between the monitoring probe and the system. For example, consider a network where two database servers exchange information with each other, causing the load on the network to increase for a 1 minute period after every 10 minutes. If network delays are monitored every 10 minutes as well, probes can become synchronized with the load fluctuation and always measure the delay when the servers are active. Another possibility is that the probes only measure the delay when the servers are not active. In either of these cases, the estimate of the network delay would not be correct. If the probes were generated at random intervals, a better estimate of the load could be obtained.

> **Note**
>
> The discussion in this section covers only a few issues with statistical measures. Before using any such measure to draw conclusions regarding SLA compliance, look closely at not only the quantity being measured but also at the techniques used to measure it. Books dealing with performance evaluation of computer systems (such as [FERRARI] [JAIN]) explain these issues in more detail.

7.6 Further Information

In this chapter, we have looked briefly at the different ways of monitoring the system and the network performance, and discussed how to validate SLA compliance using the performance tools. Further details on SNMP and MIBs can be found in the books by Rose [ROSE] and Stallings [STALL]. The latter also describes RMON. A book describing RMON2 has also been written by Miller [MILLER]. A number of RFCs describe the different aspects of protocols such as RMON , RMON2, RTFM, and so on. For systems management, useful information regarding the Tivoli framework can be found in several IBM Redbooks on the topic [TIVRED]. Computer Associates also has a book [TNG] describing systems management within their framework.

An excellent source for information related to performance of IP networks is the Web site for the Cooperative Association for Internet Data Analysis (CAIDA) [CAIDA]. The site has links to several tools that can be used to monitor the performance of IP networks. Although CAIDA has focused on the Internet, the same tools can be used for IP intranets as well.

Details on the design of measurements and evaluation of computer systems, as well as discussions on issues such as confidence intervals and synchronization can be found in books by Ferrari[FERRARI] and Jain [JAIN].

7.7 Endnotes

[APACHE] The Apache Project Web Site. Available at http://www.apache.org.

[ARMAPI] Johnson, Mark W. "The Application Response Measurement API Version 2." Available at http://cmg.org/regions/cmgarmw/marcarm.html.

[ARMCMG] Computer Measurement Group—ARM Working Group. Available at `http://cmg.org/regions/cmgarmw/index.html`.

[ARMOPEN] "Systems Management: Application Response Measurement." Open Group Technical Standard C807, July 1996. Available at `http://www.opengroup.org/pubs/catalog/c807.htm`.

[BEIGI] Beigi, M., R. Jennings and D. Verma. "Low Overhead Continuous Monitoring of IP Network Performance." Proceedings of Symposium on Performance Evaluation of Computer and Telecommunication Systems, SPECTS'99, Chicago, July 1999.

[BENNET] Bennet, L. *Multiprotocol Network Management, A Practical Guide to Netview AIX*. New York: McGraw Hill, 1996.

[CAIDA] Cooperative Association for Internet Data Analysis. Available at `http://www.caida.org`.

[FERRARI] Ferrari, D. *Computer Systems Performance Evaluation*. Upper Saddle River, NJ: Prentice Hall, 1978.

[IPMIB] McCloghrie, K. "SNMPv2 Management Information Base for the Internet Protocol using SMIv2." Internet RFC 2011, November 1996.

[JAIN] Jain, Raj. *The Art of Computer System Performance Analysis*. New York: John Wiley & Sons, 1991.

[LANE] Lane, David M. *HyperStat Online*. Web-published textbook. Available at `http://www.ruf.rice.edu/~lane/hyperstat/contents.html`.

[NTPRFC] Mills, D. "Network Time Protocol Version 3." Internet RFC 1305, March 1992.

[NTPWEB] Home Page for the Network Time Protocol. Available at `http://www.eecis.udel.edu/~ntp`.

[METERMIB] Lee, N. Brown. "Traffic Flow Measurement: Meter MIB." Internet RFC 1064, January 1997.

[MIB2] McCloghrie, K., and M. Rose. "Management Information Base for Network Management of TCP/IP-based Internets: MIB-II." Internet RFC1213, March 1991.

[MILLER] Miller, Mark. *Managing Internetworks with SNMP: The Definitive Guide to Simple Network Monitoring Protocol, SNMPV2, RMON and RMON2*. Indianapolis, IN: IDG Books, 1997.

[OPENVIEW] Lee, Jim Huntington, et al. *HP OpenView: A Manager's Guide*. New York: McGraw Hill, 1997.

[POPE] Pope, Alan. *The CORBA Reference Guide*. Reading, MA: Addison-Wesley, 1998.

[RMON] Waldbusser, S. "Remote Network Monitoring Management Information Base." Internet RFC 1757, February 1995.

[RMON2] ———. "Remote Network Monitoring Management Information Base Version 2 using SMIv2." Internet RFC 2021, January 1997.

[RMONTR] ———. "Token Ring Extensions to the Remote Network Monitoring MIB." Internet RFC 1513, September 1993.

[ROSE] Rose, Marshall T. *The Simple Book, An Introduction to Network Management*. Upper Saddle River, NJ: Prentice Hall, 1996.

[RTFM] Internet Engineering Task Force Working Group on Real Time Traffic Flow Measurements (RTFM). Available at `http://www.ietf.org/html.charters/rtfm-charters.html`.

[STALL] Stallings, William. *SNMP, SNMPV2 and RMON, Practical Network Management*. Reading, MA: Addison-Wesley, 1996.

[TCPMIB] McCloghrie, K. "SNMPv2 Management Information Base for the Transmission Control Protocol Using SMIv2." Internet RFC 2012, November 1996.

[TIVRED] IBM Redbooks for Tivoli. Available at `http://www.redbooks.ibm.com./solutions/tivoli`.

[TME] IBM International Technical Support Organization. "An Introduction to TME 10." ITSO Redbook SG-24-4984-01, September 1997.

[TME10] Lendernmann, Rolf, et al. *An Introduction to Tivoli's TME 10*. Upper Saddle River, NJ: Prentice Hall, 1997.

[TNG] Sturm, Rick. *Working with Unicenter TNG*. Indianapolis, IN: Que Education and Training, 1998.

[UDPMIB] McCloghrie, K. "SNMPv2 Management Information Base for the User Datagram Protocol Using SMIv2." Internet RFC 2013, November 1996.

[WEBLOG] Yahoo! Listing of Log Analysis Tools for Web Servers. Available at `http://dir.yahoo.com/Computers_and_Internet/Software/Internet/World_Wide_Web/Servers/Log_Analysis_Tools/`.

CHAPTER

8

Advanced Topics

In previous chapters, we have explored the different types of SLAs and the mechanisms that can be used to support them in an IP network. In this final chapter, we look at some topics that are related to SLAs. Some of these topics are still being explored within the networking research community, whereas others represent potential usage of the network that might benefit by the deployment of SLAs.

The topics we cover in this chapter are the creation of Virtual Private Networks (VPNs) using SLA support, the methods for supporting SLAs across multiple administrative domains, the applicability of multiprotocol label-switching (MPLS) to supporting SLAs, and SLA support for IPv6 networks.

8.1 Virtual Private Networks

Most enterprises have several geographically separated corporate sites. The traditional solution to interconnecting these sites has been to operate a private intranet among the sites. The private intranet may be operated by the I/T department of the enterprise, or it may be outsourced to a network provider. The network provider, in turn, may be managing the intranets of several enterprises. The provider may operate the different intranets separately, using physically different links and routers for each of the intranets. However, significant cost savings can be obtained if the network provider can share the physical infrastructure (links and routers) among the different supported intranets.

A *Virtual Private Network (VPN)* is a collection of several physically-separate, corporate-site networks that are interconnected securely over a common network shared among many corporations. VPN services are available from several network operators, including UUNET Technologies (http://www.usa.uu.net/products/vpn/) and AT&T Global Network (http://www.ipservices.att.com/worldnet/vpns/index.html).

For the customer company installing a VPN, the cost of obtaining VPN services from a network operator is substantially less than that associated with running a private network. For the network operator, the revenues associated with operating a VPN are significantly greater than the revenues obtained by offering plain connectivity to the Internet.

Figure 8.1 shows one of the possible configurations that can be used by a network provider to offer VPN services. The network provider obtains Frame Relay or ATM links from a telecommunication company and builds a physical IP network using these links. The provider then offers multiple logical networks to the customers. Each customer is connected to the provider network using access routers. The access routers are within the control of the network provider and multiplex the traffic from different customers atop the same Frame Relay or ATM links.

Figure 8.1   VPN support by a network provider.

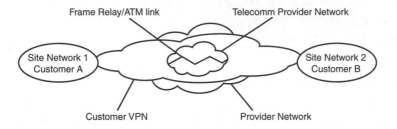

Note

The concept of a VPN as presented here is but one of many connotations associated with the term *VPN* in the industry.

The important issues a VPN solution must address are ensuring satisfactory performance of the virtual network and the privacy of communication over a shared network.

In this section, we look at the technologies that can provide the security needed for VPN communications, followed by a discussion on providing performance SLAs for VPNs. Note that security is a complex and large topic, and this section provides only a very high-level view of the issues.

8.1.1   Security Mechanisms for IP Communication

Most site networks connect to a shared network such as the Internet through *firewalls.* The firewall protects the site network from malicious users on the shared network, allowing access to only specific applications or servers in the site network. For example, access to a mail server or a public Web server may be allowed from the shared network, but not to the database servers or private Web servers.

The most common form of a firewall is a *packet-filtering firewall.* The packet-filtering firewall allows only packets with specific fields in the packet headers to cross from the Internet to the site network, and vice-versa. The packet-filtering firewalls typically operate by examining the five fields in the network and transport protocol header—namely the source and destination IP addresses, the protocol, and the source and destination port numbers. It allows only packets matching a configured set of filters to pass through and denies access to other packets. Using the packet-filtering firewall, you can allow access only to specific applications (for example, mail or UseNet news services) to communicate between the site network and the Internet. A firewall can also determine that the messages exchanged by the applications are well-formed, for example, by checking for viruses in ActiveX controls on a Web page. Such products are called *application-level gateways.*

Security can also be provided at a TCP connection level in an application-independent manner. This is done by means of the *SOCKS protocol* [SOCKSREF]. SOCKS operates by having a proxy to which all computers in the site network connect instead of to the ultimate destination in the Internet. The SOCKS proxy checks its configuration to validate that the connection is allowed, and it establishes the connection to the ultimate destination, passing data back and forth between the two connections. SOCKS can be configured to limit access to only connections originating from the site network (for example, to permit browsers in the site network to access Web servers on the Internet) or to allow connections coming from the Internet to specific servers in the network (for example, to allow external customers to access a Web server in the demilitarized zone, or DMZ). SOCKS can also be used to authenticate UDP communication across the Internet.

The filtering of packets or connections offers limited security in communication. Filtered packets or connections offer no way to authenticate the identity of the peer at the other end of the communication, nor do they offer a way to hide the contents of the messages being exchanged. Two security protocols offer both authentication and encryption in TCP/IP based communication. These include the Secure Sockets Layer and the suite of IP-security protocols.

> **Note**
> The fact that filtering firewalls offer limited security should not be construed as saying they are unnecessary. Firewalls are essential to connect to shared networks such as the Internet. Cheswick and Bellovin's book [CHESWICK] lists several types of attacks that filtering firewalls can protect against.

The Secure Sockets Layer

The *Secure Sockets Layer (SSL)* offers transport-layer security and is commonly used between Web browsers and servers. SSL operates using the notion of *certificates* (see the sidebar "Digital Encryption and Certificates"). SSL adds an additional handshake between the client and server on top of the TCP connection establishment.

The server typically presents its certificate to authenticate its identity at the time of connection establishment. The client can also present a certificate to authenticate itself, but such client authentication is not a common practice. After the authentication, the client and the server negotiate a common secret key. The message negotiations for the secret key are encrypted using public key cryptography, which is relatively time-consuming. The common secret key is used for encryption during the exchange of application data.

The SSL protocol is being standardized and has been renamed the *TLS (Transport Layer Security) protocol* [TLSREF]. Several public-domain implementations of SSL are also available on the Web.

IPsec Protocols

The IP security architecture establishes *security associations (SAs)* between pairs of nodes. The nodes could be end hosts or intermediary routes/firewalls. An SA is a logical tunnel between the two nodes and the parameters of the logical tunnel, such as the algorithms and the keys to be used for encryption and authentication. SAs are established using key management protocols, after which a user can use protocols to authenticate IP headers or to encrypt the payload of IP datagrams.

The header authentication scheme [IPAUTH] places an Authentication Header (AH) for each IP packet in order to provide information about the validity of its contents. The AH includes a digital signature of the contents of the packet. The algorithm used to compute the digital signature is called *Hashed Message Authentication (HMAC)*, which uses a shared secret and two rounds of a hashing algorithm such as MD5 or SHA. HMAC

[HMACREF] generates two keys from the shared secret, hashes the message using the first generated key in the first round, and rehashes the result using the second generated key. The hash covers the contents of the IP packet (header and payload), with the exception of some fields in the IP header that change in the network—for example, the Time to Live field.

When the originator of an IP packet includes an AH, it is located immediately after the IP header but before the payload, in what is called the *transport mode*. An alternate mode is the *tunnel mode*, where a new IP header includes the AH, the original IP header, and payload. The tunnel mode can be used to provide authenticated tunnels between two firewalls connecting two site networks of a corporation over the Internet. The tunnel mode can also be used by an end host. Both of these modes are shown in Figure 8.2.

Figure 8.2 Authenticated header in transport and tunnel modes.

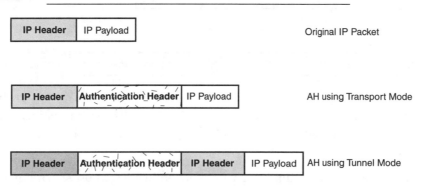

The *Encapsulating Security Payload (ESP) standard* [IPESP] specifies a method by which the payload of an IP packet can be encrypted. ESP requires the use of an ESP header, an ESP trailer, and an ESP authentication field. The header contains information identifying the SA and sequence numbers; the trailer typically contains padding bytes that are needed to encrypt the payload of the original IP packet; and the authentication field includes information to authenticate the IP header and the encrypted payload. As with AH, the authentication information typically is a hash of the payload computed using HMAC.

ESP can be used in conjunction with AH or alone. It also operates in two modes: the transport mode and the tunnel mode (see Figure 8.3). In the transport mode, the ESP header occurs right after the original IP header, but the encryption is only applied to the payload and the ESP trailer. In the tunnel mode, the encryption is applied to original IP header, the payload, and the ESP trailer.

> **Note**
>
> Encryption is normally done over blocks of fixed lengths. When a packet size is not an exact multiple of the block size, trailing padding bytes are added prior to encryption/authentication to bring the packet up to the right block size.

Figure 8.3   ESP in transport and tunnel modes.

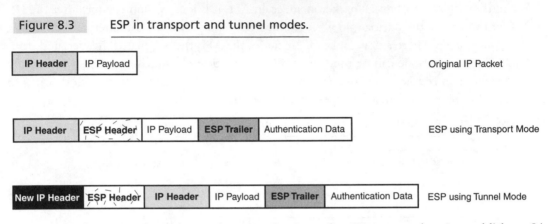

To establish a secure logical tunnel, two end points of an IPsec tunnel must establish an SA between them. To establish an SA (secure logical tunnel), the two end-points of the tunnel must exchange cryptographic keys using the IKE protocol [IKE]. The exchange occurs in two phases:

- In the first phase, communicating parties are authenticated using cerificates. (See the sidebar "Digital Encryption and Certificates"). A special SA is established in phase 1.

- In the second phase, the SA created in phase 1 is used to negotiate the cryptographic keys to be used for newly established SAs.

More details on these protocols can be found in Internet RFCs on the topic [IPSEC] [ISAKMP] [OAKLEY]. A subset of the ISAKMP/Oakley protocols that can be used for setting up VPNs constitutes the Internet Key Exchange (IKE) protocol [IKE].

8.1.2   VPNs and SLAs

In addition to security concerns, performance concerns are one of the main roadblocks in widespread deployment of IP-based VPNs. As a result, a network provider offering VPN service should also investigate offering SLAs to support adequate performance to its VPN customers.

A typical scenario for VPN communication would be as shown in Figure 8.4. Each of the site networks connects to the shared network using firewalls. Packets are exchanged among different sites using logical links established between pairs of firewalls. Each logical link consists of an IPsec tunnel created between a pair of firewalls. The firewalls encrypt the IP packets that are exchanged between the firewalls using ESP in tunnel mode. Alternatively, if encryption is not needed, the firewalls authenticate the IP packets using AH in tunnel mode.

Figure 8.4   VPN configuration using IPsec.

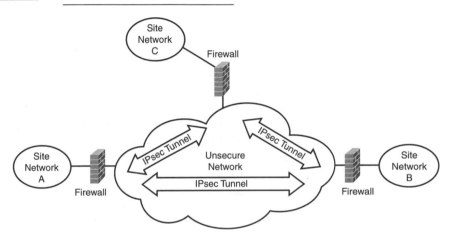

Each of the tunnels can also be associated with SLAs regarding bandwidth usage and network delay and loss characteristics.

Any of the different techniques to support network connectivity SLAs described in Chapter 6, "SLA Support in Different Network Environments," can be used to support SLAs for VPNs. Consider the case where the network operator is using Differentiated Services (DiffServ) to support SLAs. In addition to encrypting the packets with the ESP protocol, the firewalls can also mark the ToS byte in the IP header to indicate the type of service a packet should receive at the intermediate routers. Additionally, the firewall can implement other functions needed for bandwidth management, such as priority queuing and scheduling. Some firewall vendors [CHKPOINT] have started bundling bandwidth management functions with their firewalls.

Note

Marking the ToS bytes is dependent on classification rules that typically use port numbers and a field in the transport header. Encryption can hide these fields; therefore, the firewalls need to perform any functions dependent on the transport header (such as marking the ToS byte) prior to encrypting the packet.

The performance assurances offered for VPNs are valid only for the domain of a network operator. If an enterprise is connected to the same ISP at all its sites, it can ask the single ISP to provide it with VPNs that also offer performance-based SLAs. The ISP should be able to offer those SLAs using the techniques described in this book; however, some enterprises may be connected to different ISPs at different sites. In the next section, we look at the issue of supporting SLAs across the domains of different network providers.

Digital Encryption and Certificates

The goal of encryption is to transform the original digital message into an encrypted version that can be understood (decrypted) only by the two communicating parties. The methods to encrypt digital data can be roughly classified into two categories: those based on a shared secret (also called *private key*) and those based on a public key.

When encrypting data using a *shared secret*, both parties involved in the communication have some information that can be used by the sender to encrypt the data and by the receiver to decrypt the data. A simple (but relatively easy-to-break) scheme is to shift all the letters of a message by a known amount. For example, the sender and the receiver agree to shift all letters by 2; that is, change all As in the message to Cs, all Bs to Ds, ...all Ys to As and all Zs to Bs. The message would make sense to the sender and the receiver but appear as garbage to everyone else.

Practical digital encryption using a private key uses more sophisticated schemes. The *Digital Encryption Standard (DES)* is one such shared secret scheme that involves performing a series of numeric operations, such as bitwise exclusive ORing, and shifting in a number of stages with the secret key for encryption and decryption. The shared secret information is commonly called the *key*. The key would be a long bit pattern, and the number of bits in the pattern determines the difficulty in trying to decrypt the message without the key. The main issue in using shared secrets is to exchange the secret between the communicating parties in a secure manner.

In many cases, you may not want to encrypt the message but simply attach enough information to the message to ensure that no one has tampered with the contents. Such an attachment is called a *message digest* or a *hash*. The algorithms to compute the hash functions are designed so that it is easy to compute the hash from a document, but it is computationally not feasible to generate two different documents with same hash. Common algorithms to generate the message digest include *Message Digest 5 (MD5)* and *Secure Hash Algorithm (SHA)* .

A *digital signature* validates that a document originated from the sender. A hash using MD5 or SHA is computed for the document. This hash is then encrypted with a private key and included with the document. The receiver can recompute the hash and check it with the private key to validate that it was sent by the sender—the only other party who knows the secret private key.

In the case of public-key encryption, each party has a private key and a public key. The private key is kept secret, whereas the public key is made known to everyone. To send a secure message to the recipient, anyone can find the public key of the recipient and encrypt the message with the public key. The recipient is able to decrypt it with the private key. The most common algorithm used in public key is the *Rivest Shamir Adleman algorithm (RSA)*, named after the initials of its inventors. It is based on a public key that is the product of two large prime numbers and a private key consists of the primes themselves.

Usually, the private and public keys are the inverse of each other; that is, if a message encrypted with the private key can be decrypted with the public key, a message encrypted with the public key can be decrypted with the private key.

Digital signatures using the public key follow a scheme similar to that in signatures formed using the private key. The sender computes a hash of the document and encrypts it using its private key. The encrypted hash is attached along with the document as the signature. The receiver recomputes the hash and validates it with the public key of the sender.

With the public key, the challenge for the sender is to ensure that the public key indeed belongs to the recipient. The public key information is often provided in the form of a digital certificate. The *digital certificate* is usually structured in a format defined by an OSI standard—X.509. The digital certificate contains the identity of the recipient (name, address, and so on), the public key of the recipient, and the signature of a certificate authority (CA) covering the name and public key of the recipient. The CA is a party trusted by the sender and the receivers, and whose public key is widely known.

On an intranet, a corporation can set up its own certificate authority. For communication on the Internet, two common certificate authorities are Verisign [VERIS] and Thawte [THAWTE].

Details on DES, RSA, SHA, MD5, and many other cryptographic algorithms can be found in the book by Schneier [SCHNR].

8.2 SLAs on the Internet

The network connectivity SLAs enable performance bounds when all site networks of a customer are connected by means of a single network provider network. In this section, we look at the issue of extending SLAs to site networks that are connected using multiple network providers. When an enterprise obtains Internet access at different sites (for example, one in Europe and the other in the U.S.), it is quite possible that the connectivity would be provided by a different ISP at each location.

The environment we are considering is illustrated in Figure 8.5. It shows an enterprise with three site networks that are connected to two different ISPs. Two of the sites (sites A and B) are connected using the same network provider (ISP 1). The third site is connected to a different network provider (ISP 3). These two ISPs are not connected directly, but only through an intervening ISP (ISP 2) with whom the two ISPs peer at peering points P1 and P2. The enterprise can obtain an SLA from ISP 1 about the performance of the network between these site networks A and B.

Figure 8.5   Site connectivity across multiple ISPs.

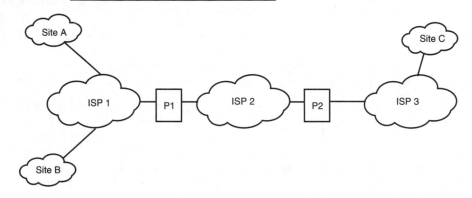

You might wonder if it is possible to obtain any SLA about communication between sites B and C that are connected to two different network operators. A related question would be which ISP would provide the SLA regarding the connectivity between points B and C. Because one or more intermediate ISPs may be present between the two sites, the SLAs that can be offered for communication between the two sites interconnected by different network operators depend on the availability of operator-to-operator SLAs. If one of the intervening ISPs is offering a best-effort service without any bounds on network delays or bandwidth guarantees, it is not possible to offer any SLAs for the end-to-end communication between the two sites.

Assume that all the ISPs are willing to negotiate SLAs for communication with their neighbors and customers. In this case, it might be possible to obtain SLAs for end-to-end communication between sites B and C. Assume that the SLA between the enterprise and ISP 1 specifies a limit on the delay and bandwidth between the two sites. Also assume that the communication delays of less than 500ms and a throughput of 1Mbps are assured. ISP 1 can ensure providing a throughput of 1Mbps and a delay of some part of the 500ms (suppose 100ms) for communication between the peering point P1 and the sites A and B. ISP 1 can also sign an SLA with ISP 2 that requires that 1Mbps of data be delivered from P1 to site C in the network with a delay of no more than 400ms.

ISP 2 ensures that a throughput of 1Mbps is available for communication between P1 and P2. It further ensures that the delay between these two points is less than, for example, 300ms. Then it can ask for an SLA from ISP 3 that 1Mbps of communication be supported between P2 and site C with a delay of no more than 100ms and a throughput of 1Mbps. If ISP 3 agrees to provide such an SLA, ISP 2 can honor its SLA with ISP 1, and ISP 1 can honor its SLA with the enterprise customer.

Although this negotiation among multiple ISPs can be done manually among a small number of cooperating ISPs, it would be fairly tedious to extend the model to a large number of ISPs. Similarly, the best way to allocate delays among different ISPs is not easy to determine.

Even if delays are not a concern, and the SLAs are only concerned about bandwidth, different ISPs may want to have separate policies for allocating bandwidth to their customers. As an example, ISP 1 may want to borrow bandwidth only in chunks of 10Mbps or more from ISP 2. A chunk bought between points P1 and P2 would be allocated in smaller portions among the different customers it supports.

Although you may not be able to resolve all the issues involved in supporting SLAs across multiple administrative domains, it is possible to reduce the tedium of SLA establishment by developing a protocol to borrow and lend bandwidth among the different network providers. A computer program that can borrow and lend bandwidth is called a *bandwidth broker* and is being explored in some universities. It is described in the next section.

8.2.1 *Bandwidth Brokers*

The *bandwidth broker* is a special program that keeps track of the bandwidth used within an ISP network and communicates with bandwidth brokers in the adjacent ISP's domains to negotiate the amount of bandwidth to be borrowed. The basic idea behind bandwidth brokers is that spare bandwidth in the network can be borrowed and lent among the different network operators. Markets analogous to bandwidth brokers are already in place for electricity as part of the deregulation of the power industry in the U.S.

The traffic load on the Internet and the loading of the router traffic can change dramatically over time. On the World Wide Web, several sites have been known to attract unusually high traffic for a limited period of time; for example, the Web sites for CNN typically get unusually high traffic during a significant world crisis. Several small companies have advertised their wares on highly watched television events, such as the Olympics, and have attracted high traffic due to that fact. Because of these surges, as well as other less dramatic traffic variations, spare bandwidth may be available along some of the parts in an ISP network, whereas a traffic overload may exist along other parts of the network.

If adjacent ISPs could detect the portions of their network with high traffic overload, they might be able to borrow excess bandwidth from some of the neighboring ISPs to deal with this situation. This process could be automated so that the borrowing and lending of excess network bandwidth could be done on a very dynamic timescale, in the order of hours. The borrowing or lending of bandwidth is implemented by adjusting the routing tables of routers at the peering points between ISPs.

Several universities are involved in prototype implementation of bandwidth brokers. One prototype implementation is being done over Internet2, and the project pages for the Internet2 implementations have pointers to the other bandwidth broker protocols. The Internet2 bandwidth broker information can be accessed via its Web site at `http://www.merit.edu/working.groups/i2-qbone-bb`.

> **Note**
>
> Internet2 is a research network consisting of several universities, research labs, and corporations that test new concepts in networking, such as support of digital video transmission and Quality of Service. More information on Internet2 can be found at `http://www.internet2.edu`.

8.3 Traffic Engineering and MPLS

One of the difficulties in supporting network connectivity SLAs on a pure IP network arises because of the static nature of IP routing. Look at the configuration shown in Figure 8.6. The SLA requirements for connecting customer sites A and B as shown in the network require that a bandwidth of 10Mbps be supported between the two sites. The shortest routing path that can be used by IP between sites A and B is shown by solid arrows in the figure. However, only 6Mbps are available on the default path between the two sites, which is clearly inadequate to meet the desired SLA. On an alternate longer path shown by dotted arrows in the figure, the additional 4Mbps are available. IP routing is constrained to follow a single path at any router for a given destination. Therefore, normal IP routing techniques are not able to use the extra 4Mbps to meet the SLA requirements of the traffic.

This problem would not arise if the SLAs were supported by mapping IP packets onto an overlaid Frame Relay or ATM network. In this case, the access router at the network can direct 6Mbps of traffic to one of the Frame Relay/ATM connections and the remaining 4Mbps to a second connection. The connections could be configured to go through the different routes. We refer to the capability to direct traffic along different paths of the network as *traffic engineering*.

Figure 8.6   Traffic engineering problems in the IP network.

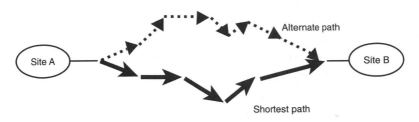

Traffic engineering can be very useful in supporting network connectivity SLAs. By direct-ing specific flows of traffic along certain paths, you can control the amount of load on each router. If one of the paths in the network is found to experience heavy loads for pro-longed periods, some of the load can be redirected to alternate paths. Traditional OSPF routing [OSPFREV] would always constrain a packet to traverse a path that is computed upon the topology of the network and some static link weights. However, OSPF does not take into account the congestion at a link or the amount of spare capacity on a link.

The initial OSPF specifications [OSPFOLD] allowed the specification of multiple routing tables, the selection among them being done by the ToS byte of a packet. This informa-tion could have been used to redirect differently marked traffic along different paths except that the option was never quite implemented, and hence it was dropped from the subsequent revisions of the OSPF specifications [OSPFREV].

Multiprotocol label switching (MPLS), a standard being defined within IETF, offers an alternative way by which traffic engineering can be supported. A network supporting MPLS would consist of several MPLS nodes, with some of the nodes being edge nodes that communicate with networks on the external domain. Several explicit routes are estab-lished within a single MPLS domain between the different MPLS edge nodes. These explicit routes are effectively connections between established edge nodes and forward packets using label swapping.

An MPLS domain appears like a single Layer 2 network to the IP layer. The domain sup-ports multiple MPLS connections between the various edge devices. These connections and the associated labels can be established by manual configuration, by extensions to routing protocols such as BGP, or by extensions to the RSVP signaling protocol.

When an IP packet is received by an MPLS edge node, the edge node determines the explicit route that is to be used for that packet. An MPLS-shim header is then attached to the IP packet before it is forwarded on to the next MPLS node. The MPLS-shim header is placed between the IP header and the underlying data-link protocol. The MPLS-shim header contains the label to be used for forwarding the MPLS data throughout the MPLS domain. The edge node can decide to use different MPLS headers for IP packets headed for the same destination, effectively enabling traffic engineering.

Figure 8.7 illustrates what an MPLS domain may look like. An MPLS edge node is connected via a FDDI ring to another MPLS node, which is connected via a Gigabit Ethernet to a third MPLS node, which is connected via a token ring to another MPLS edge node. The different types of headers in an IP packet as it traverses the network from the ingress MPLS edge node to the egress MPLS edge node are also shown for the links. By using a shim below the IP header, the MPLS nodes are able to establish a connection through disparate physical links, without any dependencies on the IP layer. The label-swapping is called *multiprotocol* because it has been defined in a manner that could support protocols other than IP.

Figure 8.7　　MPLS domain and packet structure.

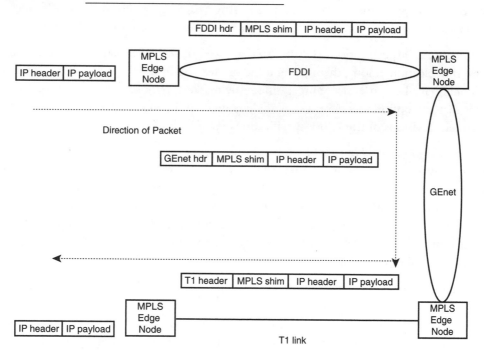

Further details on MPLS can be found throughout its various Internet drafts available at the IETF working group site [MPLSREF].

8.4 SLAs and IP Version 6

Within this book, we have concentrated on mechanisms that can support SLAs on a network based on the current version of IP—that is, IP version 4 (IPv4). IPv4 is the ubiquitously deployed version of the protocol but is facing problems because of its own popularity, and it is running out of IP addresses. The next generation of IP, IP version 6 (IPv6), attempts to resolve the problems faced by IPv4.

Although version 4 networks are expected to continue for a significant duration, you should expect to also see version 6 networks in the near future. Therefore, it would be useful to examine the type of SLAs that could be supported in IPv6 networks. We first present a brief overview of IPv6 and then examine how the different techniques for supporting SLA would apply to IPv6 networks.

8.4.1 Overview of IP Version 6

The significant differences of IP version 6 from version 4 consist of the following:

- *Larger address space*: IPv6 uses 128-bit machine addresses instead of 32-bit addresses used by IPv4. This permits more levels of addressing hierarchy and a larger number of addressable nodes.

- *Different header format*: IPv6 uses a different header format than IPv4 and eliminates many optional fields. It also provides for a different way to support header options and extensions.

- *Traffic-flow labeling*: IPv6 allows packets to be labeled as belonging to specific flows. This capability can be used advantageously to support SLAs.

The format of an IPv6 header is shown in Figure 8.8. It consists of the following fields:

- *Version*: The Version identifies the packet as an IP version 6 packet.

- *Traffic Class*: This 8-bit field is intended to contain the same field as the ToS byte in IPv4. Thus, this field can be used to enable DiffServ PHBs on an IPv6 network.

- *Flow Label*: IPv6 provides the notion of a 20-bit Flow Label field. The Flow Label can be used to identify all packets that may belong to a reserved path, for example, those established by a RSVP request and required to follow the same path. The Flow Label can also be used for functions such as traffic engineering. No particular usage is standardized.

- *Payload Length*: Payload Length indicates the length of the data carried by an IPv6 packet.

- *Next Header*: The Next Header field identifies the type of header that follows the standard header. The next header could be a transport header (TCP or UDP) or one of the several IPv6 extension headers.

- *Hop Limit*: Hop Limit serves the same functions as TTL in IPv4. It is a counter that is decremented by 1 on every hop, and the packet is dropped if the counter reaches 0.

- *Source Address*: This field contains the 12 bytes of source IP address.

- *Destination Address*: This field contains the 12 bytes of destination IP address.

Figure 8.8   IPv6 header structure.

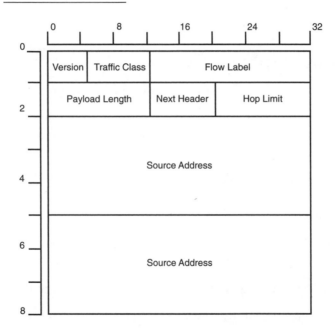

In addition to the standard header, IPv6 can contain any number of extension headers. These extension headers contain the optional headers that were present in IPv4 and provide semantics such as loose source routing or fragmentation information. Header extensions are also defined for IPsec AH and ESP header.

Fragmentation in IPv6 is done only by the source of a packet and not by an intermediary router. The source is expected to discover the maximum packet size along the current path to the destination [MTUV6] and to send out only IPv6 packets smaller than the discovered size. All IPv6 nodes are required to support packets of 1,280 bytes, so the source can also restrict itself to send packets less than 1,280 bytes to comply with the standards.

Avoiding fragmentation along the path eliminates many nasty problems that arise because of fragments in IPv4, such as difficulty in processing fragments at packet-filtering firewalls, or for DiffServ classification.

When compared to IPv4, IPv6 is a much cleaner architecture, and it offers a more elegant solution to problems such as security and QoS, techniques that require a complex array of embedded headers and assorted boxes (firewalls, network address translators, DiffServ edge devices, and so on) to work properly in IPv4. IPv6 is supported in most vendor products, but network operators have been slow to deploy it because of the large entrenched position of the current IPv4 networks.

8.4.2   SLA Mechanisms for IPv6

The basic techniques to use for SLA support for IPv6 remain the same as in IPv4—specifically, network design and capacity planning, support for QoS, and performance measurements. However, IPv6 offers features that help in the implementation of SLAs in the network.

The Flow Label header can be used as a connection identifier in an IPv6 network and can be used to enable traffic engineering by routing packets on the basis of their flow labels rather than on the destination IP address. Traffic engineering using IPv6 flow labels is independent of the traffic engineering provided by MPLS. Similarly, the Flow Label header can be used by resource reservation approaches such as RSVP/IntServ to enable a much more scalable and efficient QoS scheme.

The Traffic Class field can be used to support DiffServ in an IPv6 network.

The notion of extension headers in IPv6 enables you to provide hooks for measuring the performance of the network in an efficient manner. One of the tricky problems in monitoring network SLA compliance is measuring the delay between two routers in the network. By using an extension header that is inserted at the ingress access router of the IPv6 network and extracting it at the egress access router of the IPv6 network, you can collect information about traffic flows that can provide information about network delays and loss rates. Because the flows are uniquely identified, network performance monitoring using flows is also simplified.

8.5 *Further Information*

Several excellent books describe the issue of network security and the different security protocols. The book by Cheswick and Bellovin [CHESWICK] is considered a classic in the field of Internet security. Similarly, the book by Schneier on cryptography [SCHNR] provides very good coverage of cryptography and various algorithms such as RSA, SHA and DES. Information about SSL can be obtained from Netscape.

MPLS is still being defined in the IETF, and you can track its progress from the drafts at the working group. Because the standard is still being defined, the best source for current information is the Web site for the working group [MPLSREF]. However, a good summary of technologies related to IP switching that have led to MPLS can be found in the book by Bruce Davie et al [DAVIE]. A discussion of IPv6 can be found in the books by Loshin [LOSHIN], or you can follow the RFC that defined the standard [DEERING].

8.6 *Endnotes*

[CHESWICK] Cheswick, W. R,. and S. M. Bellovin. *Firewalls and Internet Security: Repelling the Wily Hacker*. Reading, MA: Addison-Wesley, 1996.

[CHKPOINT] CheckPoint Systems, FloodGate-1 Product. Available at `http://checkpoint.com/products/floodgate-1/index.html`.

[DAVIE] Davie, B., P. Doolan, and Y. Rekhter. *Switching in IP Networks: IP Switching, Tag Switching and Related Technologies*." San Francisco, CA: Morgan Kaufmann, 1998.

[DEERING] Deering, S., and R. Hinden. "Internet Protocol, Version 6 (IPv6) Specification." Internet RFC 2460, December 1998.

[HMAC] Krawczyk, H., et al. "HMAC: Keyed-Hashing for Message Authentication." Internet RFC 2104, February 1997.

[IPAUTH] Kent, S., and R. Atkinson. "IP Authentication Header." Internet RFC 2402, November 1998.

[IPESP] ———. "IP Encapsulating Security Protocol (ESP)." RFC 2406, November 1998.

[IPSEC] ———. "Security Architecture for the Internet Protocol." Internet RFC 2401, November 1998.

[IKE] Harkins D., and D. Carrel. "The Internet Key Exchange (IKE)." Internet RFC 2409, November 1998.

[ISAKMP] Maughan D., et al. "Internet Security Association and Key Management Protocol." Internet RFC 2408, November 1998.

[LOSHIN] Loshin, P. *IPv6 Clearly Explained*. San Francisco, CA: Morgan Kaufman, 1999.

[MPLSREF] IETF Working Group on MultiProtocol Label Swapping, Charter. Available at `http://www.ietf.org/html_charters/mpls-charter.html`.

[MTUV6] McCann, J., J., Mogul, and S. Deering. "Path MTU Discovery for IP Version 6." Internet RFC 1981, August 1996.

[OAKLEY] Orman, H. "The Oakley Key Determination Protocol." Internet RFC 2412, November 1998.

[OSPFOLD] Moy, J. "OSPF Version 2." Internet RFC 1247, July 1991.

[OSPFREV] ———. "OSPF Version 2." Internet RFC 2178, July 1997.

[SCHNR] Schneier, B. *Applied Cryptography: Protocols, Algorithms and Source Code in C*. New York: John Wiley & Sons, 1995.

[SOCKSREF] Leech, M., et al. "SOCKS Protocol Version 5." Internet RFC 1928, April 1996.

[THAWTE] Thawte Digital Certificate Services. Available at `http://thawte.com`.

[TLSREF] Dierks, T., and C. Allen. "The TLS Protocol Version 1.0." Internet RFC2246, January 1999.

[VERIS] Verisign Systems. Available at `http://www.verisign.com`.

Index

The *Macmillan Network Architecture and Development Series* is a comprehensive set of guides that provides computing professionals with the unique insight of leading experts in today's networking technologies. Each volume explores a technology or set of technologies that is needed to build and maintain the optimal network environment for any particular organization or situation.

Currently available titles in the *Macmillan Network Architecture and Development Series* include

Wide Area High Speed Networks, by Dr. Sidnie Feit (ISBN: 1-57870-114-7)

Today, conventional telephony, ISDN networks, ATM networks, packet-switched networks, and Internet data technologies coexist in a complex tapestry of networks. This book clearly explains each technology, describes how they interoperate, and puts their various uses and advantages into perspective. *Wide Area High Speed Networks* is an authoritative resource that will enable networking designers and implementers to determine which technologies to use in their networks, and for which roles.

Switched, Fast, and Gigabit Ethernet, by Sean Riley and Robert A. Breyer (ISBN: 1-57870-073-6)

Switched, Fast, and Gigabit Ethernet, Third Edition is the one and only solution needed to understand and fully implement this entire range of Ethernet innovations. Acting both as an overview of current technologies and hardware requirements as well as a hands-on, comprehensive tutorial for deploying and managing Switched, Fast, and Gigabit Ethernets, this guide covers the most prominent present and future challenges network administrators face.

Understanding and Deploying LDAP Directory Services, by Tim Howes, Mark Smith, and Gordon Goode (ISBN: 1-57870-070-1)

This comprehensive tutorial provides the reader with a thorough treatment of LDAP directory services. Designed to meet multiple needs, the first part of the book presents a general overview of the subject matter. The next three sections cover detailed instructions for design, deployment, and integration of directory services. The text is full of practical implementation advice and real-world deployment examples to help the reader choose the path that makes the most sense for their specific organization.

Designing Addressing Architectures for Routing and Switching, by Howard C. Berkowitz (ISBN: 1-57870-059-0)

Designing Addressing Architectures for Routing and Switching provides a systematic methodology for planning the wide area and local area network streets on which users and servers live. It guides the network designer in developing rational systems that are flexible and that maintain a high level of service. Intended for people who are—or who want to be—responsible for building large networks, this book offers a system and taxonomy for building networks that meet user requirements. It includes practical examples, configuration guides, case studies, tips, and warnings.

Wireless LANs: Implementing Interoperable Networks, by Jim Geier (ISBN: 1-57870-081-7)

This book provides both a context for understanding how an enterprise can benefit from the application of wireless technology, and the proven tools for efficiently implementing a wireless LAN. Based on the most recent developments in the field, *Wireless LANs: Implementing Interoperable Networks* gives network engineers vital information on planning, configuring, and supporting wireless networks.

Upcoming titles in the *Macmillan Network Architecture and Development Series* include

Local Area High Speed Networks, by Dr. Sidnie Feit (ISBN: 1-57870-113-9)

The DHCP Handbook, by Ralph Droms and Ted Lemon (ISBN: 1-57870-137-6)